Business Report Writing

Business Report Writing: A Practical Approach

Carol McFarland Baxter
The University of North Carolina at Charlotte

Kent Publishing Company
A Division of Wadsworth, Inc.
Boston, Massachusetts

KENT PUBLISHING COMPANY
A Division of Wadsworth, Inc.

Senior Editor: Richard C. Crews
Production Editor: Sarah Evans
Interior Designer: Nancy Lindgren
Cover Designer: Nancy Lindgren
Production Coordinator: Linda Siegrist

Printed in the United States of America

1 2 3 4 5 6 7 8 9 — 87 86 85 84 83

Library of Congress Cataloging in Publication Data

Baxter, Carol McFarland.
  Business report writing.

  Bibliography: p.
  Includes index.
  1. Business report writing. I. Title.
HF5719.B39   1983   808'.066651021   82-21340
ISBN 0-534-01392-9

FOR   Ken,

Mike,

and

Herb

Three profound influences on my work

Preface

Today, many of our educational programs are designed for technicians and management trainees who will need to communicate effectively through written reports. Those who enter these programs are usually pragmatic; they want to learn quickly how to perform so they can immediately apply that knowledge to their jobs. This text has been written with their needs, as well as the needs of their instructors, foremost in mind.

Of course, to appreciate the practical application of any knowledge, an understanding of some basic theory is essential. While maintaining its practical viewpoint, this text presents the most salient aspects of report-writing theory. The material throughout the text is logically organized and written in a way that makes all information readily accessible to students. Because the numerous examples that the text contains are based on actual problems encountered in business report writing, students are able to identify with the situations described and thus to appreciate the importance of writing clear, concise, and complete reports.

The text is adaptable to the needs of various groups of potential managers: the instructor may choose from among the wide variety of materials presented whatever is most practical for a particular group of students. Another important feature of the text is the classroom-tested activities at the ends of chapters. These activities quickly involve students in the report-writing process; in addition, many of the activities encourage the practice of small-group–interactive skills.

A further advantage of this text is that in their future roles as managers, students will find it a useful reference tool. For example, the lists of items to include in the various kinds of business reports (such as performance evaluation and feasibility reports), as well as the precautions to take when planning these reports, are handy checklists for managers, who are generally under pressure of time to produce effective reports.

The text is divided into three parts. Part I discusses the function of reports in an organization, the specific purposes for writing reports, and the importance of accuracy in report writing. Additional discussion focuses on understanding a problem, on the importance of analyzing the audience for whom the report is intended, on stating the objectives for writing each report, and on outlining the important points to be made in the report. The student is also introduced to sources of information for use in reports, to the various formats for reports, and finally to the verbal and nonverbal elements that are vital to good report writing. Part I concludes with a discussion of the use of graphic aids in report writing. The learning activities at the ends of these chapters, which involve students in the writing process, foster the immediate development of their writing skills. When they have completed Part I, they should have a good foundation from which to begin writing specific kinds of reports.

Part II looks at the most common types of reports that managers encounter. Discussion focuses on the purpose, format, and content of each type. Practical suggestions and common pitfalls are also discussed. Examples of each type of report are shown, and practice exercises are also included. The final chapter in Part II discusses the long formal report, which will test students' abilities to apply all the skills they have learned thus far in the course.

Many new managers will work for small companies that give competent employees other kinds of writing assignments. Part III discusses some special kinds of reports and other kinds of business writing that these managers may need to know about. Chapter 11 focuses on the corporate annual report and on how employees in the company participate in gathering the information and work together to complete the report. Chapter 12 is unique in that no other report-writing text currently on the market even mentions reporting to government agencies. This chapter discusses some of the regulatory agencies, the part they play in the free enterprise system, and some practical points to remember when preparing reports for such agencies.

The final chapter in Part III discusses other kinds of business writing, such as how to define a technical term, how to take minutes or to record proceedings of a meeting, and how to write a press release. House organs and trade magazines are discussed, and tips are given for writing for either type of publication. Examples of each of these other kinds of business writing are included, and practice exercises are provided.

Finally, the appendix provides a review of punctuation, capitalization, and words that are often confused; the glossary defines terms relevant to business report writing; and the bibliography offers interested students a list of additional references.

The following individuals served as reviewers of the manuscript, and their valuable suggestions and criticisms are gratefully acknowledged:

Lois J. Bachman
Community College of Philadelphia

Robert J. Olney
Southwest Texas State University

Jeremiah J. Sullivan
University of Washington

Barron Wells
The University of Southwestern Louisiana

Sandra E. Wolf
Portland Community College

List of Illustrations

Figure 1–1   Partial Organization Chart for ABC Theme Park   7

Table 2–1   Kinds of Information to Include in Reports   20

Table 3–1   How the SIC Number Is Assigned   56

Exhibit 4–1   Performance Appraisal Form   64

Exhibit 4–2   Performance Appraisal Form   66

Exhibit 4–3   Page Arrangement for Memorandum Reports   69

Exhibit 4–4   Heading and Introduction of a Sample Memo Report   70

Exhibit 4–5   Sample Memorandum Report   73

Exhibit 4–6   Page Arrangement for a Letter Report   75

Exhibit 4–7   Heading for a Letter Report   76

Exhibit 4–8   Sample Letter Report   77

Exhibit 4–9   Report Using a Variation of the Standard Formats   81

Exhibit 6–1   Sample Table with Its Parts Labeled   111

Exhibit 6–2   Memorandum Containing an Exhibit   113

Exhibit 6–3   Sample Pie Chart   115

Exhibit 6–4   Sample Bar Chart   116

Exhibit 6–5   Column Chart Illustrating Complex Data, with Its Parts Labeled   117

Exhibit 6–6   Student Example Showing How Data Can Be Misrepresented   119

Exhibit 6–7   Sample Line Chart   120

Exhibit 6–8   Sample Map from Annual Report   121

Exhibit 6–9   Architect's Rendering   122

Exhibit 6–10   Sample Exploded Drawing   123

Exhibit 6–11   Sample Cutaway Drawing   124

Exhibit 6–12   Sample Pictograph   125

Exhibit 6–13   Sample Pictograph   126

Exhibit 6–14 Sample Flow Chart: Paperwork System 127
Exhibit 6–15 Sample Flow Chart: Simple Computer Program 128
Exhibit 7–1 Daily Report 142
Exhibit 7–2 Weekly Report 143
Exhibit 7–3 Monthly Report 144
Exhibit 7–4 Periodic Report 146
Exhibit 7–5 Schedule of Reports 149
Exhibit 7–6 Sample 4×6 Card with Notes About an Employee's
Performance 152
Exhibit 7–7 Performance Evaluation Form 153
Exhibit 7–8 Performance Evaluation Form 154
Exhibit 7–9 Employee Commendation Form 155
Exhibit 7–10 Employee Commendation Form 156
Exhibit 8–1 Employment Interview Report 172
Exhibit 8–2 Employment Interview Report 173
Exhibit 8–3 Employment Interview Report 174
Exhibit 8–4 Employment Exit Interview Report 177
Exhibit 8–5 Information Interview Report 179
Exhibit 8–6 Information Interview Report 182
Exhibit 8–7 Unusual Progress Report 186
Exhibit 8–8 Progress Report Using Technical Outline 187
Exhibit 8–9 Progress Report 189
Exhibit 8–10 Process Chart 192
Exhibit 8–11 Flow Chart 193
Exhibit 8–12 Procedures Report 195
Exhibit 8–13 Methods and Procedures Report 198
Exhibit 9–1 Suggestion Report Using the Form Report Format 209
Exhibit 9–2 Suggestion Report Using the Memo Report Format 211
Exhibit 9–3 Recommendation Report Using the Memo Report
Format 213
Exhibit 9–4 Feasibility Report Using the Memo Report Format 216
Exhibit 9–5 Outline for a Long Feasibility Report 219
Exhibit 9–6 Sample Proposal 221
Exhibit 10–1 Long Formal Analytical Report 237
Exhibit 10–2 Long Formal Informational Report 254
Exhibit 11–1 Annual Report: Not-for-Profit Organization 277
Figure 12–1 Government of the United States — How the Executive
Branch Delegates Responsibility to Executive Agencies 292
Figure 12–2 Partial Organization Chart: Department of Treasury — How
It Delegates One Area of Responsibility 293
Table 12–1 Some Government Regulatory Agencies to Which
Businesses Report 295
Exhibit 12–1 OSHA Report: Injuries and Illnesses 300
Exhibit 12–2 Department of Transportation Route Slip 304
Exhibit 13–1 Expanded Formal Definition 309

Exhibit 13–2   Expanded Formal Definition   309
Exhibit 13–3   Definition Clarified by an Illustration   310
Exhibit 13–4   Definition Clarified by an Illustration   310
Exhibit 13–5   Definition Clarified by Illustrations   311
Exhibit 13–6   Informative Abstract of a Magazine Article   313
Exhibit 13–7   Proceedings of a Meeting   316
Exhibit 13–8   Minutes of a Meeting   318
Exhibit 13–9   Form Used to Record Organizational Relationships   320
Exhibit 13–10   Job Description   322
Exhibit 13–11   Job Description   324
Exhibit 13–12   Job Description   327
Exhibit 13–13   Press Release   329
Exhibit 13–14   Newspaper Article Based on Press Release in
          Exhibit 13–13   331
Exhibit 13–15   Article Submitted to Trade Magazine   332
Exhibit 13–16   Column from House Organ: Written by
          Employee/Reporter   335
Exhibit 13–17   Sample House Organ: Newspaper Format   336

Contents

PART I
Elements of Report Writing

1 *The Function of Reports in an Organization*   *3*

The Need for Reports   4
Communication Objectives for Reports   9
The Importance of Accuracy   10
Summary   11
Learning Activities   12

2 *Analyzing and Interpreting Information and Planning the Report*   *13*

Understanding a Problem   14
Step 1: Analyze Your Audience   17
Step 2: Write a Statement of Purpose   19
Step 3: Prepare an Outline   21
Summary   31
Learning Activities   32

3 *Obtaining Information for the Report*   *34*

Primary Sources of Information   35
Organizing and Interpreting Primary Data   48
Secondary Sources of Information   51
Summary   57
Learning Activities   59

4 *Report Formats* *62*

The Form Report   63
The Memo Report   68
The Letter Report   72
The Long Formal Report   76
Variations of the Report Format   80
Summary   80
Learning Activities   86

5 *Report-Writing Elements: Verbal and Nonverbal* *91*

The Verbal Elements   92
The Nonverbal Elements   103
Summary   104
Learning Activities   106

6 *Using Illustrations in Reports*   *108*

Tables   109
Exhibits   110
Figures   112
Points to Remember When Using Illustrations   126
Creating Illustrated Reports with Computer Graphics and Word Processing   127
Summary   128
Learning Activities   130

PART II
Preparing Managerial Reports

7 *Periodic Reports*   *137*

Purpose and Type   138
Format   138
Forms Design   139
Examples of Periodic Reports   141
Points to Remember   145
Establishing a Schedule of Periodic Reports   147
Performance Reports   148
Summary   160
Learning Activities   161

8 *Interview Reports, Progress Reports, and Methods and Procedures Reports   165*

Interview Reports   166
Progress Reports   178
Methods and Procedures Reports   190
Summary   200
Learning Activities   201

9 *Suggestion Reports, Recommendation Reports, Feasibility Reports, and Proposals   206*

Differences Among These Reports   207
Suggestion Reports: Format and Contents   208
Recommendation Reports: Format and Contents   210
Feasibility Reports: Format and Contents   210
Proposals: Format and Contents   212
Summary   222
Learning Activities   223

10 *Long Formal Reports   227*

Defining the Problem   228
Purpose   229
Prefatory Parts   229
The Body of the Report   231
End Parts   232
Examples of Long Formal Reports   236
Summary   265
Learning Activities   266

PART III
Special Reports and Other Kinds of Business Writing

11 *The Corporate Annual Report   275*

Purpose   276
Content   278
The Use of Suggestion in Annual Reports   281
How an Annual Report Is Compiled   283
Current Trends   285
Summary   286
Learning Activities   287

12 *Reporting to Government Regulatory Agencies* **290**

Organizational Structure of Government Agencies   291
The Purpose of Government Regulatory Agencies   294
Personnel Who File Reports   294
Persuasion in Government Reporting   299
State and Local Regulatory Agencies   303
Summary   303
Learning Activities   305

13 *Other Kinds of Business Writing* **307**

Formal Definitions of Specialized or Technical
        Terms   308
Informative Abstracts   308
Minutes or Proceedings of a Meeting   312
Job Descriptions (Position Descriptions)   317
Press Releases   321
Articles for a Trade Publication   323
Articles for a House Organ   334
Summary   337
Learning Activities   339

*Appendix: A Brief Guide to Grammatical Usage in Business
        Writing   341*

Glossary   355

Bibliography   363

Index   367

PART I

*Elements of
Report Writing*

The Function of Reports in an Organization

LEARNING OBJECTIVES

After reading this chapter, you should be able to:

- Define the term *report* and tell how it differs from other business communication media;
- Describe how reports are used in organizations;
- Explain how inaccuracy in reporting can cause poor decision making.

Communication is essential in conducting business. Some of the most commonly used business communication media are letters, memos, phone calls, face-to-face conversations, and desk-top computer terminals. Although much business is transacted orally and often informally, the transaction is tentative until it has been committed to writing and both parties have a copy of it. Often the written communication will be in the form of a report.

What is a report and what distinguishes it from other kinds of written communication? It is an organized, objective presentation of facts for use within or outside the organization; it is a statement about the writer's observations and experiences. Reports are usually longer and more formal than memos and letters. Furthermore, memos are used for internal communication, and letters are used for external communication, whereas reports can be used either internally or externally. A report can summarize, explain, describe, or recommend. It is a versatile communication medium because it can be tailored to fit the company's, the reader's, and the writer's needs.

As business expands through domestic and international growth, more companies will need business people who have good writing skills. For example, you may get your first important job because of your educational training and/or experience; but if you want to advance in the company, you will need more than technical skills. You will also need communication skills, one of which is the ability to report information.

THE NEED FOR REPORTS

Sometimes reported information is routine, and the decisions — based on the reports — are routine ones that keep the business operating. However, in most organizations reports serve one general pur-

"Sounds good. Can you get the report to us by next Monday?"

pose: to present facts that will somehow be used in decision making. Another reason for reports is to keep management informed about the business climate in the organization. Employees perform poorly when they are uncertain about what is going on in their company; this uncertainty breeds insecurity and prevents employees from using their energies and ideas creatively and productively. The role of reports in keeping management informed is thus sometimes called *uncertainty reduction,* and while it is not the primary reason for reports, it nevertheless is an important one.

Perhaps until now you have thought that only middle- or upper-level managers compiled reports. This is not so. Reports are generated at every level of the organization, from the clerical worker to the president. Consider these examples:

A bank teller submits a daily internal control report of the financial activity of one particular station.

A first-line supervisor in a production facility submits a weekly report of the items produced by the line.

A sales representative completes an expense report to be submitted for reimbursement of business-related activities.

A bookkeeper for Store No. 10 of a regional grocery chain reports on weekly sales volume for each department in the store.

But what becomes of these reports, and how are they used in decision making? The bank teller's report goes to the branch manager, the first-line supervisor's report goes to the department head, the sales representative's report goes to the sales manager, and the bookkeeper's report is reviewed by the store manager and forwarded to the area manager. Usually, then, reports are *upward communication* — that is, they are written for *immediate* superiors.

After receiving a report, the superior may use it in one of several ways. For example, the superior may analyze and interpret the information to make immediate decisions that affect the department, division, branch, or store. Or the superior may condense the information and report it to the next higher superior — the manager on the next rung of the hierarchy. The manager at the next level may use the information to make a decision or again may only condense or coordinate the report with other information for use at the next echelon. And so on.

Occasionally, a manager will receive and pass on information that a co-worker needs for making decisions. These reports are *lateral communications;* they are used by people on a similar level rather than by superiors or by subordinates. Furthermore, certain parts of a single report may be sent to several people at different levels of the organization for their use in making decisions. The decisions may eventually affect people at all levels through other reports; this process is *radial communication*.

The following example better illustrates how reports are used. Jack Blankenship is a food service manager at a theme park that is open year round. Figure 1–1 shows a partial organization chart for the park so you can see where Jack fits into the organization. Jack has an assistant manager who completes a daily report of food sales activities at their concession, the Main Street Ice Cream Parlor. Jack reviews the report and sends it to his superior, Mary O'Malley, an area food service manager.

Mary coordinates all activities — from settling minor personnel problems to authorizing orders for food purchases — for Jack's and for four other concessions at the park. Mary uses Jack's and the other four managers' reports to authorize orders for food supplies each day. As you can imagine, not all days at a theme park generate the same amount of revenue in food sales, so the area managers refer to past sales reports from similar periods to predict quantities of supplies needed. For example, Mary knows that on Tuesdays less revenue is generated from food sales than on weekends when more visitors come to the park. She also knows from past reports that certain seasons of the year and certain holidays generate a higher percentage of revenue than others. She must use this information to assist the managers in ordering the right quantity of food and supplies.

When Mary has compiled orders from all five of the food service managers, she submits the report to Jim Canale, Food Service Buyer, who purchases all food supplies for the park. She also sends her report and certain other information to the data processing department to be used later in computer-generated reports. As you can see from the chart, Mary and another manager make all decisions about quantities to be purchased. However, Jim contacts the suppliers and actually places the orders. He deals with local food wholesalers and with area sales representatives from other companies for certain supplies such as straws, napkins, and paper cups. Jim's greatest concern is to get the best quality for the best price with the most efficient delivery.

On some items, such as cleaning supplies that are used not only in food service but also in other operations in the park, Jack must requisition from the stores facility these supplies for Main Street Ice Cream Parlor. Another buyer, a co-worker of Jim, uses computer-based reports that are generated from the requisitions and from the stores personnel to determine the quantities of these kinds of supplies to purchase.

Jim must report to his superior, Charlene Oberholzer, Food Operations Manager, about quantities, costs, and so on. Charlene's greatest concern is that each of the park's eleven food concessions turns the profit percentage that has been established for them for each month.

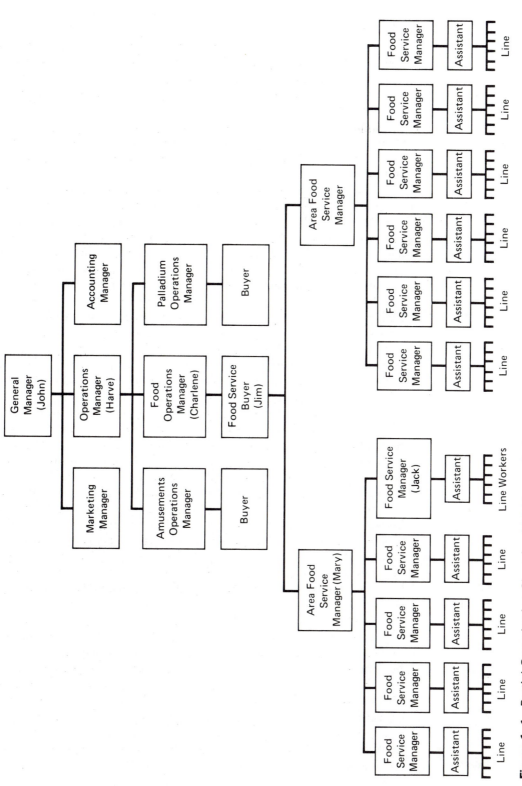

Figure 1–1 Partial Organization Chart for ABC Theme Park

Daily, she receives a computer printout of the activities of each of the concessions. If any problems occur, she can work with the area food service managers, who will work with individual food service managers to correct the problem.

Charlene reports to Harve Brown, Operations Manager; he is responsible for all operations in the park, including food service. Because food sales generate a good percentage of the park's revenue, Harve keeps close account of this area's progress. Every month Charlene submits a report to him, summarizing the activities of all eleven food concessions.

Harve reports to John Aston, General Manager of the park. Using reported information and informal meetings with Harve and other managers in accounting and marketing, John establishes policies, allocates monies for various operations at the park, and so forth. The organization chart shows only the structure of the theme park itself; however, the park is owned by a corporation that operates other such parks, so John reports to upper management at corporate headquarters.

So far, the reporting we have seen in this organization has been lateral or upward communication. However, reports can come from the top down. For example, while goals, objectives, and budgets are based on reports coming from the lower levels of management, it is these lower levels that must carry out new plans. The best way to communicate these plans is often through reports. For example, John Aston will allocate a certain dollar amount of revenue to operations; Harve Brown must then allocate that budget among all operations at the park, so he must report his allocation decision to his subordinates. Those managers also must allocate their portion of the budget among all their subordinates. For example, Charlene must allocate her budget among the eleven food concessions at the park. She will then report her decisions to the area food service managers, who will in turn pass the information to the food service managers. The eleven food service managers receive weekly computer printouts showing how well they are meeting the objectives, goals, and budgetary constraints that have been established by upper levels of management.

Similar printouts go to the upper-level managers so they can also monitor their own progress as managers. Specifically, these printouts indicate whether a superior's downward communication was successful. The superior's success is directly related to the quality of productivity by his or her subordinates, and managers know that most subordinates will perform well when told clearly and specifically what is expected of them.

This example is a simplification of the decision-making process; however, you can see the importance of reports in the process. Before leaving this section, let us remind you that although political parties, colleges and universities, governmental, not-for-profit, and other such organizations may not seem like businesses, their organizational structure *is* usually like that found in businesses. Similarly, reports are generated and used in the same way as in businesses: to make decisions.

You will have a specific objective(s) to achieve when you report information, and your objectives will fall into one or more of the following categories:

COMMUNICATION OBJECTIVES FOR REPORTS

1. *The audience should be able to make a practical decision.* Most upward communication will consider this objective as primary. The report must present to the reader all the facts that are relevant to making the decision in an accurate and clear manner. Note that the report does not try to persuade or influence the audience to make a particular decision; it merely presents the facts.

2. *The audience should be able to perform a task.* Some reports, particularly those prepared for subordinates or co-workers, must contain "how to" information if the objective is to teach them to perform a particular task. The report must present specific details in a logical, step-by-step manner. Again, note that the report does not try to persuade or motivate the audience; it merely gives them instructions.

3. *The audience should have information requiring no immediate decision.* This objective is often established for downward communication. The report gives information to keep the reader abreast of happenings in the organization; however, no decision is required, based on the information. Later, the information, along with other information, may be used to make a decision.

4. *The audience should be motivated to do something.* This objective is useful when a report must convince the reader to make a change, to accept a new idea, and so on. The report must show the reader how the new idea will be of benefit. Often this objective is used in conjunction with another objective.

5. *The audience should approve of your organization* (or of you or your ideas). This objective is often established when writing for audiences outside the organization. This objective means that you promote rather than persuade; you point out all the positive aspects. Like the preceding one, this objective is often used in conjunction with another objective.

Based on the five objectives discussed above, all reports can be grouped into three categories:

Informational reports

Analytical reports

Recommendation reports

To understand these categories better, consider the fact that managers at all levels have limited authority. They have sole decision-making power in some areas, none at all in others. The manager who is the final authority uses reports of subordinates to make immediate decisions. The manager whose decision-making power is limited gathers — usually through subordinates — condenses, or coordinates, and reports information (*informational report*) so a superior can use the data to make a decision. Informational reports also include downward reports that give subordinates information requiring no immediate decision or that give them information for performing a task. Other informational reports give customers or clients facts about the organization. Finally, informational reports giving positive details to promote the organization are often written for those outside it.

The manager who has some authority or great expertise gathers information, interprets it, and presents the analysis (*analytical report*) to a superior. The superior may base a decision on the analysis or may simply review or revise it and present the report to the superior on the next rung of the ladder. Most reports that require the reader to make decisions will interpret information — that is, show relationships among the facts for the reader.

In some cases, the manager may gather information, analyze it, and even make recommendations for implementing the plan, solving the problem, or changing the way things are done (*recommendation report*). However, final implementation of the recommendations rests with someone else in the organization who reads the report. This type of report attempts to persuade or to motivate the reader to a particular course of action.

THE IMPORTANCE OF ACCURACY

In this chapter you have seen that the original reports submitted by the bank teller, the supervisor, the bookkeeper, the sales representative, and the theme park employees never reached the upper levels of management directly. Instead, the information they reported was often condensed, put into a different form, and passed on to the next echelon. Often in their eagerness to please or impress superiors, report writers will paint a rosier picture than actually exists. Such distortion of facts — especially if done at every level — results in skewed information, which ultimately results in a poor decision. When a poor decision is made, top management must take responsibility, and rightly so. Usually subordinates who present themselves or the company in a better light than actually exists do so because they feel pressure from their immediate superior to perform well. This pressure is usually generated at the upper levels of management and is forced down through all other levels.

Of course, working for an organization where honesty, directness, and frankness are valued by top management is preferable. Only in such an atmosphere can report writers feel free to give an accurate account of facts and observations. If you are fortunate enough to work for such a company, you must learn to organize material carefully and to present it clearly and honestly. Succeeding chapters will show you how to become more skillful and accurate in reporting information.

SUMMARY

Business communication media include phone conversations, memos, letters, computer terminals, and so on. However, the written medium, particularly in the form of reports, is most often used because it provides a permanent record of business transactions.

A report is an organized, objective presentation of facts, observations, or experiences. Reports can summarize, explain, describe, or recommend; they may be used either within or outside the organization. Reports are prepared by people at all levels in an organization, from the clerical worker to the president. However, most reports are part of the upward flow of communication within an organization and are therefore prepared for immediate superiors and others up the chain of command.

The primary purpose of reports is to aid in the decision-making process required of managers at all levels; the writer's objective, however, determines the kind and treatment of information that is presented.

Many reports are routine; they are used to keep the business operating. Others are used to keep employees informed about what is happening in the organization. Still others serve more specific purposes. Generally, a report can (1) present information, (2) analyze information or a situation, or (3) recommend a plan or some action.

Since superiors depend on subordinates to assume certain responsibilities, a subordinate must be careful to report information accurately. Facts that are distorted at the lower levels will result in skewed information reaching the top management. Consequently, the ultimate decision will also be less than accurate.

LEARNING ACTIVITIES

1. Explain why report writing is usually upward communication.

2. What kinds of reports are generated at the lowest levels of an organization?

3. Once a superior has received a subordinate's report, what are the two *general* uses that may be made of it?

4. What are the differences among an informational report, an analytical report, and a recommendation report? Explain.

5. What is the role subordinates play in the accuracy of decisions that are ultimately made by top management of an organization? Explain.

6. Use your own work experience as the basis for discussing the reporting process in a particular company. Were the reports you saw upward, downward, lateral, or radial communications?

7. Go back to the example of the theme park employees in this chapter. Dissect the example and discuss which parts showed upward, downward, lateral, and radial communication. Try to develop an original illustration that shows this park's communication flows, based on the information given in the example.

8. Review the communication objectives for reports in this chapter and give examples of some types of reports that would have as their objective each of those discussed.

Analyzing and Interpreting Information and Planning the Report

LEARNING OBJECTIVES

After reading this chapter, you should be able to:

- Describe the steps in analyzing a problem;
- Explain why *audience analysis* is important in report writing;
- Explain the difference between *primary* and *secondary* audiences;
- List the three steps to follow in planning a report;
- Explain the term *statement of purpose;*
- Explain the difference between an *informal* and *formal* outline;
- List five of the many methods of organizing a report.

How will you know when you must prepare a report? Sometimes your superior will assign you, or a small group comprising you and your co-workers, to find a solution to a problem. At other times you will see things that might be improved; as an aggressive employee, you would present your suggestions to your superior in a report. On still other occasions, your work with customers or clients will necessitate preparing reports for them. As we saw in Chapter 1, some reports will require only a presentation of information; others will require solving a problem (analysis), and some will require making recommendations.

UNDERSTANDING A PROBLEM

Regardless of how the assignment comes about, you must have a clear grasp of what is expected of you before you can write anything. This is particularly true if you are to solve a problem. The following steps to understanding a problem and the example that accompanies each one will help you:

1. *State the problem.* Your engineering department is overcrowded; more work space is needed.

2. *List the needs, assumptions, and constraints surrounding the problem.* Because of one piece of equipment used in the department, ceilings in the work space must be 8 ft. high. Any new space must be larger than the current 500 sq. ft. of space; specifically, space is needed for at least one 3-ft. × 5-ft. desk for a new CRT terminal to be used in computer-created designs.

3. *List possible solutions.* All space in the building is being used to capacity; however, the company leases some office space in a building across the street. Currently, one small part of that space is not being used for offices. Another solution is to look elsewhere for space to rent.

4. *Determine the solution that has least disadvantages.* Since the company is still small, it is best to keep all operations in close proximity. Trying to use the space across the street seems to be the best alternative. You decide to test this solution. This proposed solution may be called a *hypothesis*. A hypothesis is a tentative explanation or solution for some factual question or problem — an unproven hunch. It is based on the researcher's knowledge, past experiences in similar situations, and factual information relating to the question or problem. In our example, you can see that the more you know about the company, its policies, and its goals, plus the facts from the immediate problem, the bet-

ter able you are to establish a hypothesis. The most critical step, though, is the next one: testing the hypothesis.

5. *Test the hypothesis (proposed solution).* There are several parts to this step:
   a. *Define the procedure for testing.* You decide to visit the area across the street and measure it to see if it suits your needs. If it does, you must then find out if your department could move into it.
   b. *Collect the data.* You make the following observations and find these measurements:
      i. Presently, the area is used to store old office furniture.
      ii. The main room is 20 ft. × 30 ft.; the ceiling averages 7 ft. 11 7/8 in. high.
      iii. Another small officelike area across the corridor from the main room measures 10 ft. × 10 ft.; the ceiling height averages 8 ft.
   c. *Analyze the data.* The ceilings in the main room are too low for the tall piece of equipment; however, the ceilings in the small area are higher and could accommodate it. The main room has 100 sq. ft. more space than does the present engineering area.
   d. *Draw a conclusion.* The engineering department could use the space by putting the tall piece of equipment in the small office area. There would be ample space for the new desk and CRT terminal in the large area.

More information on the four parts of testing a hypothesis can be found in Chapter 3.

Often when testing a hypothesis, the researcher will run into problems because of making incorrect or incomplete inferences. An *inference* is the connection one makes — right or wrong — between two or more facts. When an inference is made from raw data, it is called a *finding.* For example, you know the tall piece of equipment needs a space 8 ft. high (fact 1). You also know that the large storage space has ceilings 7 ft. 11 7/8 in. high (fact 2). You could infer that the tall equipment will not fit in this area; this inference is a finding because it is based on the raw data.

When a further inference is made, based on your finding, it is a *conclusion.* You could conclude that engineering cannot use the space across the street, based on the preceding finding. If a final inference is made, based on the conclusion, it is called a *recommendation.* Based on the conclusion above, you could recommend that the engineering department stay where it is since all of its equipment would not fit in the space across the street. That seems like a logical answer. However, you can see in this example that an incorrect inference was made because some of the raw data were not considered (the small officelike space).

Another problem can arise when raw data are interpreted incorrectly or too literally. For example, did you take the *exact* measurements of the piece of equipment? Does it really need 8 ft. of ceiling space, or is the 7-ft. 11 7/8-in. ceiling high enough? In this case, *specifications* must be considered; they are often stated within a small *range* of dimensions, so the equipment might fit in the large room after all.

Generally, problems are not as simple as the preceding example. In fact, if the conclusion is accurate, the real work has yet to begin: getting cost figures on repainting or redecorating the area, making an estimate of time required for the move, and establishing a timetable to make the move. The same steps would again be applied to these aspects of the problem. In fact, most problems do require performing the steps several times.

Another common mistake people make when analyzing a problem is failing to see all aspects of it and therefore not performing a complete analysis. For instance, in the example just discussed you may have noticed that some important aspects of the problem were overlooked: Are the doors in the new space wide enough to get all equipment through them? Is the tall piece of equipment exactly 8 ft. high? What are its other dimensions? Will the large piece of equipment take up so much space in the small 10-ft. × 10-ft. space that it will be hard to work in the area? Will the people using the small room feel isolated from others in the department?

Once you have thoroughly analyzed a problem and have made logical and complete inferences, you must write them so that the reader clearly sees how you arrived at the conclusion or recommendation. This example shows the various inferences:

> The small office space across the street can be used for our large piece of equipment (conclusion), *because* the ceilings are 8 ft. high and the 10-ft. × 10-ft. floor space will allow ample work space (findings). The larger area will provide more work space, including space for a desk for a CRT terminal (conclusion), *since* it has 100 sq. ft. more space than our present location (finding). *Therefore,* I recommend we pursue plans to move the engineering department (recommendation).

Sometimes with a complex problem you will automatically perform the steps discussed here on certain aspects of a problem. However, to test your analysis, run it through the steps again. Making a careful analysis of a problem will assure that you are not jumping to incorrect conclusions or recommending an infeasible course of action. Either of those errors in your report could cause someone else to make a poor decision, which in the long run could hurt your own career aspirations.

After you have analyzed a problem or gathered information for a report, you are ready to plan how to write it. The next sections discuss three easy planning steps.

Audience analysis is a conscious effort to understand the needs, thoughts, feelings, idiosyncrasies, and so forth of the person or group of people to whom you are reporting, and to give them what they want without sacrificing what you want or need. Look at the following example of audience analysis.

STEP 1: ANALYZE YOUR AUDIENCE

Yesterday, Bill Habercomb met with Sally Knudson to discuss next year's budget. He has known and worked with Sally for three years, so he understands her department's concerns, her personality, and how she reacts to various approaches in a discussion. He knows that she takes her work seriously and comes prepared to any meeting, but she seems nervous and sometimes inattentive until she has had a chance to make her presentation; then she relaxes. At this meeting, Bill let Sally begin by telling him how she proposed to budget next year's funds. When she finished, Bill gave his opinions. There was an easy give-and-take discussion, and they finally reached a compromise that was satisfactory to both of them. Bill's understanding of and *conscious attempt* to relate to Sally on her terms caused him to be successful in this meeting because he encouraged rather than antagonized his audience.

Similarly, when preparing a report, know your audience. Be empathetic; try to understand the audience's weak spot and use it in a *positive* way rather than angering or putting the other person on the defensive. For example, if you know that Jack is slightly intimidated by you because you are an accountant, do not write reports for him in language that only someone familiar with Financial Accounting Standards Board (FASB) rulings could understand. Instead, use simpler words and devise simpler ways of presenting your figures to him. Such consideration will pay off later in the good rapport you build with him; he will return the favor in many ways.

In another situation, if you know that Mrs. Wong is a perfectionist, do not insult her by submitting anything less than your best effort, even if it means staying late at the office several nights. Or, if you know that Vice-President Harrison will not read anything over five pages long, use tables, figures, and other shortcuts to make your reports brief and to the point in less than five pages.

When analyzing your audience, the most important question to ask yourself is, What does this audience want, need, or expect from me? Once you have decided on an answer, ask yourself how (by what approach) you can meet their expectations without sacrificing your own expectations or principles.

So far we have discussed reports written for use within the organization. However, reports are also prepared for customers, clients, grantors, or patrons who need detailed information before making a decision on a large purchase, a contract, or a grant. For example, a sales representative calls on a company to sell it a temperature control system for a new addition to its present building. After discussing the customer's needs, cost concerns, and special problems, the representative returns to the office to work out the details with the engineering staff. The representative then writes a detailed report for the customer; the report contains a description of the best system for the building, how much it will cost, when it can be installed, and the services that will be provided after installation.

Reports of this kind are often written for both primary and secondary audiences. The *primary audience* is the person(s) who will directly receive the report and will probably read it in its entirety. Often, too, this is the person who has the power to make decisions, based on what is in the report. The primary audience often gives the report to the *secondary audience* to read, the purpose being either to get a second opinion or to let the secondary audience know what is going on in the organization.

A skillful writer always analyzes the *primary* audience for whom a report is to be written because the primary audience will determine both the content and the tone of the report. But whether the report is written for a superior or for a customer or client, the writer should ask these questions:

What does my audience want or need to know from me?

What method of arranging the material will be best understood?

What word choices will make the most favorable impression?

Which writing style (personal or impersonal) does my audience expect?

Later chapters will help you answer these questions. However, since reports are written for decision makers, the most important of these questions is, What does my audience want or need to know from me? Once you have answered that question, you are ready for step 2.

Goals! Objectives! You have heard these two words used every day in business. No doubt you believe that unless you have goals or objectives — something very specific to aim for — you can easily get sidetracked and end up accomplishing very little. The same is true of reports: you must know what you want to accomplish if you want to write a good one.

Step 2 is to write out a brief *statement of purpose* telling what you want to accomplish. This statement will be the controlling sentence or thesis of the report. Look at the following statements of purpose:

> I want to tell Joe what the XR 500 desk-top terminal can do for us. (Purpose: to inform.)

> I will show Mrs. Jabowski how eliminating the supplemental insurance on rental cars can save us money. (Purpose: to analyze.)

> I want to suggest that we hold the regional meeting in Corning rather than in Rochester. (Purpose: to recommend.)

Be specific when writing the statement of purpose. The following sentence is not narrow enough in scope to be useful to the writer in organizing the report:

> I want to talk about the XR 500 desk-top terminal.

Because the sentence is too general, the report will either ramble aimlessly or will end up looking like the brochure the manufacturer uses to market the XR 500. In either case, the writer's superior will probably not get the pertinent information about the XR 500 — that is, what it can do for the company.

Be precise and accurate, too, when writing the statement of purpose. The following sentence does not say exactly what the writer intends to do:

> I will discuss both the XR 500 and the Savvy 6000 desk-top terminals.

A report based on this sentence may wander aimlessly from machine to machine. Again, the reader may not get the pertinent information: what each of these machines can do for the company. A more precise and accurate statement of purpose is this one:

> I will *compare* what each of these desk-top terminals can do for us: the XR 500 and the Savvy 6000.

With this new controlling sentence you can organize the report in one of two ways. One is to divide it into two parts; discuss everything that the XR 500 can do for the company in one part and everything that the Savvy 6000 can do for the company in the other (a divided comparison). The second method is to look at the major advantages of each model; then discuss one advantage of the XR 500 and the similar advantage of the Savvy 6000, and so on until all advantages are covered (an alternating comparison). Organizing a report will be discussed further in the next step.

As was mentioned earlier in this chapter, there are three basic reporting functions: to inform, to analyze, and to recommend. The statement of purpose that you write in step 2 will not only show you which of these functions your report will serve but will also help you to know what to include in the report. If your purpose is simply to inform, you will organize and present only facts or observations. If your purpose is to analyze, you will also organize and present facts or observations; in addition, you will interpret (analyze) what they mean to the reader or to the company. If your purpose is to recommend, you will organize and present facts or observations, you will interpret them, and finally, you will recommend that a particular course of action be followed. Table 2–1 shows the various layers of information required for each of the reporting functions.

A final word of advice is needed about these three types of reports: the function of the report will *not* determine its length. For example, although informational reports require only a presentation of facts or observations, you may need ten pages to discuss a complex topic. On the other hand, even though a recommendation report requires that you do three things, some topics can be discussed and analyzed and a course of action recommended in two or three pages.

Table 2–1   Kinds of Information to Include in Reports

	TYPE OF REPORT		
	Informative	Analytical	Recommendation
WHAT TO WRITE:	1. Organize and present facts and observations.	1. Organize and present facts and observations. 2. Interpret facts and observations.	1. Organize and present facts and observations. 2. Interpret facts and observations. 3. Recommend a course of action.

Have you ever written something that did not "hang together"? You knew something was wrong, but you could not pinpoint the problem? Usually when that happens, either you have not *planned* what you wanted to say or there is a fault in the planning. Step 3, preparing an outline, is an essential part of reporting; it is the plan for the report.

The introduction of your outline is simply the statement of purpose you wrote in step 2. Since this is the controlling sentence for the entire report, it also governs the preparation of the outline.

The Introduction

The body of the outline takes up the greatest amount of space and requires the most work. It must carry out the statement of purpose you used as the introduction. Each heading you write in this part of the outline has its own job to do. Since the body of the report will present facts or observations, analyze facts, and so forth, the heads of your outline should indicate the facts, analysis, and so forth that you want to discuss in the report. In short, the body is the most important part of the outline.

The Body

    The structure of the body of the outline can be handled in either of two ways, as shown here:

Standard Structure

I. First-degree head
  A. Second-degree head
  B. Second-degree head
    1. Third-degree head
    2. Third-degree head
      a. Fourth-degree head
      b. Fourth-degree head
      c. Fourth-degree head
II. First-degree head

Technical Structure

1.0 First-degree head
  1.1 Second-degree head
  1.2 Second-degree head
    1.2.1 Third-degree head
    1.2.2 Third-degree head
      1.2.2.1 Fourth-degree head
      1.2.2.2 Fourth-degree head
      1.2.2.3 Fourth-degree head
2.0 First-degree head

The main reason for using one of these forms is to check your logic when planning a report. Logical organization includes these items:

1. Each of the *first-degree heads* shows the most important divisions of the report. Since these are the key ideas, list all of them *first* to be sure you do not leave any out. Also, they should be written in similar grammatical form. *Second-, third-, and fourth-degree heads* are subheads and go in pairs; each pair refers to or explains the head under which it is placed.

2. All the subheads under any one main head should be written in similar grammatical form to give continuity to your ideas.

3. If you have only one idea as a subhead, combine it as a part of the mean head rather than having it stand alone.

There are basically two patterns for organizing information: the *inductive* (also called indirect and logical) and the *deductive* (also called direct and psychological). However, there are many variations of those patterns. In fact, all of the methods of organization discussed in this chapter are variations of these two patterns.

The inductive approach moves from the known to the unknown. For example, we may begin with known facts and use them to reach a conclusion, as can be seen in the following simple example:

Facts: 1. The outside temperature is 88°.
           2. The temperature inside our office is 82°.
           3. No cool air is circulating in the office.

Conclusion: The air-conditioning system is not functioning in our part of the building.

The deductive approach is opposite the inductive approach in that we start with the conclusion and then work back to the facts to support it as this example shows:

Conclusion: The air-conditioning system is not functioning in our part of the building *because* . . .

Facts: 1. No air is circulating in our office.
           2. The outside temperature is 88°.
           3. The temperature in our office is 82°.

These two patterns of organizing information may be used not only to construct the outline but also to develop sentences, paragraphs, or whole sections of a report.

Usually by the time we are adults, our past experience in living enables us to plan and organize our time and activities to accomplish the things we want to do. We usually do not make written plans for carrying out these activities unless our life gets very busy; we just make the plans in our heads. We can transfer this ability to outlining the body of a report. We should first think about what to do in the report. Then we should decide what should come first, second, and so on to make the report logical and easy to follow. This process usually results in utilizing one of the variations for organizing the body discussed next, although we seldom take time to analyze consciously which one we are using. The following brief discussion of each variation may give you some ideas for organizing the body of future reports.

One variation is the *problem/solution plan*. The body of the outline consists of two major parts: a discussion of the problem and a suggestion for a solution. This method is especially useful for analytical or recommendation reports. A problem/solution outline will look like this one:

Statement of purpose: This report will explore a solution to our problem of high long-distance phone call expenses.

  I. **Problem:** Give facts about problem.
    A. Long-distance calls have increased (find out exact percentages).
    B. Use of letters and teletype has not decreased (check to be sure this is still so).
    C. Currently our phone bill is over $850 a month or nearly $10,500 a year (check these figures again).
    D. Sales have increased only modestly (get exact percentage).

  II. **Solution:** Install a WATS line.
    A. Cost to us (call J. T. at phone company to review information on cost).
      1. Initial cost.
      2. Monthly cost.
    B. Cost comparison — present system vs. WATS line.

Notice that to be valid this report must cover not only the increased cost of doing business but also the volume of business generated by the increased cost. Also notice that the headings in the outline are numbered or lettered; this makes it a *formal outline*. However, you may dispense with the numbers and letters to create an *informal outline,* as long as you follow the strict logic of the formal outline. The example shown with the next plan shows an informal outline.

Another method of organizing information is the *chronological plan,* in which you organize the information according to events as they occurred in time. The body of the outline might look like this:

Statement of purpose: I will analyze our records in lending to XYZ Corporation over the past 20 years to determine if we can lend them the requested $500,000 to build a new office at their local plant.

Loan in 1959
Purpose of loan
Amount and terms of loan
Method and promptness of repayment
Financial condition of company at that time

Loan in 1965
Purpose of loan
Amount and terms of loan
Method and promptness of repayment
Financial condition of company at that time

Loan in 1971
Purpose of loan
Amount and terms of loan
Method and promptness of repayment
Financial condition of company at that time

Loan in 1978
Purpose of loan
Amount and terms of loan
Method and promptness of repayment
Financial condition of company at that time

Loan requested in 1983
Purpose of loan
Amount and terms of loan
Method and promptness of repayment
Financial condition of company at that time

Notice that again the writer has tried to consider all the data to find a valid answer to the question, "Should we lend XYZ Corp. the money?" Not only has the writer considered the previous loans and how they were repaid but also the financial condition of the company at the time of each loan. The brief mental history of the company that emerges from this chronological plan will enable the writer to predict the company's financial success.

A third method of organization is the *comparison/contrast plan,* which is useful when you want to compare or contrast two or more similar options. Earlier in this chapter we mentioned that there are two ways of handling a comparison or contrast. Using the earlier example, the two kinds of outlines might look like this:

Statement of purpose: This report will compare what each of these desk-top terminals can do for us: the XR 500 and the Savvy 6000.

Divided Comparison/Contrast Method	**Alternating Comparison/Contrast Method**

I. The XR 500
  A. Size: space needed to install
  B. Cost
  C. Application
  D. Software available for future use
II. The Savvy 6000
  A. Size
  B. Cost
  C. Application
  D. Software available for future use
	I. Size: space needed to install
	  A. XR 500
	  B. Savvy 6000
	II. Cost
	  A. XR 500
	  B. Savvy 6000
	III. Application
	  A. XR 500
	  B. Savvy 6000
	IV. Other software available for future use
	  A. XR 500
	  B. Savvy 6000

A fourth method of organizing a report is the *cause/effect plan.* Outlined the same way as the problem/solution plan, it is useful when you need to show how a current problem can affect future business or when you need to trace an effect back to its cause. The outline below uses the cause/effect plan.

Statement of purpose: I want to show the Production Control Manager the causes and the immediate effect of production being off by 8 percent in our Cord Department, and I will make a recommendation for getting back to full-capacity production.

1.0 Causes of our problems:
  1.1 Decline of 5 percent in customer demand in the entire Electronic division has hurt us.
  1.2 Decline in lead time in Electrical division has hurt our ability to meet customer time demands.

1.3 Lower overhead in Electrical division means they can sell at lower prices (check for exact figures on this).

2.0 Effect on the company:

2.1 Cost of idle capacity is $300,000 per year (check this).

2.2 Cost of employing full-capacity shift when sales are off is $100,000 per year (union contract says that we must employ a minimum of ten people in the Cord Department).

3.0 Solution to problem of idle capacity: begin making molded electronic leads in the Cord Department.

3.1 Can use present machinery.

3.1.1 New molds can be used on present machinery.

3.1.2 Cost of molds is reasonable (cite specific costs).

3.2 Can make better use of human resources.

3.3 Can increase earnings.

3.3.1 Projected earnings from new sales (get figures from Sales/Marketing).

3.3.2 Projected savings from using shift employees more productively.

Yet another way of organizing a report is the *place or location plan*. This plan works well when reporting on several locations, such as offices or plants in other countries or in several regions of the United States. It is also useful when reporting on proposed sites for new construction.

In a report to the president of a small company, the vice-president of manufacturing used the following outline to plan a report on the quarterly activities of three plants in the corporation.

Statement of purpose: This report will show production figures at our three plants during the quarter ended September 30, 1982.

I. Wyndham, CT Plant

A. Units produced/cost

B. Units scrapped/cost

C. Units salvaged/reworked/cost

II. Elmore, PA Plant

A. Units produced/cost

B. Units scrapped/cost

C. Units salvaged/reworked/cost

III. Elmira, NY Plant

A. Units produced/cost

B. Units scrapped/cost

C. Units salvaged/reworked/cost

Another method of organizing a report is the *function plan*. Such a report deals with the work done by particular segments of the organization. In the partial outline that follows, one function of a company (production) is discussed and is further broken down — again by function — into its components:

> **II. Accounting/Finance**
> **III. Production**
>   A. Production Control and Planning
>   B. Department 30
>   C. Department 20
>   D. Department 10
>   E. Shipping
>   F. Receiving
> **IV. Sales/Marketing**

A seventh method of organizing a report is the *order of importance plan*. This method is useful in preparing any kind of report in which one aspect of the report is more important than others, which must nevertheless be discussed. An example of this plan is a progress report; such a report might look like the informal outline that follows, which shows only the first-degree heads:

> *Statement of purpose:*   I will report on the progress in developing Compound T12 to replace TRIS, which was banned by the Food and Drug Administration.

> Brief summary of work already done in Phase I
> Detailed account of what we have accomplished recently in Phase II
> Brief discussion what we have yet to do in Phase III

Sometimes the only way to organize a report is by the *factor plan* — that is, discussing those factors that are significant to the reader. The following is such an outline by John Bruce, who owns a small company that installs and services in-ground pools. A prospective customer, Mr. Caldwell, asks for detailed information about putting a pool in his backyard. John knows that the way to impress a customer (and useful too in getting a bank loan to finance a pool) is to prepare a brief report for the customer.

> *Statement of purpose:*   I will show Mr. Caldwell the feasibility of installing a pool and discuss the cost.

1.0 Analysis of the proposed site of the pool
    1.1 Size and configuration of back yard
    1.2 Size and configuration of proposed pool (include diagram showing yard and pool)

2.0 Cost of the project
    2.1 Initial cost includes:
        2.1.1 Site preparation
        2.1.2 Construction cost
        2.1.3 Equipment for pool
        2.1.4 Complete list of specifications
    2.2 Cost of upkeep for one year includes:
        2.2.1 Chemicals
        2.2.2 General maintenance
        2.2.3 Cover and winterization

3.0 Financing options (at personal bank)
    3.1 Home improvement loan
    3.2 Refinancing home
    3.3 Second mortgage on home

A final method of organization is by the *quantity plan*. Like the others mentioned, this plan can be used to organize the major divisions (first-degree heads) of a report, or it can be used to subdivide the major divisions. For example, a report could be organized first by function and then subdivided by quantity as this partial outline shows:

Statement of purpose: This report will analyze the decline in sales volume in both our retail and wholesale divisions during the first quarter.

Retail Sales Division
    Departments with sales under $10,000/week
      1. _____
      2. _____
      3. _____
      4. _____
      5. _____
    Departments with sales under $15,000/week
      1. _____
      2. _____
      3. _____

Departments with sales under $20,000/week

1. _____
2. _____

Wholesale Division

A conclusion results from an investigation of a problem. The conclusion comes at the end of the outline and prepares the reader to take some kind of action. If the report is analytical, only a conclusion is needed; if it is a recommendation report, both a conclusion and a recommendation are needed.

As you can see from the outlines shown earlier, sometimes the outcome or conclusion cannot be predicted until all the facts have been gathered and the report written. Specifically, the outline under the factor plan is such an example. Until he has analyzed the site and costed the labor, materials, and overhead, John cannot predict what the pool will cost. However, he knows that the kind of conclusion he wants will look like this:

Conclusion: We can build a 20-ft. × 40-ft. pool on this property at a cost of $_____.

When the report is finished, John will be able to supply the final dollar amount.

Here is another outline that shows a conclusion. The two stockholders in L & M Heating and Air Conditioning, Inc., a 35-year-old company, want to sell the company because they plan to retire; they have no relatives who want to continue the business. Jim Blakey and Jack Sprunkel are commercial heating and air-conditioning representatives who presently work for a large electric utility company. They heard about L & M and would like to purchase the business. They ask their accountant to determine the financial position of the company, based on figures given to them by L & M's accountant. Jim and Jack's accountant prepares an informal outline:

Statement of purpose: I will show my clients the financial position of L & M Heating and Air Conditioning, Inc., based on financial records from 1978–1982.

Evaluate financial position by comparison with industry averages:

Quick ratio
  Brief explanation of the ratio
  Comparison with industry averages
Current ratio
  Brief explanation of the ratio
  Comparison with industry averages
Fixed assets/net worth
  Brief explanation of fixed assets/net worth
  Comparison with industry averages
Total debt/net worth
  Brief explanation of total debt/net worth
  Comparison with industry averages
Sales/receivables
  Brief explanation of sales/receivable
  Comparison with industry averages
Sales/working capital
  Brief explanation of sales/working capital
  Comparison with industry averages
Net worth/profit
  Brief explanation of net worth/profit
  Comparison with industry averages
Profit/total assets
  Brief explanation of profit/total assets
  Comparison with industry averages
Return on working capital
  Brief explanation of return on working capital
  Comparison with industry averages
Sales per day
  Brief explanation of sales per day
  Comparison with industry averages
Collection period
  Brief explanation of collection period
  Comparison with industry averages

(Construct table to show comparison of each ratio with industry averages for each year)

Conclusions: Closing statement on L & M's financial position.

    Again, the reporter cannot write a specific conclusion until the facts have been gathered and analyzed.
    Finally, let us remind you that time spent preparing an outline is time well spent. With a clear plan on paper, the report is much easier to write. The planning steps are easy to remember and only somewhat more difficult to implement:

Step 1: Analyze your audience.

Step 2: State your goal or objective.

Step 3: Outline your strategy for achieving the goal.

SUMMARY

Before you can prepare a report, you must understand what the audience needs from you. If that means solving a problem, you must understand it completely. The following steps are used to analyze a problem: (1) state the problem, (2) list the needs, assumptions, and constraints surrounding the problem, (3) list possible solutions, (4) determine the solution that has fewest disadvantages, and (5) test the hypothesis (proposed solution). Testing the hypothesis includes four parts: (a) define the procedure for testing, (b) collect the data, (c) analyze the data, and (d) draw a conclusion.

In planning a report, follow this three-step procedure: (1) analyze your audience, (2) write the statement of purpose, and (3) prepare an outline of the report. Audience analysis requires a conscious effort on the part of the writer to understand the needs, feelings, predispositions, and idiosyncrasies of the audience for whom a report is written. The writer must then attempt to satisfy that audience's needs and desires without sacrificing personal objectives, wants, and needs. In audience analysis the writer should plan the report for the primary audience — that is, the person(s) who has decision-making power. Secondary audiences are those who have a general interest in the report or an interest in a particular section of it; the primary audience usually passes the report on to a secondary audience for their general information.

The statement of purpose is the controlling sentence or thesis that states specifically what you want to accomplish by writing the report. The statement of purpose should be unified, specific, and accurate since it determines the direction the report will take. If the statement of purpose indicates that the aim is to inform the reader, the report will present facts and observations. If the purpose is to analyze, the report will present facts and observations, and it will interpret them for the reader. If the purpose is to recommend, the report will present facts and observations, interpret them, and recommend a course of action. The outline for the report is the plan for carrying out what the statement of purpose says the report will do. The outline may be informal or formal. The two types of formal outlines are the standard and the technical. A formal outline has three parts: the introduction, the body, and the conclusion. The introduction is simply the statement of purpose, written in step 2. The body of the outline consists of the major points that will be used to prove the statement of purpose.

There are two patterns for organizing information in the body of the outline: the *deductive* and the *inductive*. There are, however, several variations of these patterns. Some of these variations are the problem/solution plan, the chronological plan, the comparison/contrast plan, the cause/effect plan, the place or location plan, the function plan, the order of importance plan, the factor plan, and the quantity plan. The conclusion of the outline states what you think the analysis of the facts will show or states what the relationship is between the facts that are presented.

LEARNING ACTIVITIES

1. To help you understand the concept of audience analysis, bring some popular magazines to class. In small groups, you and your peers should try to answer these questions about the audience for whom one or two magazines are written:

    a. Is there a particular age group that reads this magazine?
    b. What is the socioeconomic level of the readers of this magazine? What evidence do you find in the magazine to support your answer?
    c. What is the life-style of the people who read this magazine? Again, what evidence supports your answer?
    d. Look at the writing style of the articles and answer these questions:
        i.   How long are the sentences (number of words) in an average paragraph?
        ii. How many one-syllable, two-syllable, three-syllable words are used in an average paragraph?
        iii. What is the level of the vocabulary used in the average article?
        iv. What is the educational level of the reader of this magazine?
    e. What do you think the purpose of this magazine is, and why does this particular group of readers read it?
    f. Write a summary of who reads this magazine.

    Suggested magazines to analyze: Cosmopolitan, Good Housekeeping, Business Week, Glamour, Inside Sports, Reader's Digest, Teen Beat, Omni, Gentlemen's Quarterly, People, National Geographic, and Newsweek.

2. Prepare an informal outline for an oral presentation of the findings of your group in the previous exercise. Show the statement of purpose (thesis/introduction), the body, and the conclusion in your outline.

3. Using the steps listed early in this chapter, analyze the following problem. Begin by listing the five steps (and the four parts of step 5); then write your analysis beside the steps. You may have to do some research about shrinkage (shoplifting, employee theft, and so on) to list some possible solutions. You may make any assumptions about the business that you wish. However, list those assumptions so you can check the validity of your analysis of the problem.

BJ's Fashions has had a 15 percent increase in shrinkage this year. The shop is small, and the owner cannot afford to install computerized deterrents. As the owner's consultant, what can you do to solve the problem on the budget of $2,500 that has been allocated?

Obtaining Information for the Report

LEARNING OBJECTIVES

After reading this chapter, you should be able to:

- Describe the difference between *primary* and *secondary* sources of information;
- List four kinds of primary sources of information;
- Explain what kinds of information can be found in indexes, annuals, and business directories;
- Explain how to find information about government agencies and government publications;
- List other sources of information useful in preparing business reports.

Joe Schultz has just completed a report, but he is not very happy with it. He analyzed his audience, wrote a statement of purpose, and prepared an outline. He knew what kinds of information he needed to report, but when he looked at each first-degree heading in his outline and at the second-degree headings under them, he had no idea where to get the information he proposed to discuss; he laid the outline aside. A few days before the report was due, he talked to some of the people in his department and browsed for a while in the company library. Finally, he wrote the report, based on sketchy facts and several hastily contrived "observations." This chapter will help you avoid the pitfalls Joe encountered by discussing where to get material for a report.

Many business reports are based on firsthand information learned by the reporter, whose information is based on the results of experiments and surveys, on observations of a procedure or event, on interviews with experts, and so forth. Such firsthand sources are called *primary sources*. Information from primary sources is usually "raw" — that is, it is purely factual and has not been previously analyzed or interpreted.

PRIMARY SOURCES OF INFORMATION

One of the best sources of information — and one of the most often overlooked — is the information interview with a specialist who works with a particular subject every day. In fact, some reports — for example, those submitted by insurance claims adjustors or by market surveyors — are based entirely on interviews.

Information Interviews

Many people in your organization have expertise you can use; most are willing to share their knowledge if you explain that you do not know much about the subject but want to learn. Add that the specialist's name will be used in the report so that he or she will not think you are trying to steal ideas or information. Including the name of your expert source will also lend credibility to your report. The same rules apply if you are interviewing people outside your organization who can give you information. Of course, do not overlook *any* primary source, especially the local or regional offices of such government agencies as the Small Business Administration and the County Agricultural Extension Service.

Preparation for interviews is important. Sometimes interviews can be conducted by phone; others are best conducted in person so you can benefit from the nonverbal communication that occurs in interpersonal communication situations. Regardless of the method you use, here are some things to do *before* the interview:

1. *Be sure the interviewee is an expert.* For example, if you need information on sales of a particular product last quarter, talk to the sales manager, not the manager's secretary. Even though the secretary may have access to the figures you need, the manager may be able to give you important background information that the secretary may not know about.

2. *Do your homework.* Find out as much as possible about the interviewee's department, position, and idiosyncrasies before the interview. This background work will help you plan how to conduct the interview. Decide what specific questions you want answers to. Open-ended questions — those that require more than a yes or no answer — are best because they encourage the interviewee to talk at some length. An example of an open-ended question is, "What kinds of problems might this present?"

3. *Make an appointment with the interviewee* and give him or her a list of the questions you need answers to. You will be perceived as a thoughtful, organized person in contrast with the one who rushes in and expects the interviewee to drop everything to answer a few spur-of-the-moment questions.

The interview itself also requires some planning. After you have set up an appointment and done your homework, there are other points to remember *during* the interview:

1. At the beginning, *ask how much time the interviewee can spend with you;* then be considerate enough not to overstay that time limit.

2. *Be sure your facts are accurate.* Do not carry them in your head; instead, write them down, along with the name and job title of the person interviewed. If an interviewee talks too fast for you to get all the facts on paper, ask for a moment's pause to catch up. Do not hesitate to ask for something you don't understand to be repeated or explained. Of course, if the interviewee does not object, use of a tape recorder is the best means of capturing the answers to your questions.

3. *Start the interview with small talk.* This technique makes the interviewee believe you are interested in him or her as a person, not merely as a source of information, and it puts both of you at ease. Cover the easier questions before asking those that are more difficult or controversial; this sequence allows each party to learn

more about the idiosyncrasies of the other. The resulting feedback will aid in determining how to phrase the hard or controversial questions.

4. *Inspire confidence by appearing confident.* Act as if you have every right to obtain answers to your questions. For example, instead of asking, "Would you mind if I . . ." or "Would it be all right if I . . . ," say, "I'd like to ask you about . . ." Also, give the impression that you know where you can find additional information if your source declines to answer. Later, try to rephrase the unanswered question; you may receive the response this time.

5. *Use listening responses to your advantage* to show interest in the interviewee and what he or she is saying. One type of response is the use of nonverbal communicators such as nodding your head in agreement, pausing at strategic places during the discussion, and leaning forward toward the interviewee as he or she talks. Another technique involves verbal responses such as casually remarking, "Really" or "Is that so!" or using the echo response of repeating important phrases verbatim. Another verbal response is to paraphrase an answer so you make it clear that you understand what has been said. Do be sure to vary your listening responses, though, for the repeated use of one technique can become annoying to the interviewee.

6. *At the end of the interview, thank the interviewee* for his or her assistance and offer to reciprocate if such an occasion arises.

Some or all of the following questions might be used to gather information during an interview. Of course, the interviewee's responses will probably bring to mind other questions you would like to ask too.

1. Ms. Jones, what is your official title?
2. How long have you worked for XYZ Company?
3. How long have you held the position you have now?
4. What position did you hold before you took this position?
5. Would you tell me about your background in _____.
6. We have had a problem with _____. What has been your experience in handling this kind of thing?
7. We have tried _____ without much success. Can you suggest another (method/idea/plan)?
8. If we were to try _____, what do you think the outcome might be?

9. How might this affect (the consumer, our employees, the accounting function, our rapport with the Nuclear Regulatory Commission, and so forth)?

10. I have read/heard about _____. Have you had any experience with it? Are there reasons why this would/would not work for us?

Company Records

Company records are considered primary sources of information because they usually have not been published outside the organization and are not available to the general public. In some cases, the material may even be "raw" facts or figures that have not yet been analyzed. Company records are an excellent source of information; they include computer printouts, data on microfilm, letters, reports, contracts, and so forth. The best way to gain access to them is through the person who works with these records every day; that is why it is important to cultivate a good rapport with *everyone* you come in contact with in your organization. You never know when you will need some information, and the clerk that you speak to regularly as you pass her desk may be just the person to help you find the facts you need in a hurry. When using company records, follow the rules set down in our discussion of interviewing.

Questionnaires and Surveys

Sometimes you may need to get a sampling of similar information from many people, and a questionnaire is probably the easiest way to do this. The questionnaire may be mailed to prospective respondents, or the questions may be asked over the phone or in person.

When mailing a questionnaire, the researcher should develop a cover letter explaining the purpose of the research and asking for the respondent's assistance. A stamped return envelope should be enclosed to further encourage the respondent. The advantages of mailing a questionnaire are the ease in getting information from diverse geographic areas and the relatively low cost of obtaining the information. Another advantage is that sound sampling techniques can be applied if the mailing list is representative. A major disadvantage is the generally low response to mailed questionnaires: they are often read and forgotten. Another disadvantage is the slowness in getting the returns back because of the mail turnaround time and because respondents may not answer right away. In addition, the mailed questionnaire eliminates observation of nonverbal communication.

Telephone questioning has the advantages of speed and relatively low cost. One disadvantage is that phone subscribers do not truly represent all of American society; low-income people may not have phones. Another disadvantage is that most nonverbal communication elements cannot be observed by phone. Sometimes gestures or facial expressions help a researcher gauge respondent's sincerity, truthfulness, and so on.

Personal face-to-face surveys have two advantages: the opportunity to observe nonverbal communication and the chance to establish rapport with the respondent. Disadvantages include the possibility for human error unless the questioner is highly trained. In addition, this method of gathering data can be quite expensive unless the respondents live within a very narrow geographic area.

One thing to remember about questionnaires is that people dislike filling out forms and answering lengthy sets of questions. Here are some suggestions if you are composing a questionnaire or phone survey:

1. *State the questions clearly.* Ambiguous, misleading, or otherwise confusing questions will hinder your efforts to get accurate information. Questions such as, "Do you use a calculator often in your work?" are poor because *often* is a vague word. Instead, ask, "How often do you use a calculator in your work?" Then list several choices such as "Never," "Every day," "Two or three times a week," and so on.

2. *Phrase the questions so they can be answered easily and tabulated easily.* Open-ended questions such as, "How much interest do you have in home computers?" are poor. First, respondents may not answer because to truly express how much interest they have in home computers would take too much time. Second, if people do respond to the question, tabulating the responses accurately would be difficult and time-consuming. Usually, multiple-choice questions are easy to tabulate, especially if you have access to computer tabulation. Writing a good multiple-choice question, however, does take time and careful thought.

3. *Don't ask questions that "set up" the respondent.* Questions such as, "Are you adventurous enough to try a new concept (electronic tellers) in banking?" are poor. They involve an emotional appeal that may cause the respondents to answer the way you want them to, rather than telling you their true feelings. A better question would be, "Would you try the new electronic tellers being introduced by banks?"

4. *Avoid personal questions.* Some questions such as, "What is your age?" are personal and may cause people to be untruthful; giving several age ranges and asking respondents to check the range they belong in is a better approach. Also, be careful how you phrase

questions about income, sexual preferences, morals, values, and personal habits.

5. *Devise an attractive easy-to-read format.* Allow plenty of white space around each question and a generous amount of space for responses. This is particularly true if you are using a rating scale such as the following one:

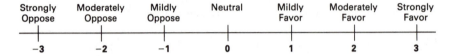

What is your opinion of deregulating the banking industry?

Strongly Oppose	Moderately Oppose	Mildly Oppose	Neutral	Mildly Favor	Moderately Favor	Strongly Favor
−3	−2	−1	0	1	2	3

THE PROCESS OF GATHERING DATA FROM QUESTIONNAIRES AND SURVEYS

If you are using the questionnaire to collect information for a report, there are several steps in the process. First define the population you will survey. The *population* is the entire group a researcher wants to study. The following are three examples of a population:

1. All chain drugstores east of the Mississippi

2. All working women between 19 and 65 years of age in the United States

3. All families within the city limits of Savannah, Georgia

After defining the population, define the variables you want to measure. If the variables are not definable, they cannot be easily measured. The following are three examples of variables that have been defined:

1. We want to determine *how many* chain drugstores east of the Mississippi stock NO-Bite insect repellent.

2. We want to find the *median income* for all working women aged 19 to 65 in the United States.

3. We want to learn *how often* all families within the city limits of Savannah eat at fast-food establishments.

Once the variables have been defined, select a design for sampling. This involves determining who will take part in the sample, determining sample size and sample items, and estimating the characteristics of the population from sample data that are collected.

The idea of sampling is probably already familiar to you. When bakers enter cakes in competition, they expect the judges to cut them and examine a small slice of each one — to judge the whole by inspecting and tasting a small portion of it. Buyers of tobacco pull out a few leaves from a farmer's lot and smell and inspect them to judge the quality of the whole lot. The idea of sampling underlies the thought that one part of the whole is representative of the whole.

The *general theory of sampling* is that a sufficiently large number of items taken at random from a larger quantity of the item will have the same characteristics as the larger group. The reason the sample must be sufficiently large is to guarantee reliability. Small samples might contain some chance errors, but as the sample size increases, the likelihood of errors becomes smaller. Of course, if the number of items is small, there is no need to sample; the researcher can examine all of them.

A second principle of sampling is that it must be representative of the population. The size of the sample has nothing to do with its being representative. For example, suppose a researcher used the phone book from a city of 100,000 people and phoned 10 people — or even 10,000 of them. The sample would not be representative of the town's population because numerous people, particularly low-income families, would not be represented, regardless of the number called. In other words, representative means that the sample must cover the whole range of responses from the population surveyed.

Random sampling is preferred over other sampling methods. The sample is random if everyone within the whole population has an equal chance of being selected for the survey. Another kind of sampling is *stratified random sampling*, in which the population is divided into subgroups and a random sample is taken from each subgroup.

Getting a random sample of some populations, particularly human ones, is often difficult. However, to continue with the three examples used earlier, the following choices might be made to determine who will be questioned:

1. We know that many chain drugstores have a regional purchasing office that orders inventory in quantity for all its stores in the region. We could survey the purchasing managers at the regional offices of every major chain drugstore. We could identify these chains from various secondary publications containing information on each region.

2. If the U.S. Department of Labor needed to find the median income for working women, it might first use stratified random sampling to establish several age categories to be certain that all age groups were equally represented. Within each age group, women

might be selected randomly by Social Security number to participate in the study. If a recent census had been taken, the department might also be able to obtain figures from that source.

3.　To determine which families in Savannah to survey, we could go
to the chamber of commerce, which publishes, for a small fee, a
listing of all households in every subdivision or section of the city.
We could select families at random from this listing to participate
in the survey.

As you can see, researchers often must be creative in finding
approaches to obtain random samples. Sometimes the problem of getting a random sample can be nearly eliminated if the researcher
knows — from experience or from published sources — some of the
characteristics of a particular population. For example, the researcher
who knows that 15 percent of the United States' racial mix is black
could specify that 15 percent of the respondents to a particular questionnaire should be black.

Once you have defined your population, defined your variables,
and selected a design for sampling, you are ready to start constructing
the questions to be included on the questionnaire. When constructing
questions, you must consider these problems:

1.　Do the questions get the information needed by the researcher?

2.　Do the questions mean the same thing to the researcher as they do
to the respondents? Do they mean the same thing to all the respondents?

3.　Are the questions asked in the right sequence?

4.　Are the questions objective, making no attempt to influence the
respondent's reply?

To create a good questionnaire, follow these steps:

1.　Determine what information is wanted.

2.　Determine the type of questionnaire to be used (personal survey,
mailed, phone).

3.　Determine the content of individual questions by asking, "Is this
question necessary?" "Are several questions needed instead of
just one?" "Does the respondent have enough information to give
a response?" and so on.

4.　Determine the type of question to ask. *Open-ended* questions
such as, "Why do you use X shampoo?" generate more subjective

answers but are difficult to tabulate. *Multiple-choice* questions such as, "What is the total annual income earned in your household? Under $10,000, $10,000–$15,000, $15,000–$20,000, $20,000–$25,000, $25,000–$30,000, $30,000–$35,000, Over $35,000," limit the respondent's reply but are easier to tabulate. When using this type of question, be sure to allow for "Other" responses when applicable. Questions using the *ranking method* are often best when measuring attitudes; an example of this type is found on page 40. Sometimes the *dichotomous* question (which gives a choice between only two responses) is appropriate. An example of a dichotomous question is, "Was it new or used when you got it?"

5. Use simple words and sentence structure to avoid ambiguous questions.

6. Avoid questions that suggest to the respondent how to reply. An example of such a question is, "Is Dove your favorite complexion soap?"

Once you have prepared the questions, you should do a *pilot survey* to pretest your questionnaire. In this pretest, ask several people from the particular population you want to survey to answer the questionnaire. From their responses you will be able to determine if the questions are clear, if the responses look promising, and if you need to make corrections, additions, or deletions to the original.

**SOME GUIDE QUESTIONS FOR CONDUCTING A PHONE SURVEY
FOR A DISCOUNT DEPARTMENT STORE**

Introduction: May I speak to Mr. Charles Brown? Mr. Brown, my name is Mary Smith. I am a researcher with Evans, Caldwell, and Bronson. We're doing a study for a local store, and your answers to a few questions would help our client give shoppers better service. Would you have a few moments to answer some questions about your shopping habits?

(*Note:* The researcher identified herself immediately.

The researcher appealed to Mr. Brown's desire to help others to encourage him to answer the questions.

The researcher was courteous and specific about what she would ask.)

1. How many times a month do you shop at discount department stores? Discount department stores are ones like K-Mart, APCO, and Ayr-Way.

(*Note:*   A specific time frame [one month] was used to obtain uniform responses from all respondents.

Discount department stores was defined so respondents knew exactly what kind of store the researcher had in mind.)

2.   Which particular discount department stores in your area do you shop at?

(*Note:*   This question will allow the researcher to determine who the client's strongest competitors are.)

3.   What are your main reasons for shopping at discount department stores?

(*Note:*   This question will allow the researcher to see if the client's/ the industry's perception of why people shop at these stores is accurate.)

4.   What is your biggest complaint or problem with these stores?

(*Note:*   This question will allow researchers to find out if the consumer feels the client and its competitors are doing anything wrong so that the client can either correct its problems or perhaps capitalize on the competitors' problems.)

5.   What kinds of merchandise do you purchase at discount department stores?

(*Note:*   Again, the researcher can uncover perceptions about these stores.)

6.   Are there any kinds of merchandise you would not purchase from a discount department store?

(*Note:*   Again, the researcher seeks consumers' perceptions of these stores.)

Closing: Okay, Mr. Brown, that's all. You've been very helpful. Thanks for your time.

(*Note:*   As you can imagine, this type of survey is costly; the researcher must be highly trained to listen for and record the responses given.

This survey was purposely brief because phone respondents will spend less time talking to a researcher than those who talk to researchers in person. Also, even though the questions are few, they are open-ended ones, which allow for numerous comments from the respondent. These are time-consuming both for the respondent and for the researcher.)

Experiments, Personal Experience, and Observation

An *experiment* is a technique in which the researcher systematically manipulates one variable of a problem while keeping all other variables constant. The researcher then measures any changes that occur from manipulating the one variable. For example, after studying the problem, the Bistro Company hypothesizes that a new packaging design would improve sales of a mature product in its line. A researcher designs an experiment to test that hypothesis.

First, the researcher selects two cities that are as nearly alike as possible in the characteristics that might affect purchasing habits. Since the Southeast is a major market for the product, the researcher chooses two southeastern cities that are similar in population and in the fact that both have few manufacturing facilities but numerous regional offices for companies as well as other service-oriented businesses. The median family income in both cities is approximately $32,000 annually, and 65 percent of both cities' employees hold white-collar jobs.

For a three-month period, the researcher will record sales of the product in these two cities. At the start of the fourth month, the new package design will be introduced in only one of the cities; the old packaging will continue to be used in the other city. During the next three months, the researcher will again record sales of the product in each of the two cities. Also during this time the researcher will make sure that all of the other variables — amount of advertising, economic conditions, the competition, and so on — remain the same. At the end of this three-month test period, the researcher should be able to see whether or not the new packaging had any effect on sales.

Of course, the most important aspect of experiments such as this is to *keep all but one variable constant*. In much business research this is difficult because of circumstances beyond the control of the researcher. If that difficulty arises, the researcher must try in some way to compensate for the unwanted changes in variables; the outcome of the experiment should at least be qualified by an explanation of the changes.

In designing an experiment, the researcher must make it fit the requirements of the problem. Generally, the basic design will either be the *before-after design* or the *controlled before-after design*. In the former, the researcher follows these steps:

1. Selects the test group;

2. Selects and measures one variable;

3. Introduces the experimental factor for a specified time;

4. Measures the one variable again after the specified time;

5. Assumes the difference in the measurements was caused by the experimental factor.

An example of this method was used in the production department of a small wire and cable manufacturing company. One machine extruded a plastic jacket onto television lead-in wire. Engineers hypothesized that they could increase the speed of the machine to run the wire 50 ft. per minute faster than it had been running in order to produce more wire in the same time period. In the experiment they kept all other variables — plastic compound used, temperature of compound, extrusion technique, and so on — the same; they merely speeded up the machine. This experiment lasted for one week. At the end of the period, the engineers measured the results of the experiment against the measurements taken when the machine had run at normal speeds. They checked for quality as well as quantity. The results showed that the machine produced less usable wire when it was speeded up. The conclusion was that the machine could not produce more wire at higher speeds. Obviously, this experiment had some shortcomings: it tested only one machine, it did not consider that the machine operator may have contributed to lower output, and so on.

A better method is the *controlled before-after* design. To help filter out the effects of influences other than the experimental factor, this design attempts to measure these influences by means of a control. Instead of selecting just one group, the researcher selects two. The steps carried out in this method are as follows:

1. One group is designated as the control group, the other as the experimental group.

2. The variable to be tested in both groups is measured beforehand.

3. The experimental factor is introduced into the experimental group only — to be tested for a specific time period.

4. The variable in both groups is again measured after the experimental time period.

5. The measurements are studied to derive a conclusion.

Since the control group did not contend with the experimental factor, the difference in measurements can be explained only as other factors, while the difference in the experimental group can have two causes: the experimental factor and other influences. Earlier in this section, the Bistro Company researcher used the controlled before-after design.

Because of the nature of the scientific experiment, it is limited to problems that deal with the effects of change on a given set of conditions. Many kinds of business problems are of a different nature. Therefore, other kinds of original research must often be used.

One of these, the *personal observation,* means looking at or for something with a predetermined purpose in mind. In the observation, unlike the experiment, the researcher does nothing to manipulate what naturally occurs. Rather, the researcher merely watches closely and records exactly what he or she observes. An example of research using personal observation is the market researcher who visits three sports stores on busy Saturday afternoons to observe what brand of running shoe consumers are buying.

The major advantages of the personal observation are its objectivity and its accuracy. One disadvantage is that the observer records only what can be seen — not the psychological reasons why those being observed behave as they do. Also it is sometimes more costly to pay an observer to collect data than to use another method of collection. For example, the market researcher may be paid by the hour but will not be equally busy during the entire observation period.

Generally, the most important aspect of the observation is to determine the procedure for obtaining the desired information. For example, the researcher must consider such things as on what days and at what times and places the observation should take place. In addition, details such as where the researcher will sit or stand must also be worked out. Next, the researcher must develop a form that can record quickly and easily what is observed. For example, a market researcher might use a form that lists all major brands of running shoes so that information as it is observed can be easily checked off. Such a form could also be tabulated with ease at a later date. The form used might look like this:

Market Sample #5132—Consumer Preference in Running Shoes

Observer _____ Date _____

Location _____ Hours _____

	BRANDS						
	Adidas	Converse	Mercury	Nike	Puma	Staly	Tru-T
Price							
$30							
$40							
$50							

Selecting the site for making the observation is important. In some cases site selection will be automatic: the industrial engineer must go to the location where work is being done in order to record the time and motion exerted to do a particular job. On the other hand, the market researcher will need to determine which sport stores in which parts of the city will give a clear, unbiased picture of running shoe sales.

In a few cases, mechanical devices are used to "observe" situations. For example, you have seen the device used to count the number of vehicles that pass in a certain area.

Observation as a source of information is valuable in a report if you remember a few rules when using it:

1. *Be sure the conditions under which you make your observation are valid.* For example, assume that your task is to recommend which of two makes (similar models) of automobiles the company should select for company cars. By using written sources and by talking to dealers, you have gathered information on all aspects except handling and actual gas mileage. You decide to test-drive the two makes. To be valid, the experiment should test cars of similar weight and engine size, and they should be driven under the same weather and road conditions. Also you should drive more than one vehicle of each make.

2. *Be sure your observations are accurate.* Make observations when there are few distractions to divert your attention from the task and when you are rested and alert.

3. *Record all details, such as names, dates, times, quantities, and equipment.* Once the observation is over, reenacting it can be difficult.

This may be your only source of information or the best one if you are asked to analyze or recommend a course of action for which there are no precedents in the company. Sometimes, though, you may need to refer to sources other than primary ones for information to support a report thesis.

ORGANIZING AND INTERPRETING PRIMARY DATA

When organizing primary research data, the researcher looks for a way to classify the data. In surveys the data are best organized according to broad quantitative groups or according to broad categories of answers. For example, if 500 people responded to the question, "How many magazines do you subscribe to?" the researcher could organize the 500 pieces of data along the ranges from the questionnaire: 0, 1–2,

3–4, 5–6, more than 6. In a case in which many different answers are given to a question such as, "What do you eat for breakfast?" the data can be grouped along broad categories, based on a sampling of the responses: don't eat breakfast; beverage and toast; cold cereal and beverage; fruit and beverage; bacon/other meat and eggs; meat, potatoes, eggs, toast, beverage. The researcher must organize the data for each question separately.

After the data have been organized, the researcher must edit and tabulate the responses. Editing means looking at all the data for errors, inconsistencies, omissions, and so on. If the data are to be tabulated manually, a tabulation sheet must be developed. Often a copy of the questionnaire itself is used, and the categories of responses are listed if they do not already appear on the questionnaire. Then hash marks (**卌**) are used to designate each separate response. If the data are tabulated by computer, each response must be keypunched or otherwise entered so that the resulting printout will be accurate and easy to interpret.

Because people are at times prone to strange quirks and irrational or inconsistent moments, problems can arise in interpreting data. The following problems are some of the common ones:

Common Problems with Interpreting Primary Data

1. The desire to produce something spectacular or outstanding may lead the researcher to exaggerate or misinterpret the data.

2. The belief that every problem has a solution may cause the researcher to draw a conclusion that cannot be justified. Or the data may yield more than one possible conclusion. The data may even be inconclusive. Whatever the result, data should be reported accurately.

3. The lack of data to prove a particular proposition may cause the researcher to assume — incorrectly — that the opposite proposition is true. Remember, every conclusion must be supported by evidence.

Sometimes using incorrect procedures to interpret data can cause problems too. Here are some pitfalls to avoid:

1. *Being biased toward a particular outcome of the research.* All of us have ideas and opinions about how things ought to be. These biases can cause us — consciously or unconsciously — to interpret the same set of data differently from another researcher. We must keep a truly open mind, always questioning ourselves, when interpreting data.

2. *Being confused about cause and effect.* It may appear that one thing caused another when in reality, the relationship was only coincidental. Again, we must test all such relationships to see if there truly is a cause-effect tie.

3. *Basing conclusions on unreliable data.* Refer to earlier discussions about how to determine reliability of data.

4. *Neglecting to see all the factors in a complex problem.* We may believe that only one factor influenced our data when in reality one or more others may also have influenced the data.

5. *Not testing conclusions.* Verifying that our conclusions are correct is probably the most important part of our research.

We can work toward preventing these problems by cultivating a critical attitude toward all research, by developing a logical mind set, and by discussing our research with others since one person cannot possibly know all there is to know about any subject.

When interpreting data for an audience via a report, we must state the problem, relate the data to the problem, discuss all the interpretations that relate to the problem, and then draw conclusions from those interpretations. This logical pattern will help the reader to accept our conclusions.

Once you have collected the raw data, you will tabulate the responses and analyze what they mean. You can, of course, merely report the number of responses to each question and draw simple conclusions from these numbers. However, you will probably need some background in statistics to understand the significance of the responses. The following brief discussion may be useful in describing the typicality of the responses you receive on a questionnaire.

Probably the most common indicator of typicality is the *mean,* a simple arithmetical average arrived at by adding up all the numbers and dividing by the total number of responses. For example, if we wanted to find the mean number of absentee days for employees at the ABC company last year, we would total the number of absentee days of all the employees and divide by the number of employees.

Sometimes knowing the *median* may help someone understand the typicality of your responses. The median value is the one in the exact middle of the whole range of scores; one-half of the responses will be below that number, and one-half will be above it. For example, to find the median score on a mechanical aptitude test taken by a group of people applying for jobs as machine operators throughout a company, coast to coast, we would list all of the scores in rank order. The score that falls in the exact middle of the ranking is the median score.

We might also want to look at the *mode*, which is the value that occurs most often in the distribution. We could have found the mode in the aptitude test example above, or we can find it in the following example. If on the responses to a particular question on a questionnaire, 55 people chose response (a), 10 chose response (b), 2 chose response (c), and no one chose response (d), the mode is the preference for response (a).

If your background in statistics is limited, you may want to ask someone in your organization to make suggestions about your questionnaire to help you determine the validity of your sampling, and so on. Usually the data processing department will have at least one such specialist who could assist you. Remember, the key element in using primary sources for a report is to seek other people's help in their areas of expertise. Most people enjoy sharing their knowledge if the recipient seems grateful and gives them credit and praise for their assistance.

SECONDARY SOURCES OF INFORMATION

Occasionally a report will require information that you must obtain from a published source. Material that someone else has compiled, analyzed, and made available to the general public is called a *secondary source*. This type of information is available in the company library or at public libraries. Never be reluctant to ask librarians for assistance; their job is helping people find the information they need.

However, you may want to have a personal copy of a good source book such as *How to Use the Business Library, with Sources of Business Information*, 4th ed., by H. Webster Johnson (Cincinnati, Ohio: South-Western Publishing Co., 1972). Such handbooks not only tell you how to use the library but also list and describe various business yearbooks, directories, financial services, trade publications, almanacs, forecasting services, and many other sources of information for the business person.

Indexes

Indexes are volumes that list all of the material published during a particular period of time so you can find the names of several articles on a single topic at one sitting. Some indexes, such as *Books in Print*, list all books published in a particular period of time. Others, such as the *Readers' Guide to Periodical Literature*, list all the popular magazine articles published during a particular period. More useful for the business person is the specialized index of magazine articles in the general business field, the *Business Periodicals Index*. It lists articles by general subject matter, including the names of well-known people in business, industry, and politics. Issued monthly, it is accumulated and bound in annual volumes. Each entry in the *Business Periodicals Index* will tell you the name of the article related to the topic under consideration; the name of the author; the name of the periodical in which to find the article; the volume number and the inclusive page numbers; and the month, day, and year of the issue. For more specialized indexes in specific business fields, the following sources may be valuable: the *Accountant's Index*, published by the American Institute of Certified Public Accountants, index books, pamphlets, and articles in that field. The *Journal of Economic Literature*, published by the American Economic Association, covers both periodicals and books. *Best's Insurance Reports: Life-Health* and *Best's Insurance Reports: Property-Liability* are issued annually, but weekly and monthly supplements are also published; these give information about United States and Canadian insurance companies and their financial position.

For locating newspaper articles in the most widely read business paper, use the *Wall Street Journal Index*. This publication is issued monthly and cumulated annually. It is organized in two sections, "Corporate News," which lists articles by the name of the company in the news, and "General News," which lists articles by topic, including names of well-known people who have been the subjects of articles. For more general newspaper articles, use the *New York Times Index*, which is similar to the *Wall Street Journal Index*. If you don't know how to use an index, check the front pages inside the cover for instructions. If you are not sure which index to use, ask the librarian to suggest where to look for the information you want.

Annuals

Annuals are yearly compilations of data. The *World Almanac and Book of Facts* is one that contains general facts and statistics. A more specialized annual for business people is the *Statistical Abstracts of the United States*, which gives information on population, production, and consumption. Most of the information is presented in easy-to-read tables. Another source is the *Economic Almanac*, published by the Conference Board, a not-for-profit research association in management and economics.

Business Directories

Directories can give you bond ratings, tell you names of associations, products, companies, and much more. One of the best-known *financial* directories is *Dun and Bradstreet's Million Dollar Directory*, which lists businesses with net worth of $1 million or more, tells the type of product or service, and shows gross sales annually. For businesses with net worth between $500,000 and $1 million, Dun and Bradstreet also publishes the *Middle Market Directory*. Another publisher of financial directories is Standard and Poor; their financial directories include *Stock Reports: American Stock Exchange*; *Stock Reports: N.Y. Stock Exchange*; and *Stock Reports: Over the Counter*. Another important publication of Standard and Poor's is *Industry Surveys*.

A directory that can tell you names and addresses of corporations — large and small — the names of top management, the product or service offered, and so on is *Standard and Poor's Register of Corporations, Directors, and Executives*. Business people use this source in many ways including the following:

To verify names of top managers and spellings of names;

To find the location of corporate headquarters;

To locate guest speakers;

To find contacts for fund-raising campaigns;

To obtain contacts for selling group policies.

Another directory is *Moody's Industrial Manual*, which covers companies listed on the New York and American Stock exchanges as well as regional companies listed on the regional American exchanges. The information is obtained from the corporations, from reports to stockholders, and from Securities and Exchange Commission (SEC) reports. This source gives a brief history of the company and tells its business or products, its officers, and varying amounts of financial data, including bond ratings. The *Thomas Register of American Manufacturers* is especially useful to purchasing agents or others who need to find the names of companies that manufacture a specific item. There are several volumes, with services and products listed alphabetically by "modified noun" headings. For example, if you need a 5 mm coil spring part, look in the volume containing *S* under "Springs: Coil." The *Thomas Register* is actually an advertising medium for manufacturers; they pay to be listed in it. Manufacturers may also include a copy of their catalog in separate volumes, called the *Thom-Cat*, which has over 800 catalogs listed alphabetically by company name.

Numerous other general and specialized directories are available in libraries. Or you may obtain specialized directories from publishers of trade magazines. Examples of the latter include the *Directory of Hotel and Motel Systems, Hardware Age "Who Makes It" Buyers Guide*, and the *Directory of the Canning, Freezing, and Preserving*

Industries. If you don't know the best source to use to find the information you need, the reference librarian can help you.

Business Services and Newsletters

Business services and newsletters are often published more frequently than other sources of information and are geared to specialized business functions and activities. Many are loose-leaf publications that can be collected in binders. Individuals as well as companies and libraries are likely to subscribe to at least one business service or newsletter. In fact, in recent years so many of these services and newsletters have sprung up that it is impossible to cover all but the oldest and most respected ones here:

> *Moody's Bond Survey* is a weekly publication that reports on the entire bond market and gives comments and recommendations on individual issues.

> *The Kiplinger Washington Letter* appears weekly and presents data on such topics as business forecasts, economics, labor, and finance.

> *Value-Line Investment Survey* is published weekly in loose-leaf form. It provides data on selected stocks and gives them ratings. Many individual investors use this service to determine what to buy and sell from their portfolios.

> *U.S. Master Tax Guide* is a service to assist tax managers with current information on recent additions to, deletions from, and new rulings on tax law. This collection is available in a bound edition at year-end.

A check of your library may turn up some of the newer, popular, and usually less expensive newsletters and business services. Usually those that have been in existence for twenty years or more are the most reliable.

Government Publications

Government documents are important sources in researching problems in a particular industry since the government closely monitors the nation's economy. Many libraries have extensive government document sections with trained librarians to help you find the right source.

The federal government (Government Printing Office) publishes numerous articles, pamphlets, reports, and books that may be purchased by individuals as well as by libraries. Especially valuable to business people is the *Monthly Catalog of U.S. Government Publications,* an index that lists publications by author, title, and general subject. A large library will have many of the listed publications in its government documents section, so you may not need to order a particular publication. The *Index to U.S. Government Periodicals* is another index that lists articles by author and subject. Both these periodicals are published by the United States government.

Another important source of government records is the *Federal Register.* Issued daily (Monday through Friday), this source contains all new regulations and notices issued by federal agencies, including executive orders and presidential proclamations. The format is an 8½ × 11 "newspaper" that is collected and bound into volumes. In addition to these general sources, many government agencies publish special reports about their activities. Examples are the volumes of *Federal Trade Commission Decisions,* which give the alleged FTC violation, the history of each case, the decision reached, and whether or not it was appealed; and *General Accounting Office Documents,* which gives similar details of cases dealt with by that office. Of course, some agencies publish specific documents based on their research. An example is the *Pesticide Series,* published by the Environmental Protection Agency. Another useful source, one of the regular publications of the Department of Labor, is the bimonthly *Area Labor Summary,* which shows data on labor trends, unemployment, and job outlook for specific Standard Metropolitan Statistical Areas (SMSA's) within every state.

When you are looking for information about a particular agency, the best source is often the agency itself; you can write for information about responsibilities, programs, and so forth to the agency's information office in Washington, D.C. The address of any agency's information office can be found in the *U.S. Government Manual,* an annual publication available in any library. This publication also contains information and addresses for all branches of the federal government, government agencies, independent government corporations, and regional offices.

Another important government publication for business people is the *Standard Industrial Classification Manual,* which gives the code number for any industry from amusement parks to zipper manufacturers. Originally, the Standard Industrial Classification (SIC) Code was developed for government use. Its purpose was to allow departments to compile statistics that would accurately describe various facets of the nation's economy and to allow them to spot trends, predict growing industries, and so on. Now, however, private industry also uses the code for classifying its customers, clients, suppliers, and so forth. In addition, it is used in market research and by trade associations and professional organizations. And of course, in many government reports, the reporter must list the company's SIC number for use by the government for its original purpose — gathering statistics.

The SIC Code is organized in the following way:

1. Several major *divisions,* denoted by letters, show broad categories such as A — Agriculture, B — Mining, C — Construction, D — Manufacturing, and so on. These are seldom used today; the numerical parts of the code are preferred.

2. Each division is broken down into *major groups,* each indicated by two digits. For example: 01 — Agricultural Production-Crops; 02 — Agricultural Production; 07 — Agricultural Services; 08 — Forestry; and 09 — Fishing, Hunting, and Trapping.

3. Each major group is further divided into group numbers, and each of these is represented by the third digit of the code. For example: 011 — Cash Grains; 021 — Livestock except Dairy, Poultry, and Animal Specialties; 071 — Soil Preparation Services; 081 — Timber Tracts; 091 — Commercial Fishing.

4. Finally, the group number is broken down into the industry number, indicated by the fourth digit, as in 0111 — Wheat; 0211 — Beef Cattle Feedlots; 0711 — Soil Preparation Service; 0811 — Timber Tracts; and 0912 — Finfish (there is no 0911).

Table 3–1 shows how the SIC number is assigned.

Other Sources

Sometimes there are quick and easy routes to finding material for a report. Before running out to search for facts, think about every possible source of information available to you and use the most convenient one. For example, the local Employment Security Division may be closer than the nearest good library. If so, you can obtain there the

---

Table 3–1   How the SIC Number Is Assigned

Division (letter is usually deleted)	B				Mining
Major Group Number		14			Mining and quarrying of nonmetallic minerals except fuel
Group Number			2		Crushed and broken stone, including riprap
Industry Number				2	Crushed and broken limestone (complete number: 1422)
				3	Crushed and broken granite (complete number: 1423)

same recent labor statistics compiled by the U.S. Department of Labor that can be found in the library.

Other sources are bulletins that come out periodically from various financial or management services that your company subscribes to such as the monthly Conference Board reports. And of course, do not overlook the trade magazines you read regularly. They are excellent sources of specialized information for reports.

As with primary sources, be sure to list the title, date, author's name, page numbers, and so on if you use information from a secondary source. Also, to avoid charges of plagiarism, enclose in quotation marks the words you take directly from the source. To learn more about documenting your reports, refer to Chapter 10.

SUMMARY

Sources of information for reports are either primary or secondary. Primary sources consist of anything that is firsthand information and include experiments, surveys, observations, interviews with experts, company records (unpublished), and personal experiences. If using any of these sources, be sure that the source is reliable, that you ask for specific information well in advance of your need for it, and that you write down facts rather than carrying them in your head. You may want to tape-record interviews. Often someone in your company will be responsible for maintaining certain primary information. Since you never know when such information will be needed, you should cultivate a good rapport with everyone who might possibly be able to assist you sometime in the future.

If you use questionnaires to gather information, conduct a *pilot survey* and correct any deficiencies in the questionnaire. Randomly select a *representative sample* to answer your questionnaire. Be sure to write questions that are clear, that can be answered easily and quickly, and that can be tabulated efficiently.

Observations and personal experiences can also be useful primary sources of information. Be sure that the conditions under which you make the observations are *valid*, that your observations are *accurate*, and that you record the data *exactly*.

Secondary sources consist of material that has been compiled, analyzed, and published for use by the public. Many such sources are available in the company library or in public libraries. Your personal library should include a business handbook that describes and explains how to use various yearbooks, directories, financial services, trade publications, and so on. Some of the secondary sources you will find useful are indexes, annuals, business directories, government publications, and other published sources.

INDEXES

Accountant's Index

Best's Insurance Reports

Business Periodicals Index

Journal of Economic Literature

New York Times Index

Readers' Guide to Periodical Literature

Wall Street Journal Index

ANNUALS

Economic Almanac

Statistical Abstract of the United States

World Almanac and Book of Facts

BUSINESS DIRECTORIES

Dun and Bradstreet's Million Dollar Directory

Moody's Industrial Manual

Standard and Poor's Register of Corporations, Directors and Executives

Thomas Register of American Manufacturers

BUSINESS SERVICES AND NEWSLETTERS

Kiplinger Washington Letter

Moody's Bond Survey

U.S. Master Tax Guide

Value-Line Investment Survey

GOVERNMENT PUBLICATIONS

Federal Register

Index to U.S. Government Periodicals

Labor Area Summary

Monthly Catalog of U.S. Government Publications

Standard Industrial Classification Manual

U.S. Government Manual

1. Conduct an interview with a "specialist" in a field that interests you. You may have one of these objectives in mind when arranging the interview:

   To obtain information for an oral or written report
   To explore opportunities for starting your own business
   To learn how one business interacts with another
   To learn what a particular product can do for you (or your company)
   To find out what a particular job entails day to day
   To learn about the kinds of reporting activities of a particular company

2. Go to the nearest library and explore the Business Reference section:

   a. Check to see how many of the references discussed in this chapter are in your library.
   b. Locate one other business reference that interests you and prepare a short oral report about it for class.

3. Use the *U.S. Government Manual* to find the address of the information office of a government agency that interests you and write requesting free pamphlets about the agency. Chapter 12 mentions some government regulatory agencies you may want to contact.

4. Use the *Thomas Register* to find the names of the companies nearest you that manufacture one of the following:

soft-drink vending machines	solar heating plates
temperature controls	license plates
trash compactors	band and choral risers
dental office supplies	terry cloth
cutting dies	needle nose pliers
soft-serve ice cream dispensers	depilatories
handrails	pay envelopes
jail cell doors	pneumatic drills
heat exchangers	golf ball enamel
grain dryers	emblems for clothing

LEARNING ACTIVITIES

5. Use the *Standard Industrial Classification Manual* to find the SIC Code for each of the following:

   a. accounting firms
   b. plumbing, heating, and air-conditioning contractors
   c. architectural firms
   d. Federal Reserve banks
   e. TV broadcasting stations
   f. poultry producers
   g. rubber tire manufacturers
   h. life insurance companies
   i. automotive parts suppliers (wholesalers)
   j. state credit unions

6. Go to the government documents section of the library nearest you to use the *Labor Area Summary* for your area. Prepare an oral report on the unemployment rate, the number of people employed in each type of work, and projected needs for each job category in the next few years.

7. Howard Ruff, a conservative business analyst, publishes a newsletter called *Ruff Times*, one of the new newsletters that have been started recently. Try to find out the date of the first issue of this publication, obtain a copy of any issue, and analyze the kinds of financial advice it gives.

8. Use the *Business Periodicals Index* to compile a bibliography of ten recent magazine articles on one of these or other topics:

   word processing centers
   unions for clerical workers
   TRS-80 or Apple computers (or others)
   the Procter & Gamble Company (or other company)
   synthetic fuel plants
   Eurodollars
   factoring (as related to business)
   American Express credit cards (or other credit card agencies)
   health care containment costs
   Microprocessors

9. Using *Standard and Poor's Register of Corporations, Directors and Executives*, find the location of corporate headquarters of the following companies. Also locate the major product/service, and the number of employees for each:

   a. Armour-Dial Corp.
   b. Belden Corp.
   c. Burroughs Corp.
   d. Celanese Corp.
   e. Carter, Hawley, Hale Stores, Inc.
   f. Deere and Company, Inc.
   g. Eastern Airlines, Inc.
   h. Knight-Ridder Newspapers, Inc.
   i. Kraft, Inc.
   j. Martin Marietta Corp.
   k. Nucor Corp.
   l. Nabisco, Inc.
   m. Phelps Dodge Corp.

n. Philip Morris, Inc.
o. Playboy Enterprises, Inc.
p. Purolator, Inc.
q. Revlon, Inc.
r. Ralston Purina Company
s. Roadway Express, Inc.
t. The Sherwin Williams Company
u. SCM Corporation
v. White Motor Company
w. Wm. Wrigley Jr. Company
x. Western Pacific Industries, Inc.
y. Zale Corp.
z. Zayre Corp.

10. One group of five to seven people should develop a question-naire to be given to the members of the class to establish a profile of the group. You may want to include questions about age, class standing, university major, job experience, hometown location (state or region of the state), residence (on or off campus), marital status, and other items. Pilot test your questionnaire on a second group of people in the class and make revisions in it.

   Distribute the questionnaire to the class and ask a third group of students to tabulate the responses and report them to the class. In a class discussion, determine the best method of discussing the typicality of this information if it were to be presented in a report.

Report Formats

LEARNING OBJECTIVES

After reading this chapter, you should be able to:

- Describe the *form report* format and tell how it differs from other formats;
- Describe the *memo report* format and tell how it differs from others;
- Describe the *letter report* format and tell how it differs from others;
- Describe the *long report* format and tell how it differs from others;
- Explain what kinds of report are best suited to each format.

Information can be reported in a variety of ways. This chapter will discuss the most common formats and will describe some techniques for using each one.

Perhaps the most often used format is the *form report*. Some reports are used to present routine information at regular time intervals — daily, monthly, quarterly, and so on. These periodic reports are frequently submitted on a form that has been devised by the company to save time and money in reporting routine information. Periodic reports will be discussed in more detail in Chapter 7.

THE FORM REPORT

The *form report* requires the use of check marks, single words, phrases, figures — any brief means of communicating other than the traditional complete sentences and paragraphed information. Some form reports are easy to complete because of the specific, detailed organization of the form; others are more general and allow more latitude for self-expression but require more writing skill to report the information accurately.

Exhibit 4–1 shows a sample report form used by the personnel department of a small company to evaluate an employee's performance each quarter. Although the top portion can be filled out quickly, traditional sentences, paragraphs, lists, and so forth are required to complete the main part. If you must use a similar form to submit your report, follow these general guidelines about what to write:

1. First, outline the important points you want to cover, no matter what type of report it is (for example, a performance report or an administrative report).

2. In writing the report, state its purpose in the first sentence and give any background information needed to understand the report.

3. Next, write one or two sentences about each of the main heads from your outline.

4. Draw a conclusion or make a recommendation if one is justified.

For examples and comments about actual reports made on the form in Exhibit 4–1, see Chapter 7.

Another company uses the more specific form shown in Exhibit 4–2 to report employee performance. Note that this form states the purpose of the report, shows the reporter what to evaluate, and in general requires fewer skills to organize the information because it

EXHIBIT 4–1
Performance Appraisal Form

PERFORMANCE APPRAISAL

XYZ Corporation

Employee—————————— Date Submitted——————————

Division—————————— Quarter Ending——————————

Department—————————— Submitted by:

——————————————————
(Supervisor must sign)

COMMENTS BY EMPLOYEE BEING EVALUATED

——————————————————
Signature of Employee

FORM S–311
Revised 3–31–83

has already been arranged by headings. Notice, however, that space is provided for some paragraphed remarks.

Both of these examples are form reports used *within* organizations; however, form reports are used for external purposes too. For example, the reports submitted by businesses to government agencies are often form reports. Government reporting will be discussed in Chapter 12.

Since form reports are usually used for reporting routine information, less audience analysis is needed. Forms reflect the fact that they have been carefully planned and designed for particular audiences and their needs. Therefore, *accuracy* is the most important consideration in completing them. Often your subordinates will complete form reports. When training them to use the form, teach them the specific kinds of data to list on it; also, make sure they follow these guidelines:

Training Subordinates to Use Form Reports

1. *Always proofread your work.* This is especially important if the report contains figures or if a secretary will type the report. Keep in mind that the data will likely be entered into a computer and ultimately will affect other data that may be based on the report; thus accuracy is a must.

2. *Make the report neat and legible.* Some reports can be completed in longhand. If your subordinates must fill out such reports frequently, ask them to *print* rather than write the information. Many business people have learned to print as rapidly as they can write — and it's usually more legible. Another thing to remember is the importance of the nonverbal message conveyed by a report: the report that is neat says that the writer is organized and efficient.

3. *Complete all the blanks.* To subordinates submitting a form report, some information may seem unnecessary, tedious, or repetitious because they don't understand how the information will be used in the decision-making process. Remember, however, that if information is included in the form, someone needs the information; if you can explain its use, that will help your subordinates to do a better job too. If vital information is omitted, the decision will be delayed because the report will be returned for completion. Giving complete information is especially important when reporting to government agencies.

4. *Limit yourself to the information asked for.* Psychologically, when people are given a limited space to write in, they suddenly think of a hundred things to put in it. When this happens, remind

EXHIBIT 4–2
Performance Appraisal Form

                                                                   CONFIDENTIAL

FORM 16511 (1-80)

DUKE POWER COMPANY
LEGAL AND FINANCE
EMPLOYEE PERFORMANCE EVALUATION

EMPLOYEE _____   CURRENT DATE _____

CLASSIFICATION _____   DEPARTMENT _____

EMPLOYMENT DATE _____

INSTRUCTIONS

    The purpose of this report is to provide a summary of information relating to the progress of employees in Legal and Finance. Essentially, the objective is to assist you and others in effectively counseling and developing each member of our department. We should be mindful of the fact that a careful preparation of this report will lead to an honest and impartial appraisal. Employees are to be rated according to the standards of their **present assignments.**

Check Applicable Column

	Superior	Commendable	Competent	Fair	Requires Improvement	No Basis for Evaluation
A. PERSONAL QUALIFICATIONS						
1. Attendance						
2. Leadership						
3. Dependability						
4. Relationship with fellow employees						
5. Relationship with employees of other departments						
6. Demonstration of self-confidence						
7. Effectiveness of oral expression						
8. Effectiveness of written expression						
B. EVALUATION OF WORK PERFORMED						
1. Quality (how good is the product?)						
2. Quantity (was enough accomplished in time expended?)						
3. Accuracy						
4. Completeness						
5. Neatness and legibility						
6. Inclusion of essentials and elimination of nonessentials						
7. Creativeness						
8. Efficient use of assistants						
9. Effective training of assistants						
10. Efficient use of time						
11. Willingness to accept responsibility						
12. Ability to follow instructions						

EXHIBIT 4–2 (Continued)

Legal and Finance
Employee Performance Evaluation

Check Applicable Column

	Superior	Commendable	Competent	Fair	Requires Improvement	No Basis for Evaluation

B. EVALUATION OF WORK PERFORMED (continued)

13. Willingness to keep supervisor advised of project status
14. Working up to capabilities in present job
15. Understand own talents and limitations
16. Making every effort to broaden his (her) experience
17. Ability to foresee and solve problems
18. Involvement in self-improvement activities

C. JOB KNOWLEDGE (is employee's knowledge sufficient?) —
Rate where appropriate

1. Accounting principles and their application
2. Systems design
3. Programming
4. Use of equipment (computer and all other business equip.)
5. Application of sound rate design principles
6. For employees to whom the above items do not apply, note overall job knowledge and list appropriate comments below

The majority of employees will perform at the competent level. Clarifying comments must be inserted for qualifications other than competent. Your suggestions for the betterment of satisfactory performances will be most helpful. Your opinions with respect to any outstanding performances or attributes will also be beneficial. **This appraisal must be discussed with the employee.** This does not necessarily mean that the employee must review the details on this evaluation form, but must be fully aware of the results. Compliment the employee on work well done and be constructive in your suggestions in areas where improvement is required.

REVIEWER'S COMMENTS: _____

_____

_____

_____

_____

_____

EMPLOYEE COMMENTS OR COMPLAINTS: _____

_____

_____

_____

In relation to his experience the   ☐ Complex   I have discussed this evaluation
work assigned to employee is: ☐ Moderately difficult   with employee on _____
                             ☐ Relatively easy

Employee Reaction to Discussion

☐ Receptive
☐ Indifferent
☐ Antagonistic

Prepared by _____   **Approved by** _____

Date _____   **Date** _____

Source: Reprinted by permission of Duke Power Company, Charlotte, North Carolina.

your subordinates to give only the pertinent information, nothing more.

Although these suggestions apply to form reports in general, we will talk more about this format and how to design forms in later chapters.

THE MEMO REPORT

As was mentioned earlier, many reports are used for decision making within the organization. Another means of transmitting short, internal reports — those written for your immediate superior and less than five pages long — is via the *memo report*. This format uses the traditional memorandum heading: the date, the name of the person to whom the report is being sent, the name of the writer, and the subject of the report.

Often the memo report will say "Memorandum Report" at the top to tell the reader that this is more than a short, routine memo (see Exhibit 4–3). The next piece of information — the date line — should consist of a combination of words and figures. For example, write "9 June 1982" rather than "6/9/82." Today, business is often conducted with multinational corporations, and in most other countries 6/9/82 would be read "September 6, 1982"; we must therefore write so as to avoid ambiguous information.

The subject line of a memo report should be brief and specific so the reader knows what to expect in the report. Study these examples:

> *Poor:* Subject: Car Insurance
> *Improved:* Subject: Proposed Change in Rental Car Insurance

The first thing the reader looks for in a report is the name of the person who wrote it; the second thing is the subject of the report. Do not disappoint the reader by using a vague subject line. Exhibit 4–4 shows the heading and introduction of a sample memo report.

Statement of Purpose

Recall from Chapter 2 that establishing a goal or objective is important in the planning stage. When writing the report, this statement of purpose remains important. In the first paragraph of a memo report, simply reuse the statement of purpose you wrote in the outline. This introductory statement may be one or two sentences in a short report or a couple of paragraphs in a longer report, but it should never be lengthy. The statement of purpose on the form in Exhibit 4–4 is good because it is clear, concise, and complete.

EXHIBIT 4–3
Page Arrangement for Memorandum Reports

MEMORANDUM REPORT

DATE: _____

TO: _____

FROM: _____

SUBJECT: _____

(Statement of Purpose:) _____

_____

Section Heading

_____

_____

_____

Section Heading

_____

_____

_____

_____

Section Heading

_____

_____

_____

_____

EXHIBIT 4–4
Heading and Introduction of a Sample Memo Report

```
                    MEMORANDUM REPORT

    DATE:     October 2, 1983
    TO:       All Store Managers
    FROM:     J. M. Cone, Operations
    SUBJECT:  New Procedures for Unloading Grocery Trucks

    Unloading grocery trucks is an important function in
    the B&M Company. Using the new procedures suggested
    in this report will result in greater worker
    efficiency and higher productivity.
```

In addition to the statement of purpose, you may need to provide some background information for the reader in the first paragraph. Or you may indicate the major divisions the reader can expect to find in the report. The following introductory statement briefly and clearly combines a statement of purpose with information about the main divisions in the report:

This report discusses the current problems in the Southwest branch, makes recommendations to correct them, and offers suggestions to prevent future occurrences of the same problems.

You have heard it said that if you get the day off to a good start, the whole day will be good. The same applies to memo reports: if you get them off to a good start with a clear, concise introduction, the whole report will be easier to write.

Section Headings   Section headings show the main divisions of the report and call the reader's attention to the most important ideas. In the planning stage you made an outline of the report. From that, simply pull out the first-degree heads to use as section headings. You may need to shorten them, though, so only the most important words remain to convey what the section is about. These headings may be centered above each section or they may be placed to the far left; they may be underlined or capitalized. Chapter 5 discusses these choices in more detail.

Headings are important for two reasons. First, the report with headings looks less formidable than one with only paragraphed information. For example, a five-page report without headings may look verbose and dull to a busy manager who skims written information to ascertain whether or not to spend time reading it in more detail. Headings can tell the manager at a glance what the major concerns are in the report; you save your boss valuable time, and in turn the boss thinks you are efficient and well organized. Second, the headings will help you stay on the subject rather than wandering off on tangents. An idea that doesn't fit under any of the headings may not be important enough to include in the report at all. Remember to give the reader everything necessary but nothing more.

Avoid empty headings such as "Discussion" or "Comments"; because these do not tell the reader what the section will contain, they are usually a waste of both the writer's and the reader's time. Headings should be parallel in structure — that is, similar in grammatical form. For example, you could begin each heading with a verb or you could write each one as a question beginning with *who, what, where,* and so on. Headings such as the following from a short procedures report are poor because they are not parallel:

Prepare the Surface

Installation

Miscellaneous Instructions

This particular report could be improved by using nouns (the *-tion* words that follow) to make the headings parallel:

General Instructions

Preparation of the Surface

Installation

Conclusions and Recommendations

You will remember from our three planning steps in Chapter 2 that the outline you made had a conclusion. When using the memo report format, you can pull out the conclusion from your outline and use it in the report. In an informational report, a conclusion is not used, but you may choose to summarize the main points. In many reports, the writer needs to make the reader feel that all the facts have been presented and that the report is formally finished. If your report is analytical, you can draw some conclusions so the reader knows how you feel about the relationships among the facts you presented. As with the introduction, the conclusion should be brief and simple. Here is such a conclusion:

> Although Ms. Blossom is not yet the "perfect" salesperson, she understands her weaknesses and has agreed to work to eliminate them.

If your report is a recommendation report, you may draw conclusions; you might also make recommendations that you would like to see implemented. Often, when drawing conclusions or making recommendations, a good idea is to *list* them. This technique makes each idea stand out in the reader's mind. Following are two good recommendations, the first in sentence form, the second in list form:

Recommendation

On the basis of this study, I recommend that Park Road Union 76 not add high-test gasoline to its product line. At this time all statistical information shows that adding high-test would be infeasible.

Recommendations

1. Deposit all receipts in the bank daily.

2. Pay only with checks.

3. Establish a petty cash fund for small expenditures.

4. Implement bar-coded, computer-scanned inventory labels.

Regardless of the form you use for stating conclusions and recommendations, remember to keep them simple, direct, and clear so the reader knows exactly what you think. Exhibit 4–5 shows you a complete memo report. Note the memorandum heading, the introductory paragraph, the section headings, and the conclusion.

THE LETTER REPORT

The letter report format is used when sending a *short* report to someone outside your organization — for example, to a customer, a client, or a grantor. The format includes a *heading*, an *inside address*, a *subject line*, and a *salutation* and *closing* like any other letter.

At the top of the page comes the name and address, city, state, and zip code of your company (or a letterhead) and the date. Several spaces below and to the left is the *inside address*, which includes the name and title of the person receiving the report, the name of the company and its address, city, state and zip code. Two spaces below

EXHIBIT 4–5
Sample Memorandum Report

```
                        MEMORANDUM

DATE:     February 5, 1983
TO:       Crime Department Underwriter Trainees
FROM:     Department Manager
SUBJECT:  Acceptance or Declination of a Fidelity Bond Risk
```

The marketplace for fidelity insurance in this territory is very competitive and fast paced; therefore, a crime underwriter has to accept or decline a fidelity bond risk as quickly as possible after reviewing data and exercising individual underwriting business judgment.

The decision for acceptance or declination can be reached only after the underwriter has considered the following: (1) the method by which the agent presented the risk — by telephone, by mail, in person, or any combination of these methods; (2) the available information concerning a particular risk and/or class of similar risks; (3) the department's current guidelines; and (4) the effect the decision will have on the department's relations with the agent.

The Method

A majority of risks are presented by telephone. This is the least desirable method of trying to evaluate a risk, but the agent often has no choice because of time constraints. The underwriter must be a good listener and be able to ask the right questions when the agent fails to provide necessary information. Printed matter, such as applications, descriptions, and so on, is much more concise in presenting a risk. A one-on-one conversation will sometimes be most revealing, because an agent's ''body language'' can bring attention to certain parts of a risk that may need special consideration. Regardless of how a risk is presented initially, the underwriter determines at this point if there is enough information and interest to continue.

The Information

Besides the initial information presented by the agent,

EXHIBIT 4–5 (Continued)

the underwriter consults as many of the following sources as possible: (1) <u>Dun & Bradstreet</u>; (2) <u>Moody's</u>; (3) other departments; (4) any other appropriate information source, and (5) the underwriter's own general knowledge and experience.

<u>The Guidelines</u>

Once the risk has been analyzed as closely as possible, the underwriter decides whether or not it falls within the department's underwriting and budgetary guidelines. Naturally, the budgetary guidelines are stable on an annual basis, but the underwriting guidelines can be very fluid. The underwriter's judgment will determine if the risk is acceptable or not.

<u>The Effect</u>

Whether the risk is deemed to be acceptable or not, one very important point to consider is how this decision will affect the department's relations with the agent. Does declining the risk mean the agent will be upset and never submit another piece of business? Or does accepting the risk mean it will open up more business for the department in the future? Just what are the ramifications — both present and future? This concern is probably the hardest area to interpret correctly. The agent's mind cannot be read, and the underwriter has to make a decision that will be acceptable.

<u>Conclusion</u>

The underwriter does not have to follow this sequence of considerations in every case. It is given only as a guideline, and we realize that the demands of the job will necessitate skipping and/or changing parts of the overall sequence. This is the underwriter's decision.

that comes the *subject line,* which gives the title of the report. Another two spaces down is the *salutation* or greeting to the reader. Exhibit 4–6 shows the page arrangement, and Exhibit 4–7 shows the heading of a letter report.

Like memo reports, the letter report needs a brief introductory statement of purpose. Also, like memo reports, it should have section headings for ease in reading and a conclusion when needed. And like other business letters, the letter report needs a *complimentary close*

EXHIBIT 4–6
Page Arrangement for a Letter Report

LETTERHEAD

_____

_____

Date _____

Inside Address _____

_____

_____

Subject: _____

Salutation:

Statement of Purpose _____

_____

Section Heading

_____
_____
_____
_____
_____
_____

Section Heading

_____
_____
_____
_____
_____
_____

Closing,

Typed name

EXHIBIT 4–7
Heading for a Letter Report

National Printing Company
24361 Westlake Avenue
La Habra, CA 90631

October 19, 1983

Ms. Jane Cougill
Purchasing Agent
J. B. Crane Company
Edson, IN 47361

Subject: Report on the Development of Special
          Order #653106

Dear Ms. Cougill:

such as "Sincerely," "Sincerely yours," or "Cordially," as well as the *signature* of the writer. Exhibit 4–8 shows a complete letter report.

All of the formats we have discussed so far will be useful in preparing *short reports* — that is, those that require five pages or less of typed material. Remember that the term does not refer to the purpose or kind of report but only to its length. When a report is longer than five or six pages, whether it is to be used within or outside the organization, it is usually submitted in a different format.

THE LONG FORMAL REPORT

Long formal reports are sometimes used within an organization, but more often they are written for customers, clients, the public, or some other audience outside the company. Long reports, however, are not simply lengthier than short ones; they are also more formal. For example, they usually contain *prefatory material* (table of contents, letter or memo of authorization, letter or memo or transmittal, and abstract) and *end material* (end notes, bibliography, and appendix) not usually found in short reports. These sections are useful because they help the reader quickly locate pertinent parts.

Long reports are also presented in a binder, which often displays the company name and/or logo. The purpose of the binder is not only to promote the company but also to hold together a bulky set of pages so they can be read easily and to protect the report from damage and

EXHIBIT 4–8
Sample Letter Report

Charlotte Management Consultants
First Union Plaza, Suite 2400
Charlotte, North Carolina 28288

October 27, 1983

Mr. James Sewell
Barrington's
6101 Long Horn Drive
Houston, Texas 61204

SUBJECT: Report on Management Problem at Barrington's
Southwest Branch

Dear Mr. Sewell:

This analysis of the management problem at the
Barrington's Southwest Branch is based on my observations
during a recent three-day visit. Also, this report is a
follow-up to our recent meeting and outlines the basic
problems and recommendations we discussed.

MAJOR PROBLEM: LACK OF ORGANIZATION

Organization is one of the fundamental functions of
management, and it is also the basic problem of the
Barrington's store. Organizing deals with (1) what is to be
done, (2) by whom it is to be done, and (3) who decides what.
These issues need to be determined by (1) setting objectives,
(2) telling people what is expected of them, and (3) monitoring
progress.

I recommend that James Monroe, area manager, begin
immediately by conducting individual meetings with each of the
department heads. He should cover their job descriptions in
detail and explain how the office work should flow.

Job descriptions help define and establish job
responsibilities. Each department head should have a clear
knowledge of job responsibilities and the reporting
procedures. This helps establish Monroe's position of

EXHIBIT 4–8   (Continued)

authority and clearly sets objectives and expectations of the
department heads.

The major part of the office work should be located in the
departments and handled by the department heads. Certain
office work is centralized under Monroe. Monroe's main job is
to counsel department heads and help them accomplish their
work rather than to do the work for them.

A manager who establishes goals and clear policies can get
the work done efficiently and can clearly monitor the process.

AREA MANAGER'S PROBLEM: LACK OF DELEGATION

James Monroe, the area manager, is a people-oriented
person. He has a compromise-characteristic personality and a
teamwork spirit. Above all, he wants to get work accomplished
adequately and to maintain a continuity of satisfactory work
achievement. Monroe's problem is that he has not delegated
responsibility to the department heads. He feels that by
giving up some of his responsibility he will lose authority.
This is typical of a person who has worked up through an
organization, and it is an easy problem to solve once it is
recognized.

I recommend that James brush up on his management skills
as well as his writing by enrolling in management and business
communications courses at one of the local colleges. A
management course will help him realize that delegating
responsibility is also a way of establishing his authority and
leadership. A business communications course will help him
develop better written communication skills.

I would further like you to consider Monroe's span of
control. He may have too many department heads reporting to him
even after he has implemented the organizational
recommendations I suggest. I recommend the combination of like
departments under a coordinator. Monroe would have fewer
people reporting to him and would still maintain the
effectiveness he needs.

MINOR PROBLEM: TELEPHONE CALLS

Telephone calls have an unprescribed way of circulating
back to Monroe. The main points to remember about telephone

EXHIBIT 4–8   (Continued)

calls is that they build goodwill, expedite information, and provide help.

I recommend that Monroe talk with a Southern Bell representative to obtain some helpful advice on the way calls and messages can be received and circulated in this department store. Meanwhile, Monroe should reinstate the company's prescribed way of handling calls during the meeting he has with department heads.

OTHER RECOMMENDATIONS

I recommend that sales personnel have an opportunity to rotate to other departments in the store. Perhaps every fifth day a sales employee could work in a different department. This would provide cross-training and cross-checking, improve employee morale and the quality of work, and encourage teamwork and a lower absenteeism rate.

Also, I suggest that Barrington's provide a Christmas party for the employees at the Southwest branch. This is a point I did not mention in our meeting, but it is an important way of expressing thanks to the employees for a job well done.

SUMMARY

Organizing enables managers to enlarge their scope of influence. Activities are placed in manageable units, areas of responsibility are clarified, decision-making areas are clearly established, and teamwork is encouraged.

Thank you for the opportunity to work with you. I look forward to hearing about the progress on these recommendations.

Sincerely,

Sharyn S. Elder
Management Consultant

Source: Reprinted by permission of Sharyn S. Elder.

soil. Usually much time is spent in preparing long reports, and they are often read by several people within the organization, so they must be durable. Chapter 10 deals in detail with the preparation of long, formal reports.

VARIATIONS OF THE REPORT FORMAT

Not all business reports that you will have to write will fit neatly into one of the four formats just discussed. You may, for example, need to write a long informational report that contains only *some* of the parts usually associated with long formal reports. Or you may need to write a report that seems unlike anything we have discussed. In that case, usually someone in the organization has previously prepared a similar report, and you will be able to look at it to see how it was done.

Exhibit 4–9 is an example of a report that does not fit any of the formats discussed earlier. Since it is a sales report, the figures in it are most important; and since there is little need for words, this format allows the numbers to stand out. Because the title of the report and the section headings clearly tell what the report is about, no formal introduction is used. This format is very efficient for presenting numbers; however, its greatest disadvantage is that the reader does not know for whom it was written. Also, the writer seems anonymous until he signs his name on the last page of the report.

If your superior likes a particular format that is not very effective, you may suggest changes; but if they are rejected, follow established precedents even if they are not the best way. As any effective business person knows, "When in Rome, do as the Romans do."

SUMMARY

This chapter discusses four formats for reports: the form format, the memo format, the letter format, and the long report format.

The *form report* is usually used to report routine information or information that is needed at regular time intervals to make decisions. The form is designed so that the statement of purpose is clear and the required information can be given quickly. This format requires few skills in writing or organizing material because of its design; however, as with all reports, accuracy is an important consideration. Usually only check marks, phrases, numbers, or short sentences are needed to complete a form report.

The *memo report* format is for reports that will be used within the organization and are less than five or six pages long. It uses the traditional memorandum *heading* (date, to, from, subject). The *subject line* shows the topic of the report; it should be brief and specific. Unlike the form report, the memo report does not have the *statement of purpose* already prepared for the writer; thus this statement is the first thing that should be written. The remainder of the report should cover the ideas from the outline that was prepared in the three-step plan presented in Chapter 2. Since these reports may seem lengthy to the reader, the writer should use *section headings* to break up the text as well as to organize the material so the reader immediately sees the important points. Be sure that section headings are descriptive, clear, and concise; avoid empty headings such as "Comments" or "Discus-

EXHIBIT 4–9
Report Using a Variation of the Standard Formats

VIPCO FILMS
Monthly Sales Report
November 1982

I. SALES STATISTICS

Nov. 1981 YTD Sales	Nov. 1982 YTD Sales	Nov. 1982 YTD Quota	% 1982 YTD Quota	Share of Market
1,528,282	2,262,635	1,466,663	154.27%	33%

COMMENTS:
1. Branch Farms warehousing program is completed. Product is already in stock in the Weston warehouse. Branch Farms will be pulling stock out in December.
2. Southern Packaging, Inc. has started working the Virginia market. I made joint calls with Bob Callahan in November; we expect new business and orders in 1983.
3. Boone Supply, Inc. has moved a salesman to Charlotte. I will make joint calls with Dave Stinson in December.
4. We have replaced Gladstone at Babson & Brown, Hickory. I am currently making presentations to B & B in Charlotte.

II. CURRENT MONTH SALES ACTIVITIES
A. Major Customers — 50M Pounds Plus
    1. Account: Boone Supply Inc. — Bubbling Spring, NC
        Type Product: Supermarket Films Distributor
        1981 YTD Sales: 483M lbs.
        1982 YTD Sales: 700M lbs.
        Share of Business: 90%
        Status: Excellent
        Comments: Account continues to expand sales growth with our films. They have extended their sales force and located new representatives in Charlotte and Richmond.
    2. Account: Packaging Materials Corporation — Millville, NC
        Type Product: Supermarket Films Distributor
        1981 YTD Sales: 225,141 lbs.

EXHIBIT 4–9   (Continued)

```
        1982 YTD Sales:      264,692 lbs.
        Share of Business:  10%
        Status:             Good
        Comments: This distributor represents our interests
        through brokers in Greenville, SC, through M. R. Hanes
        and in Norfolk and Richmond, VA, areas through Jim Sims
        Brokerage.
        Joint calls are to be made week of December 14, 1982 in
        Virginia.
    3.  Account: Branch Farms Poultry — Weston, NC
        Type Product:        Fresh Wrap–P
        1981 YTD Sales:      318,762 lbs.
        1982 YTD Sales:      785,809 lbs.
        Share of Business:  35%
        Status:             Excellent
        Comments: Warehouse program is in complete operation.
        This will increase our sales substantially in 1983.
    4.  Account: Dixon–Morrison — Charlotte, NC
        Type Product:        Top Wrap, PWGS
        1981 YTD Sales:      –0–
        1982 YTD Sales:      97,332 lbs.
        Share of Business:  100%
        Status:             Good
        Comments: This account has started closing stores in
        this market. Two were closed in Charlotte in November.
    5.  Account: Briston Special Products — Durham, NC
        Type Product:        Supermarket
        1981 YTD Sales:      67,838 lbs.
        1982 YTD Sales:      58,820 lbs.
        Share of Business:  100%
        Status:             Good
        Comments: Supra Film may open new opportunities. I will
        make the Supra presentation in December.
    6.  Account: Packaging Materials — Winston–Salem, NC
        Type Product:        Fresh Wrap–P
        1981 YTD Sales:      36M lbs.
        1982 YTD Sales:      26M lbs.
```

EXHIBIT 4–9 (Continued)

Share of Business: 10%
Status: Good
Comments: Printing for Branch Farms. Fresh Wrap–P has
been successfully run and account is hoping that Branch
will begin requesting to develop a competitive spirit
at this account. Gladstone is having difficulty here,
and Branch is not ready to cut us loose. I will follow
up monthly.

7. Account: Candus of Carolina — Newberry, SC
Type Product: Fresh Wrap–P
1981 YTD Sales: 20M lbs.
1982 YTD Sales: 43M lbs.
Share of Business: 20%
Status: Fair
Comments: Direct account. We are receiving only 24″
business. We must pursue other sizes; I will make a
presentation in December.

8. Account: Southern Packaging – Gastonia, NC
Type Product: J–H Tuf–Wrap
1981 YTD Sales: 30M lbs.
1982 YTD Sales: 145M lbs.
Share of Business: 100%
Status: Excellent
Comments: This account is fully supportive of us and
has expanded into the Virginia market. I will work
closely with this account to expand our pallet wrap
sales.

B. Major Prospects — 50M Pound Potential
1. Prospect: Halsey–Taylor — Charlotte, NC
Type Product: Supermarket Films
Estimated Annual Potential: 125M lbs.
Our Sales Prospects: Fair
Comments: Account is loyal to present source. I will
make Supra presentation in December with Dave Stinson
of Boone Supply, Inc.

2. Prospect: Delsey Foods — Wilkesboro, NC
Type Product: Supermarket Films

EXHIBIT 4–9   (Continued)

Estimated Annual Potential: 75M lbs.

Our Sales Prospects: Fair

Comments: Poor past experiences with us. I will make
Supra presentation in January 1982.

3. Prospect: Allston Supply, Inc. — Hickory, NC

   Type Product: Supermarket Films

   Estimated Annual Potential: 250M lbs.

   Our Sales Prospects: Poor

   Comments: A buyer change will be made in January. Joint
   call on Supra Film will be made in December.

4. Prospect: Candus Foods — Virginia City, VA

   Type Product: Supermarket Films

   Estimated Annual Potential: 250M lbs.

   Our Sales Prospects: Fair

   Comments: Amcros is a major key to this account. Joint
   calls by us, by BBC, and Jim Sims Brokerage are set up
   for week of December 14, 1982.

5. Prospect: Berger Supply — Norfolk, VA

   Type Product: Supermarket Films

   Estimated Annual Potential: 50M lbs.

   Our Sales Prospects: Excellent

   Comments: Karen Brown of Packaging Materials advises
   that this account successfully tested Top Wrap in early
   September. I will follow up on broker with this in
   December.

6. Prospect: Callis's — Asheville, NC

   Type Product: Supermarket Films

   Estimated Annual Potential: 100M lbs.

   Our Sales Prospects: Fair

   Comments: Currently Ramco has strong rapport at this
   account. I will work with PMI and make Supra
   presentation in December 1982.

7. Prospect: Best Brands — Mauldin, SC

   Type Product: Supermarket Films

   Estimated Annual Potential: 60M lbs.

   Our Sales Prospects: Poor

   Comments: Prior administration advised that Ramco

EXHIBIT 4–9 (Continued)

price reduction to this account is making sales
difficult. I will make Supra presentation in January
1983.

8. Prospect: <u>Foodland — High Point, NC</u>
    Type Product: Supermarket Films
    Estimated Annual Potential: 75M lbs.
    Our Sales Prospects: Fair
    <u>Comments</u>: Account currently having some problems with
    Haber & Associates. I will try for an appointment for
    Supra presentation in December.

C. <u>Accounts Sold in October and November 1982</u>
    Rubican & Bush — Hickory, NC

D. <u>Accounts Lost in October and November 1982</u>
    No accounts lost in October and November 1982.

III. COMPETITIVE ACTIVITY

1. Ramco is testing at Foodland. They gave three weeks' supply
    of film for test. I should have results by the middle of
    December.
2. Gladstone having difficulty at Packaging Materials.
    Account complaining about poor quality, specifically
    varying width and edge hang; lack of sales contact and sales
    support.
3. Haber & Associates have sold stretch meat film to Foodland
    in High Point. Quality is poor.

IV. SALES NEEDS FROM MARKETING

Harry Hanes of Southern Packaging has suggested a carrying
bag for pallet wrap or supermarket films. This would give our
product an added professional touch.

It would also give our samples added protection from the
elements.

In addition, it would help keep our business a private
matter between buyer/broker and our sales force.

EXHIBIT 4–9   *(Continued)*

V. NOVEMBER YEAR–TO–DATE
BUDGET RECAP

1982 YTD Actual Expense	1982 YTD Expense Budget	Variance
$575.56	$600.00	$24.44 or 4% under

Austin Davis
Austin Davis, Field Representative

sion." The conclusions in a memo report may be *listed* or written in *paragraph form* under the section heading "Conclusions."

The *letter report* format is used for reports to people outside the organization — customers and clients primarily. It is useful for reports that are less than five or six pages long. The letter report contains the basic parts of the business letter, including a *subject line* for listing the topic of the report. This subject line may be placed *before* the salutation of the letter. Since the main difference between the letter and memo report is the work relationship between writer and receiver, the same comments about statement of purpose, section headings, and conclusions apply to both formats.

The *long formal report* may be used either within or outside the company. This format is not only lengthier but also more formal than other formats. The long report contains *prefatory material* (table of contents, letter or memo of authorization, letter or memo of transmittal, and abstract) and *end material* (end notes, bibliography, and appendix), items not found in shorter, less formal reports. Chapter 10 discusses the long formal report in detail.

LEARNING ACTIVITIES

1. The form report is used extensively, especially at lower levels of an organization. Explain why this format is very effective at these levels.

2. If you are employed, bring to class samples of the various kinds of report formats that your company uses. Be sure to ask permission

from your superiors to show the report to your class, especially if it contains privileged information. If you are not employed, ask a friend or relative who does work to let you borrow sample reports from his or her company. Be prepared to tell your peers:

a. The name of the company;
b. The format used and why;
c. The kind of information reported;
d. Good and poor points about the organization or writing in the report;
e. Any unusual details about the report.

3. The following exercises are very simple; they merely provide you with an opportunity to practice the formats discussed in this chapter. Problems in later chapters are more sophisticated and should challenge your ability to research, organize, and write good reports.

a. In a memo report to your superior, Anne Browne, show the following facts about the racial composition of the United States population in the censuses of 1960 and 1970. Using the table, also show Ms. Browne the percentage of each group that comprised the entire population.

U.S. Population

Year	Total Population	Caucasian Race	Negro/Other Races
1960	179,323,000	158,832,000	20,491,000
1970	203,212,000	177,749,000	25,463,000

b. In a memo report to your superior, Joe McDowell, Director of Advertising, present the information in the following table about leading United States advertisers and their expenditures for advertising, as well as the percentage of total sales spent on advertising.

Advertising Costs

Ranking	Name of Company	Advertising Costs	Total Sales	Advertising as % of Sales
1.	Procter & Gamble	$614,900,000	$10,772,186,000	5.7
2.	General Foods	393,000,000	5,959,600,000	6.5
3.	Sears, Roebuck and Co.	379,313,000	17,514,000,000	2.1
4.	General Motors Corp.	323,395,000	66,311,200,000	0.5
5.	Philip Morris	291,201,000	8,302,892,000	3.5

c. In a letter report to regular outpatients at Bradenton Clinic, explain that the cost of physical therapy treatments will increase by 9 percent beginning June 1. Present reasons for the increased fees (budget cuts in state funds, new equipment, or other reasons). Be persuasive and convince the patients that good medical care is a bargain at any price.

d. Refer to Exhibit 4–2. Send a memo report to all supervisors in both of these departments. Remind them of the following things about completing the upcoming evaluations:

    i. Be sure that *all* questions have been answered; if a question is not applicable, write n/a.

   ii. Complete the "Comments" section on *all* employees.

  iii. Most importantly, this year we are asking that *all* employees sign the evaluation somewhere in the space provided for employee comments or complaints. Report to the supervisor that this change is being made because of allegations by an employee that she has never seen an evaluation of her work in the two years she has been employed by the company. Explain the significance of this case.

e. In a letter report to the members of the Farmers Organization of America, discuss the dollar amount of agricultural and nonagricultural products exported in the past year. The total dollar amount in exports was $181,802,000. Of that amount, $35,209,000 was expended for agricultural commodities while $146,428,000 went to nonagricultural commodities. Compute and show the percentage for agricultural commodities of total dollars in exports. Also discuss the outlook for exports this year and the reasons for it. Discuss how all these considerations will affect the farmer.

f. In a memo report to your superior, recommend that Mary Bliss, a clerk IV in your department, be transferred to the purchasing department as of May 1. Give reasons for Mary's request and for your recommendation.

g. You are a paralegal working in the legal department of a large corporation. Your superior asks you to prepare a letter report to a student at the local university responding to his questions about the training, responsibilities, and salary for entry-level jobs in this field (you will need to research this information before you can write the report for this exercise).

h. In a letter report to Mr. John Carson, inform him that he may use a number of renderings (which you will list in the report) from your architectural firm in a forthcoming book. Explain that the company wants full recognition (name of company and name of design architect on renderings), that he must obtain permission from the State Department for the renderings of two government buildings designed by your firm, and that he may *not* use two other renderings (list these too) because your contracts with the firms prohibit any use of them except by persons designing and constructing the buildings.

i. Chris Zutek is Director of Investor Relations for Raybrod, a company that manufactures radio broadcasting equipment. Raybrod wants to diversify by acquiring Automated Business Concepts, a two-year-old company that produces computerized business systems for radio broadcasting stations. Raybrod would market the systems to stations to handle their internal billing and accounting functions. In a letter report to stockholders, Zutek must explain Raybrod's intentions to acquire ABC and present some facts about the new company. Write the report that Zutek should submit, remembering to make the acquisition appear financially sound to the stockholders. Include the following information in your report:

ABC is located in San Diego.

Raybrod currently has equipment in 1,000 radio stations in the United States.

Fewer than 5 percent of the 8,900 AM and FM stations in the United States now use computerized business systems (how does the market look?).

Raybrod's sales for the current year were $54.1 million.

Expected sales of computerized billing systems could bring in an additional $1.2 million in the first year ABC is owned.

j. You work in the personnel department of your company. Your superior heads the wage and salary administration area. She has asked you to prepare an informational report on the wages earned by tool and die makers in your particular area of the state for comparison with company wages, which are given in the following table. You decide to use the *Labor Area Summary* plus an informal interview with someone in the local Employment Security Division to get the information for the report. Then you will compare the data from those sources with the wages paid to tool and die makers by your company. Use the memo format for this report.

Company Wages for Tool and Die Makers

	Low	High	Weighted Avg.
Tool and die maker — Grade 2	$7.33	$7.83	$7.51
Tool and die maker — Grade 3	7.04	7.43	7.46
Tool and die maker — Grade 5	5.72	5.72	5.72

k. Submit an informational report in memo form to your superior, Mary C. Haynes, a Washington lobbyist for a national association. Include the following table in your report and discuss the enrollment patterns in 1970 and 1978 in public and private schools. Predict future trends for each level of education, based on (1) the figures from the table and (2) economic conditions during that period.

Total Enrollment in Public and Private Schools, 1970 and 1978

1970 TOTAL = 60.4 MILLION STUDENTS			**1978 TOTAL = 58.6 MILLION STUDENTS**		
Educational Level	Public	Private	Educational Level	Public	Private
	(in millions)			(in millions)	
Nursery	.3	.8	Nursery	.6	1.2
Kindergaten	2.6	.5	Kindergarten	2.5	.5
Elementary	30.0	3.9	Elementary	25.3	3.2
High school	13.5	1.2	High school	14.2	1.2
College	5.7	1.7	College	7.4	2.4

Source of data: Statistical Abstract of the United States.

l. You are product manager of Bolger's coffee at Pector and Gumble's food division. Send a memo report to your superior, Mr. Randolph Greene. Interpret the latest figures (see table) on the continued drop in coffee consumption and the increased costs of advertising to maintain market share. P and G acquired Bolger's in 1963, and coffee consumption has declined each year since.

Coffee Consumption and Advertising Costs

	1960	1970	1980	Projected 1982
Consumption in lbs. per person	11.6	10.4	8.6	8.0
Market share	14%	15.5%	15.9%	16%
Advertising costs (in millions)	$1.1	$2.5	$3.1	$3.2

Report-Writing Elements: Verbal and Nonverbal

LEARNING OBJECTIVES

After reading this chapter, you should be able to:

- Define the term *verbal;*
- Define *connotation* and give examples of words and phrases with *positive, negative,* and *neutral* connotations;
- Explain the difference between *concrete* and *abstract* words;
- Explain the *four levels of diction* and why only the *popular* level is suitable for business writing;
- Define *jargon;*
- Explain the differences between *strong* and *weak* verbs;
- Explain when to use *active* and *passive* voice verbs;
- Explain the two most important *positions for words* in a sentence;
- Explain how to keep *sentence structure* simple and easy to understand;
- Explain the difference between the *personal* and *impersonal* writing styles;
- Explain how *nonverbal elements* can be used to communicate effectively in a report.

**THE VERBAL
ELEMENTS**

The term *verbal* refers to the use of words or language — written or spoken. Once you know what you need to report, you must decide what words to use and how to put them to work for you in sentences and paragraphs. Words help create tone in a report. *Tone* is the total impact created by the choice of words, the writing style, and the content of a report. It is the feeling the reader has as he or she reads — confusion, anger, pride, pleasure. You should not choose words arbitrarily; instead, analyze the audience and put yourself in their position to determine what words will offend or please, clarify or obscure a point. The following suggestions will help you create the tone you desire.

**Choose Words
with
Appropriate
Connotations**

If the purpose of your report is to make the reader feel guilty, there are words to create that tone; or if you want to persuade or present information accurately, there are other words. *Connotation* is the feeling — the positive, negative, or neutral emotional responses — that a word evokes in the reader or listener. Some words cause you to recall experiences from your past; these associations make you feel good or bad about the word that reminded you of the experiences. Adjectives and adverbs in particular evoke emotional responses, but other words, or phrases, can also call up such feelings. For example, "profits" may sound too crass (negative connotation) to be effective in reporting to the consumer advocate but may have just the positive connotation you need to address the owner of a small business. For similar reasons the large corporation refers to "net income" or "earnings" rather than "profits." Or let's say you are writing a report that includes references

"Mr. Eiler, I have a tiny suggestion. Instead of saying that the new Mishka cloth is made by our foreign subsidiary, why not call it our latest imported line!"

to business done with a foreign manufacturer. If you say "foreign goods," many Americans will have a negative feeling about the expression. However, if you make reference to our "goods imported from . . . ," the feeling is neutral or even positive for many people.

Sometimes such words as *no, not, failed, reject,* and so forth have denotative meanings (dictionary definitions) that are negative. Therefore, you should avoid using them unless you want to create a negative tone. For example, a not-for-profit organization had an advertising agency prepare a brochure about its activities for the upcoming season and to solicit funds. The design of the brochure was attractive, the information was clear, and even the subtle persuasion seemed effective. But the positive tone was ruined by this sentence:

> *Mailing of tickets:*   Do not expect to receive tickets until after November 15.

It made the reader feel like a child who has been reprimanded for asking, "How long till Christmas?" That negative sentence could have been phrased in a more positive way:

> *Mailing of tickets:*   All tickets will be mailed after November 15.

If you remember the importance of connotation, you can avoid errors that can alienate or offend your audience.

Use Concrete Words

As stated earlier, reports present information for use in decision making. In choosing words to report that information, you should be very specific rather than generalizing about what you want to say. That means that you should choose *concrete* (specific) words rather than *abstract* (general) words. In this sentence, *prohibitive* is an abstract word:

> The cost of the cards should not be prohibitive.

To the manufacturer of the cards, $15 per 1,000 cards may seem prohibitive. However, to the purchaser, $10 per 1,000 cards may be prohibitive. To eliminate any doubt about what you mean, use a concrete expression:

> The cost of the cards should not exceed $10 per 1,000 cards.

Here is another example of the importance of using concrete words:

> *Abstract:* My employees are *lethargic* because the temperature in our office is *extremely* high.
>
> *Concrete:* The temperature in our office today was 88°, and my employees *got little work done because of the heat.*

Notice that the words *prohibitive, lethargic, high,* and *extremely* were adjectives and an adverb, respectively. Generally, when reporting information, avoid using these two parts of speech. Not only are they abstract, but they are also "carriers of emotion," as we said earlier. Usually your purpose in reporting information is to give facts, not to call up emotions that will distract your readers from your prime objective.

Of course, adjectives and adverbs are useful on some occasions. For example, the adjective and adverbial forms of colors, directions (east, west), and sizes can be helpful in writing methods and procedures reports, which are discussed in Chapter 8.

Another kind of abstraction to avoid is imprecise words. The English language usually offers several words that loosely define any particular thing; some are abstract, some are concrete. Look at the levels of precision here:

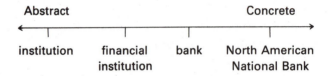

Because there are many kinds of institutions, that term is abstract. *Financial institution* makes a more concrete impression, but there is more than one kind of financial institution. The word *bank* further clarifies the kind of financial institution, and *North American National Bank* is the most concrete of all because it tells which specific bank we mean. Always try to use the most precise word available, as this example shows:

> *Abstract:* NANB is the largest *institution* in Illinois.
> *Concrete:* NANB is the largest *bank* in Illinois.

Use Popular Diction

Another consideration in choosing words is the level of diction. Most words in our language can be classified under one of four *levels of diction:* learned, popular, colloquial, or slang. *Learned* words are scholarly words; used by our best educated people, they include those unfamiliar words you often see in books and may understand the general meaning of but never know well enough to use in your own speech or writing. *Popular* diction includes words that the majority of our population uses and understands; this level of diction includes words used by the mass media — popular newspapers and magazines, TV, and radio. *Colloquial* diction refers primarily to the spoken language and includes words, phrases, and pronunciations that are peculiar to a particular region or area of the country and, therefore, are not used by people outside that region. *Slang* is vivid, expressive language that has a short life span; today's slang expression will undoubtedly seem old-fashioned five years from now.

Although the distinction between levels is not always clear-cut, and although there is some overlapping of words in the various levels, you can usually tell the level of diction of a particular word. Look at these examples:

Learned	Popular	Colloquial	Slang
to depart	to leave	none	to split to book
transport me	take me	carry me	none
none	you (plural)	y'all, you guys, youse guys	none
inebriated	intoxicated drunk	none	smashed schnockered
to cleanse	to wash	"warsh" (a pro- nunciation)	none

Use the popular level of diction in report writing to ensure that the reader will understand you. Colloquialisms are too limited to be valuable in business that is transacted nationally or internationally; slang changes too rapidly and becomes outdated too soon. In addition, foreign business people usually cannot understand slang expressions. The learned level of diction should also be avoided unless you are certain your audience understands all your learned words. Even then, popular words are often assimilated by the mind faster than learned ones because the audience has seen and heard the popular words more often.

One category of words that does not belong in our discussion of levels of diction but that is important in reports is *specialized language*. Specialized words are those used by a particular business or trade group or by a particular work function within an organization but are

Use Specialized Words Only with Other Specialists

not familiar to the general population. For example, the letters *ID* at the popular level of diction are an abbreviated form of the word *identification*. However, to specialists such as engineers, plumbers, and pipefitters, ID means *inside diameter* (of a pipe, drain, etc.). Or consider this example: the accounting department of a meat packing plant knows exactly what a *yield control statement* is, but if the accountants mention this report to the personnel department, they may get a blank stare. Therefore, it is both ridiculous and rude to use *specialized* words with people who will not understand what you mean. You may impress them with your knowledge of the field, but you won't achieve your main objective — informing them of your ideas. If you must use a specialized term with lay people, define it before using it in the report. Chapter 13 discusses how to define specialized words.

Avoid Jargon

Another kind of writing that is meant to impress rather than to express the writer's ideas is *jargon*. Jargon is riddled with bursts of learned words strung together by unnecessary prepositions and other parts of speech. This pretentious, often meaningless, language should be omitted from your report writing. The following example of jargon is a directive that came across the desk of former President Franklin D. Roosevelt:

> In those establishments where suspension of labor is possible, direct those parties of management to the termination of the illumination.

FDR rewrote it in a clear, concise way:

> In buildings where work can be stopped, tell the managers to turn off the lights.

Often writers of government reports are guilty of this misuse of the language; and in the past, documents such as sales contracts and insurance policies used jargon. Recently, though, laws such as the Truth in Lending Act and pressure from consumer groups have caused writers to make documents more understandable. Remember, if you want to impress your superior, the best way is to write clear, concise sentences that say what you mean.

Use Strong Verbs

You may have noticed that the verbs used in a sentence carry much of the meaning. You can make your reports clearer, more concise, and more direct if you use *strong verbs*. Strong verbs consist of a single word, as opposed to weak verbs, which are joined with other parts of speech to form a phrase. Look at these examples:

Weak Verbs	Strong Verbs
is a discussion of	discusses
placed an order	ordered
has the job of operating	operates
is inspector of	inspects

You can eliminate weak verbs — and other unnecessary words — from your reports by learning to edit your own writing. That means you should write a rough draft of a report, then set it aside while you do other tasks. Later, pick up the draft and reread it carefully; delete anything wordy and revise things that are not clear to you now that the writing is "cold." Be ruthless. Do not keep anything that is poorly written even if, for example, a particular word or phrase sounds impressive, "has a nice ring," or whatever other weak excuse you might be tempted to use.

Use the Active Voice When Possible

Another aspect of verb usage is active and passive voice. The *voice* of a verb describes its relationship with the subject. If the subject performs the action stated by the verb, the verb is in the active voice. However, if the subject does not perform any action but rather is acted upon by someone or something else, the verb is in the *passive voice*. Study these examples:

Active: President Hawkins *visited* the lab yesterday.
Passive: The lab *was visited* by President Hawkins yesterday.

Active: Beecher Wholesale *distributes* six brands of beer in the Austin area.
Passive: Six brands of beer *are distributed* by Beecher Wholesale in the Austin area.

Active: Figure 1, page 3, *shows* the proposed location.
Passive: The proposed location *is shown* in Figure 1, page 3.

The active voice is preferred in most reporting because it is more direct and forceful than the passive voice. Look at these sentences from a request for a report:

> Please indicate below the prerequisites that you enforce for each of the courses you teach in the undergraduate program. Your reply before Wednesday, November 21, would be appreciated.

The second sentence is written in the passive voice. Notice that it is weak when compared to the active voice verb in the preceding sentence and that it is inconsistent to use both voices within the same paragraph. The second sentence is more consistent and more direct when written in the active voice:

> We would appreciate your reply before Wednesday, November 21.

Notice in the revision that the most important piece of information — the date the report is needed — is now last in the sentence. You will see later in this chapter that this final position is one of the most important in a sentence.

Lest you be tempted to avoid the passive voice at all costs, let's look at some occasions when it is useful. You may need it when the agent of the action is unknown. For example, if you don't know the subject to be used with an active verb, you may have to use the passive. Here is such an example:

> The invoice *was paid* on March 5.

Also use the passive voice when you must be tactful. Because it takes more words to write it, the effect is a "slowing down" or softening of the statement, as in this example:

> This problem *should be taken up* with our legal department.

The same statement made in the active voice is more direct and confident and would be used only by someone whose opinion carried a lot of weight:

> We *should take up* this problem with our legal department.

Remember that your choice of active or passive voice will be determined by the effect you want to create for the reader.

**Put the Most
Important Ideas
First or Last
in the Sentence**

People tend to remember best the ideas that are presented either at the beginning or at the end of a sentence. Since efficiency and clarity are most important in reporting information, put the most important ideas first or last in the sentence. In short, avoid beginning sentences with empty words such as "There is . . ." or "It was . . ." Look at these examples to see how eliminating these expressions creates more economical and forceful sentences.

Empty beginning:	There are only two types of mortgage available now: the conventional and the VHA.
Economical beginning:	Only two types of mortgage are available now: the conventional and the VHA.
Empty beginning:	There are two significant disadvantages to industry in converting to the metric system.
Economical beginning:	Industry faces two significant disadvantages in converting to the metric system.
Empty beginning:	It is important that we save time and money in handling new bank card requests. The following procedure is more efficient.
Economical beginning:	By using the following procedure, we can save time and money in handling new bank card requests.

Keep Sentence Structure Simple

In any sentence in our language, nouns and verbs carry the bulk of the meaning. For that reason, the clearest sentence patterns are the subject-verb (noun-verb) pattern and the subject-verb-direct object (noun-verb-noun) pattern. The more extra words (modifiers) that are inserted between each part of a pattern, the greater the likelihood of a misunderstanding of the meaning. The best sentences, then, are those that keep the S-V or S-V-O as close together as possible. Of course, that does not mean you must write uninteresting or choppy sentences. Simply put the modifiers *before* or *after* the basic pattern and keep the basic elements close together. Look at these examples to see how the placement of the modifiers *before* the basic pattern improves the sentence:

Original sentence:	The most important task, before you write the direct mail letter, is audience analysis.
Modifier before basic pattern:	Before you write the direct mail letter, the most important task is audience analysis.

These additional examples show how you can enlarge a sentence by placing the modifiers before or after the basic elements.

<table>
<tr><td></td><td>   **S**   **V**   **O**</td></tr>
</table>

Basic sentence:	**S V O** Mr. Monroe lacks skills in business writing and communication.
Enlarged with modifiers:	Judging from the tone and appearance of his written communications to his staff, I **S V O** would say that Mr. Monroe lacks skills in business writing and communication.
Basic sentence:	**S V O** (You) Sort the completed forms into two piles.
Enlarged sentence:	**V** At 4:00 P.M. each day, sort the completed **O** forms into two piles, one for snap and one for continuous forms.

Even when you use other sentence patterns for variety in your writing, the information will be clearer if you keep the basic elements that carry the meaning close together.

Use the Appropriate Writing Style

Careful audience analysis, as well as precedents that have been set in your organization, will help you decide whether to use the personal or impersonal writing style.

The personal style is preferred for letters and memos. It is also used in other types of reports, particularly if they are to be read by a single individual and will not be used again sometime in the future. The *personal style* is characterized by the use of the first- and second-person pronouns: *I, we, you, my, our,* and so on. These make the reader feel personally involved in the report:

> On October 1, 1982, I interviewed Robert Barnes of M & M Wholesale in Charlotte. Our discussion focused on the kinds of reports written and received at M & M. The interview was informal and lasted approximately 45 minutes. This report discusses the information gathered during that interview.

Most reports, however, are written in the impersonal style. Technical reports or any other kind that will be filed and referred to in the future should use the *impersonal style,* characterized by the use of the third-person pronouns — *he, she, they,* and so on — or by the use of the impersonal pronoun, *one.* Generally, reports written in the impersonal style will sound less stiff and aloof if you use nouns such as *the engineer, the marketing specialist,* or *the hospital administrator* rather than the impersonal *one.* This example shows the impersonal style:

> Each employee in the order department should be able to handle the breakdown and distribution of order forms. This job is vital because these forms are the detailed instructions given by the sales and sales-service people to the manufacturing managers so they can produce goods.

Be equally careful not to change from one style to another in a report as this person did:

> *Organizational Relationships:* The manager or assistant manager of the store is in direct control of all employees of the store. Each employee is also under the supervision of his/her department manager. At this level of *our* organization, *you* are not responsible for anyone else. (Note the shift in style in the last sentence.)

People who have self-confidence inspire confidence in others and generate credibility for themselves and their ideas. Such confidence comes through in reports too. When writing a report calling for a stand on an issue, be sure you know what you are to report and research it carefully. Then take a stand and report the information directly without hedging. State the facts and let them speak for themselves; avoid such expressions as *I think, I feel,* and *I believe.* The following example shows a bad case of hedging:

Take a Firm Stand

> I cannot help but think that Mike was somewhat unprepared. It is my belief that the information that he asked me for would have been of little value in the selection of a substitute for MX-31.

This writer could have expressed these same thoughts more concisely and firmly and could have done so tactfully. Here is one possible revision:

> Mike seemed unprepared in that the information he asked me for has little value in selecting a substitute for MX-31.

If you have thoughtfully studied the facts and have carefully presented the information, your recommendations are probably sound.

Avoid Sexist Language

Businesses are attempting to rid their written documents — manuals, handbooks, reports, and so on — of sexist language. Words are sexist if they refer only to men or only to women. Examples include *chairman, her, husband, he, wife,* and *women.* If you are writing about a situation in which either men *or* women may be involved, use nonsexist language to talk about it. For example, a job description for a secretarial position might use the job title *secretary* (nonsexist), but it should not use words such as *she,* which imply that only women are secretaries. Neither should a job description use a title such as *fireman,* since it implies that only someone of the male sex could do such work.

Of course, if you are speaking about a *specific* man or woman, it is silly to use nonsexist language, which will sound abstract. Use the most concrete words possible — man, woman, and so on — to describe the person.

Several ways can be found to avoid sexist language, as these examples show:

Sexist Language	Nonsexist Language
chairman	chairperson
maid	housekeeper
foreman	overseer, supervisor
policeman	police officer

Another way to avoid sexist language is to use both masculine and feminine words in describing a situation involving either men or women, as this example shows:

Discuss the employee's work, not *his or her* personality.

Occasionally you will need to recast a sentence to avoid sexist language, as these examples indicate:

Sexist: In situations in which the manager is the final authority, *he* must assume responsibility for *his* decisions.

Nonsexist: The manager who is the final authority must assume responsibility for any decisions.

You will have to make a conscious effort to avoid sexist language, since many language habits are unconsciously ingrained and must be unlearned.

As we have seen, the verbal elements of report writing are important for many reasons; the nonverbal ones, however, also play a part in preparing a good report.

The term *nonverbal* refers to devices other than words that can communicate in a report. This section discusses several of these devices, most of which deal with the psychological impact on the reader.

THE NONVERBAL ELEMENTS

The amount of blank space around a word, a sentence, or a paragraph can convey a positive or negative feeling to the reader. Think of your own reaction when confronted with several pages of crowded material in fine print. Your first thought probably is, "I'll never be able to wade through this boring stuff," and you may even put it aside. Even though the material may contain an exciting narrative, the psychological impact of the way it looks on the page is negative. A good idea, then, is to use white space liberally.

White Space

Look back at Exhibit 4–5 to see how white space was created in the heading of a report. Leaving ample blank space between parts of a heading and using double spacing between paragraphs are two ways of creating white space. In Chapter 4 we saw that section headings can be used to create the impression that a report is shorter than it really is. Part of the reason is the white space that is left around a heading. You will find other places to use white space, such as in indentations for lists, and in numerous places in illustrations (see Chapter 6).

Underlining important words or phrases in a report is another device that improves communication by enhancing psychological impact. Paragraph headings, for example, might get lost among the other words in the paragraph unless they are underlined. This technique also signals to the reader which ideas you consider important.

Underlining

Another device to call attention to important ideas such as main headings is to use capital letters for the entire word or phrase. In other cases, you may choose to capitalize only the first letter of the important words in a heading. In either case, the psychological effect is much the same as with underlining.

Capital Letters

Listing means arranging items one per line, perhaps using numbers, letters, dashes, or other markers to set off some information from the regular paragraphed information in a report. This technique is shown

Lists

in the recommendations under "Conclusions and Recommendations" in Chapter 4. Listing creates the feeling that a report is shorter than it really is and that the writer is well organized and can present ideas concisely.

Listing also serves the function of breaking the material into easily absorbed parts so the reader can assimilate it more readily. A third advantage of listing is that it provides a means of physically or mentally checking off the items on the list as they are read. Finally, we know the human mind can easily recall up to seven items of information. So, for example, if you *list* five steps in a process, the reader will remember them more easily than if you describe the same steps in longer, more detailed paragraph form.

Paper and Binders

Even the kind of paper used for a report can be a nonverbal communicator. Thin, slick paper is often used for forms on which routine periodic reports are made. These are for in-house use, so they need not be on impressive paper. However, if a report is being prepared for a customer, client, or grantor, heavier bond paper will give the impression that the company is prosperous, professional, and businesslike. Also, the report that goes outside the organization will likely be presented in a heavy paper or acrylic binder that displays the organization's logo. Again, this nonverbal communicator indicates that the company is businesslike. In addition, the binder serves the practical purpose of protecting the report from becoming damaged or soiled in handling.

All of the nonverbal communicators are useful. You may use every one of them in some reports; in others you may use only white space and underlinings. Be creative. Nonverbal factors are the silent communicators!

SUMMARY

This chapter deals with the verbal and nonverbal elements of report writing. The term *verbal* refers to the use of words or language. *Nonverbal* refers to means other than words or language that can be used to communicate. *Tone* is an important verbal element in writing. It is the total impact created by word choice, writing style, and content. Another verbal element is *connotation*, the feeling — a positive, negative, or neutral emotional response — that a word or phrase evokes in the reader. Choose words carefully to create the proper tone in a report.

Use *concrete* rather than *abstract* words in reports. Concrete words are those that have specific meanings, while abstract words are general and leave the reader free to infer various meanings from a single word or phrase.

Use the *popular level of diction* in reports. Most words in our language fall under one of these levels of diction: learned, popular, colloquial, and slang. *Learned diction* includes those words used by the best educated people and may include words you've heard or seen but don't know the meaning of. These are usually not suitable for reports because many people will not know their meanings. *Colloquial diction* includes both spoken and written words peculiar to a particular region or narrow area; they are therefore not suitable in reports. *Slang* is vivid, short-lived language that is unsuitable for reports because it soon becomes outdated. Furthermore, foreign business people cannot understand slang. In this era of numerous multinational corporations, we must be able to write so English speakers everywhere will understand us. The *popular* level of diction is language that will be understood by English speakers throughout the world. It is the language used by the mass media — the newspapers, TV, and radio. This is the level suitable for reports.

Use *specialized words* only with other specialists. Specialized words are those used by a particular business or trade group, a particular industry, or even a particular work function within an organization. Use these terms only in reports to other specialists who will understand them.

Avoid *jargon*, bursts of learned words strung together with unnecessary prepositions and other parts of speech. This kind of writing attempts to impress with the learned words but actually makes the writer look foolish since the prime concern in report writing is to express ideas, not to impress someone.

Use *strong* verbs in writing reports. These are single verbs in the active voice. Weak verbs are formed from a verb plus some other part of speech; the result is wordiness and an indecisive tone.

Use verbs in the *active voice* when you want to convey information. Use the *passive voice* when you want to sound tactful. Voice identifies the relationship between the subject of the sentence and its verb. With verbs in the active voice, the subject performs the action expressed by the verb. In the passive voice, the subject is acted upon by someone or something. Fewer words are used to write the active voice, so a sentence sounds decisive. Sentences in the passive voice require more words, so the effect is a "slowing down" of the sentence.

Put the most important information first or last in the sentence because information in either of these locations is remembered better than if it were in the middle.

There are two choices of writing styles — the *personal* and the *impersonal*. The personal style makes the reader feel involved in the report; it is characterized by the use of the personal pronouns *you, I, we,* and so on. The impersonal style is used when a report will be used and referred to by many readers, present and future. It is characterized by the use of the personal pronouns *he, they, she,* and so on, of the impersonal pronoun *one*, and of nouns such as *the engineer* or *the nurse practitioner*.

The nonverbal elements in report writing create a psychological impact on the reader. Such things as the kind, color, and quality of paper on which a report is typed tell us something about the professionalism and financial status of a company. Such things as the appearance of a report — does it look cramped on the page? — also communicate. Skillful use of white space on a page, underlining, capital letters in headings, and other such nonverbal communicators enhance the verbal elements in a report.

LEARNING ACTIVITIES

1. What is the difference between the terms *oral* and *verbal?*

2. Look at these phrases. Each consists of an adjective and a noun. Tell whether the connotation of each is positive, negative, or neutral. Would different audiences feel differently about the connotation of these phrases? Explain.

   a. a small woman
   b. a petite woman
   c. a little woman
   d. the little woman
   e. the tiny woman
   f. the wee woman

3. How can you make these abstract sentences more concrete?

   a. It is more economical to purchase the larger quantity.
   b. The company library subscribes to one business newspaper.
   c. The level of pollutants from the stack was too high to meet Environmental Protection Agency standards.
   d. During the heat wave in July, the demand for electricity reached an all-time high.
   e. The new plant is expected to open soon.

4. What is the level of diction of these words and phrases?

   a. prognosis
   b. mortgage
   c. hey (meaning hi or hello)
   d. jump the gun
   e. prestidigitator
   f. commercial

5. Change the weak verbs in these sentences to more direct strong verbs.

   a. She is supervisor of the entire accounts payable section.
   b. The treasurer has control over all financial decisions.
   c. Section V is a review of all previous complaints.
   d. Mr. DiGirolamo has the job of handling all requisitions for materials.
   e. In January we made a request for two additional calculators.

6. Tell whether the verbs in these sentences are in the active or passive voice:

   a. The shipment will be sent from our Bridgeport factory on September 1.
   b. Continued bad weather caused a decline in sales.
   c. Accountants often handle special work such as pension funds and profit-sharing accounts.
   d. The shares were issued in 1945.
   e. Please check the camera, the monitor, and the recorder before you store them.

7. Change the personal writing style in this paragraph to the impersonal writing style.

   Progress Thus Far: I have interviewed the manager of the store. I have also questioned employees at the Better Business Bureau of Anson County, Inc., the Richmond Chamber of Commerce, and the Merchants Association. On the 13th of November I will meet Peter Santano from the Crime Prevention Department of the Richmond Police Department. In addition, I have obtained information from books and microfilm in the library to incorporate in the report.

8. Enlarge these sentences by using modifiers before or after the basic sentence pattern:

   a. The company's position can be strengthened.
   b. CSC Ltd. presented the lowest bid.
   c. I have sent the copy to the printers.
   d. Please return the parts return request form within 30 days.
   e. The Federal Reserve branch bank is on South Fifth Street.

9. Read the article, "War on Gobbledygook — Report from the Front," in *U.S. News & World Report*, September 14, 1980, pp. 71–72.

10. Collect two writing samples for analysis. One should be a paragraph from a popular business periodical or news item; the other should be a paragraph from an academic journal. Make an analysis of the following:

    a. The number of one-syllable, two-syllable, and three-or-more-syllable words.
    b. The number of technical words that you — a business person — do not know
    c. The number of learned words in the passage.

    After tabulating the results, draw some conclusions about the two pieces of writing.

CHAPTER

6

Using Illustrations in Reports

LEARNING OBJECTIVES

After reading this chapter, you should be able to:

- State why *illustrations* are important in writing;
- Identify the *three types* of illustrations, based on the way they are labeled;
- Define each type of illustration and describe what each is best suited for;
- Construct *tables* and the simpler *figures* for your own reports;
- Explain the use and labeling of *exhibits;*
- Recognize the importance of using a *source note* when the illustration is not your own creation;
- Describe how *word processing* and *computer graphics* are changing reporting procedures.

Time is money in the business world. Therefore, any method of communication that saves time — for the reader or for the writer — saves money. The writers who put what they have to say in the briefest form will stand out in the crowd of mediocre, verbose business people. In previous chapters we studied several ways to say what we mean economically. Now let's add another method to that list — the use of illustrations.

Illustrations are useful for several reasons. For example, many of our business associates have grown up with TV and movies and are visually oriented. An illustration is often a better way to communicate with these people than are words alone. Also, imagine for a moment turning to the sports page in your newspaper and finding the baseball or basketball statistics written in sentence and paragraph form. This notion is ridiculous because sorting out and retaining the important information would be difficult and time-consuming. Sports statistics, as well as numerous kinds of business statistics, are usually presented in tabular form (tables) for ease in assimilating the information. This chapter will discuss tables as well as other kinds of illustrations that can be used in business reports.

An *illustration* is any kind of visual element that can save time or words or that can present a fact more dramatically. There are three kinds of illustration: tables, figures, and exhibits.

In most cases, illustrations should be integrated with the rest of the report. Time is wasted if the reader has to keep a finger stuck in one page while leafing to the back to find an illustration. In general, put illustrations on the same page or as close as possible to the page where they are mentioned.

TABLES

We are all familiar with tables. Look back at Table 2–1. A *table* is any set of related numbers and words grouped together in rows (horizontal) or columns (vertical) for ease in reading and understanding. Tables are arranged in some logical form, and the rows and columns are given headings to make the information clear. Tables can be integrated with the text of the report to provide vital information. Used in this way, they should be referred to by table number. However, tables can also be used as *supplementary* material in the appendix of the report; if used this way, in the body of the report refer the reader to the table in the appendix.

Tables can be used for many kinds of statistical data and can be organized in numerous ways. The following paragraphs describe the usual parts of a well-planned table.

Table numbers are needed if more than one table is included.

Number the tables consecutively as they appear in the report; the number can be placed above or below the table.

Titles are used so the reader immediately knows the subject matter of the table. The title may be placed beside or below the table number, and the important words should begin with capital letters. For more emphasis, the entire title may be capitalized. Titles should be as clear, concise, and complete as possible. Here is an example of a table number and title:

Table 3.   Number of Subscribers by District to HBO in 1982

Column headings are phrases that tell what kind of information the reader will find in a particular column. Column headings must be clear and concise. Column totals are usually placed at the bottom of the column but can be put at the top if the total is more important than its parts. Also, if there is no information on a particular item, the space in the column should be filled with a (0) or "n.a." (not available) to avoid confusion to the reader.

Stubs are the phrases on the left-hand side of a table that explain what the figures in a row represent.

End data, such as footnotes, are placed below the table to tell the source of borrowed material, to explain material in the table, and so forth. Usually an asterisk beside the information in the table indicates a footnote in the end data. Other symbols or letters may be used if several footnotes are needed. Exhibit 6–1 shows the parts of a table.

When setting up tables, you must also decide how to use lines (called *rules*) to separate some information in the table from other information. Generally, use *horizontal rules* between important headings. Do not use them between each item in the table or the information will look choppy and unrelated. Use *vertical rules* sparingly, too. You can use them to separate column headings that are completely unrelated. However, if plenty of white space surrounds the data, even those rules may be omitted. Refer to Table 2–1 and Exhibit 6–1 for examples of the use of rules.

EXHIBITS

A second type of illustration is the *exhibit*. Sometimes — to explain or clarify what we mean in a report — we will include a copy of a form used by our department or division. Or we may include a copy of an invoice or other documentation as proof of a statement in the report. At other times we may attach a sample of a component of one of our products: small items such as yarns, labels, or small wires. These can be very effective illustrations when discussing the product in a report. Whenever we use a real object, an original or a copy of a business

EXHIBIT 6–1
Sample Table with Its Parts Labeled

TABLE NUMBER → TABLE 1

TITLE OF TABLE → AVERAGE WEEKLY EARNINGS OF HOURLY WORKERS 1967–1970
(excluding overtime)

COLUMN HEADINGS
STUBS
END DATA

Year	Hours Worked	Hourly Earnings	Gross Earnings Weekly*	Net Earnings 0 Dependents*	Net Earnings 3 Dependents*
1967	40.6	$2.72	$115	$ 93	$101
1968	40.7	2.88	123	98	107
1969	40.6	3.06	130	102	111
1970	39.8	3.24	134	107	116

* Figures have been rounded to nearest whole dollar.
Source of Statistics: World Almanac.

Important points to note about this table:

Years are in *even* increments of 1 year (rather than showing 1960, 1963, 1965, 1968, 1969).

A sensible number of lines are used to separate the information to make it readable (lines drawn between each year would have been excessive).

form, letter, memo, or other item, we call these illustrations *exhibits* and label them as such.

If the exhibit is an integral part of the report, it should be placed on the same page or on the page just after the one on which it is mentioned. Of course, exhibits may also be used in the appendix of a report as supplementary material.

Since exhibits vary so widely, there is no specific format as there is for tables. But each one must be given an *exhibit number* to help the reader locate the item in the report. The number may be placed at the top or at the bottom; however, if the exhibit is printed horizontally on the page, place the exhibit number at the bottom of the page so it will not be covered when the report is put in a binder.

If the exhibit is a form, memo, letter, contract, or the like, it will probably have a heading that tells the reader what it is, so you will need to give it only an exhibit number.

Exhibit 6–2 shows a brief methods and procedures report that uses an exhibit as an illustration.

FIGURES

The third type of illustration, figures, is the most common. If the illustration you want to include in your report does not qualify as a table or as an exhibit, as we discussed them, it will be labeled as a *figure*. There are many kinds of figures, each created to present a particular kind of information concisely and dramatically.

Once you know the kind of figure best suited to your needs, draw it in pencil on graph paper so it will be accurate. When it is perfect, transfer it to the report, using black ink.

The following sections describe the most common kinds of figures and the information they best illustrate.

Pie Charts

Pie charts are circular illustrations used to show the percentages of the parts that comprise a whole thing — 100 percent. For example, a pie chart could show the total number of people employed by a company as well as the percentage of that number in each division of the company. Or it could show the total expenditures of one division as well as the percentage of the whole that was spent on each kind of expense. These charts should have a figure number and title placed either above or below the chart.

When making a pie chart, you should remember these points:

1. The whole "pie" represents 100 percent of something, so the parts that comprise it must be in percentages and must equal 100 percent when totaled.

EXHIBIT 6–2
Memorandum Containing an Exhibit

MEMORANDUM

DATE: 5 February 1983
TO: All Buyers and Expediters
FROM: John Jones
SUBJECT: Telephone Call Memo

    The Telephone Call Memo shown in Exhibit 1 is a convenient
method to report the content of telephone conversations to all
interested personnel.

EXHIBIT 1
TELEPHONE CALL MEMO

Telephone Call

Route _____ ⑤ _____

By _____ ① _____ Co. _____   _____

To _____ ② _____ Co. _____   _____

Date _____ ③ _____ Time _____ ③ _____   _____

Subject _____ Job. No. _____ ⑥ _____

④

EXHIBIT 6–2   (Continued)

```
Preparation
     Although this report of the telephone conversation is
intended to be informally written, it should contain the
following information (the numbers listed refer to the
numbered spaces on Exhibit 1):
     1. Give the name, title, and company of the person making
        the call. If the call was made by the person writing the
        report, the title and company may be omitted.
     2. Give the name, title, and company of the person called.
     3. Record the date and time the call was made.
     4. Write a brief statement of the important points
        discussed. Often simply listing purchase order numbers
        will suffice. Avoid unnecessary details and the
        repetitive use of ''I said,'' ''He replied,'' etc.
     5. List the names of all personnel who will get a copy of
        this report.
     6. Show the five-digit company project number the report
        applies to.
Distribution
     1. Send a copy of the report to all personnel listed on the
        ''Route'' section.
     2. File the original in the purchase order file.
     3. Put a copy in the memorandum log.
     The Telephone Call Memo is useful in communicating
information that is brief and not detailed.
     Use a typewritten memo report when detailed background
information is necessary or when client or upper-management
personnel are included on the distribution.
```

2. Start at the 12 o'clock position and measure off the segments clockwise. To ensure that the percentages are accurate, try the following suggestion. As you draw the rough copy of the chart on graph paper, divide the pie into quarters; then divide each quarter into eighths; finally, divide each eighth into sixteenths. You will now have sixteen equal segments, each representing 6.25 percent of the whole pie. The smaller slices make it easier to get the right amount allotted for each item.

3. Label each segment of the pie. You can put the label inside or

EXHIBIT 6–3
Sample Pie Chart

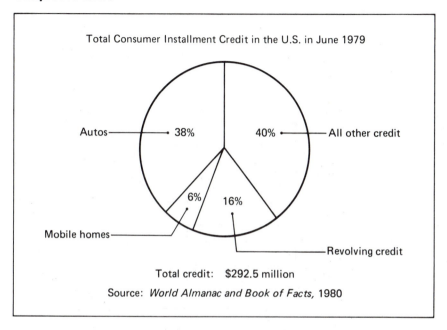

Total Consumer Installment Credit in the U.S. in June 1979

Autos——•—— 38%　　40% ——•——— All other credit

6%　　16%

Mobile homes———————

————————Revolving credit

Total credit:　$292.5 million

Source: *World Almanac and Book of Facts,* 1980

outside the segment, but be consistent in your method. Also type or print the label *horizontally* so it is easy to read.

Because pie charts are easy to read and assimilate, they are useful not only in written reports, but also in oral presentations of a report if they are enlarged so the audience can see them clearly. Exhibit 6–3 shows a sample pie chart.

A *bar chart* is used when you need to show two variables. Time and quantity are the most common ones, but others can be shown as well. Since there are two variables, the bar chart has two axes, the vertical and the horizontal. Also, the bars on the chart run *horizontally.* When constructing bar charts, remember these points:

Bar Charts

1. Select the scale to use for the chart.

2. Mark off *equal* segments on each axis and label them accurately.

3. Draw the bars accurately to reflect the amounts shown by the segments on the horizontal axis. You can show exact amounts by typing or printing in the exact figure at the end of each bar.

Exhibit 6–4 shows an example of a bar chart.

EXHIBIT 6–4
Sample Bar Chart

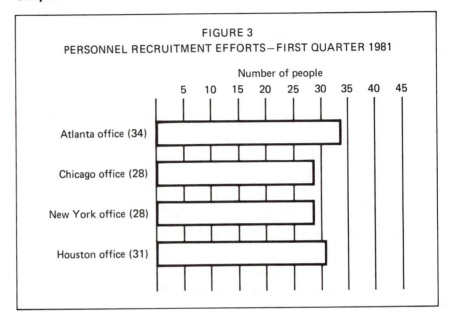

FIGURE 3
PERSONNEL RECRUITMENT EFFORTS—FIRST QUARTER 1981

Number of people

Atlanta office (34)

Chicago office (28)

New York office (28)

Houston office (31)

Column Charts

The *column chart*, like the bar chart, is used to show the relationship between two variables. Also like the bar chart, it needs a figure number, a title, and clearly labeled segments on each axis. The column chart, however, has *vertical* columns rather than horizontal bars (see Exhibit 6–5). Sometimes many facts can be presented on both bar and column charts by using a key or different colors to represent different items or by segmenting the bar or column to show several parts that comprise the whole bar or column. For example, study the complex data that follows; then look at Exhibit 6–5 to see how such data can be presented more succinctly and clearly than in the paragraphed form by using a key to represent the different states.

> Per capita personal income per state is figured by dividing total personal income in each state by its total population. Through the years 1970–1973, the per capita personal income increased throughout the United States; however, Mississippi still ranked lowest of all states, and the District of Columbia highest.
> Indiana lay about midway between the two extremes. For example, in 1970 the per capita income for Mississippi residents was $2,630 compared with $3,768 for Indiana and $4,938 for residents of Washington, D.C.

EXHIBIT 6–5
Column Chart Illustrating Complex Data, with Its Parts Labeled

FIGURE 6

PER CAPITA PERSONAL INCOME

FOR MISSISSIPPI, INDIANA, AND WASHINGTON, D.C. —1970–1973

Stub
(Notice the zeros to indicate thousands)

Vertical Axis
(Notice the equal increments)

Horizontal Axis
(Notice the equal increments)

Key

Figure Number

Title of Figure

While all three areas reported increases in personal income the following year, Mississippi's was smallest at $2,832, while D.C. reported the largest at $5,357. Again, Indiana was between the extremes at $4,051.

In 1972, both Indiana and Mississippi reported similar increases (approximately $300 per capita), while D.C. again reported a larger one (about $500 per capita). The actual figures were: Mississippi, $3,188; Indiana, $4,364; Washington, D.C., $5,827.

By 1973, Indiana recorded the largest per capita increase of the three areas at $4,987; Washington, D.C. reported $6,337; and Mississippi reported $3,556.

It appears that, even with substantial increases in per capita income each year, the so-called poor areas of our country are unlikely to catch up to the rich ones such as Washington, D.C. or New York.

Before we look at other figures, let's add one more thought about bar and column charts: be sure you understand clearly what you want your illustration to show. In the problem illustrated by Exhibit 6–5, the last sentence indicates that the reader should understand the relative disparaties in per capita income among the states. A student who didn't understand the meaning of the data created the illustration shown in Exhibit 6–6. Instead of showing the disparities, this chart shows the yearly increase for each state; however, it does not dramatize the fact that Mississippi is always far behind Washington, D.C. What other problems make this illustration difficult for the reader to understand quickly and easily?

Line Charts

A *line chart*, like a column or bar chart, shows the relationship between two variables. Also like other charts, a line chart needs a figure number, a title, and clearly labeled segments on each axis. The points of intersection of the two axes are plotted, and a line is drawn to connect the points. Line graphs are best suited for showing the ups and downs of the facts being illustrated. Again, the line chart can be used to show several items in a single illustration by using a key to explain the kinds of lines used — for example, dotted, broken, solid, dot/dash. The line graph in Exhibit 6–7 shows how the same information used for the column chart in Exhibit 6–5 can also be shown dramatically by a line chart.

EXHIBIT 6–6
Student Example Showing How Data Can Be Misrepresented

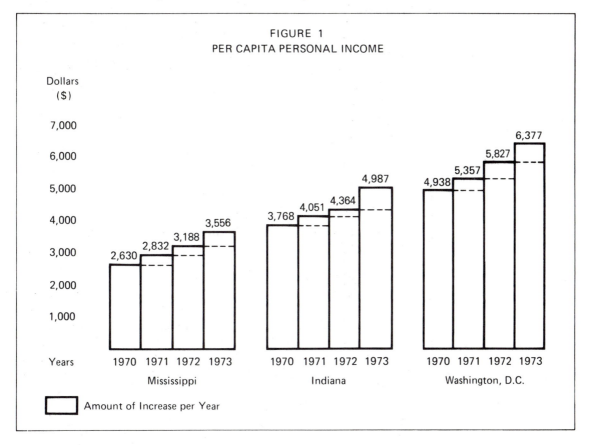

FIGURE 1
PER CAPITA PERSONAL INCOME

A map can show a geographical location more simply and quickly than several hundred words can. If using a map in your report, give it a figure number and title it clearly so your readers know exactly what they are looking at. If you borrow the map from another source, be sure to give credit for it in a footnote, unless, of course, the source appears in plain view. A large map can be folded so that it opens easily when it is attached to the report. A large map should be placed on the page following the one on which you refer to it. Small maps can go on the same page on which they are mentioned. Also remember that if you use an *actual* map, you should label it as an exhibit rather than as a figure. Exhibit 6–8 shows a map used in an annual report.

Maps

EXHIBIT 6–7
Sample Line Chart

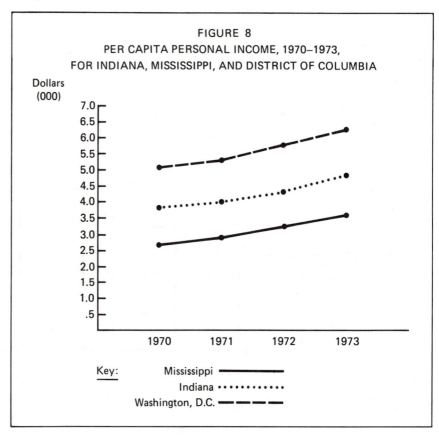

FIGURE 8
PER CAPITA PERSONAL INCOME, 1970–1973,
FOR INDIANA, MISSISSIPPI, AND DISTRICT OF COLUMBIA

Dollars
(000)

Key:
Mississippi ——————
Indiana ••••••••••••
Washington, D.C. ——— ——— ———

Photographs and Architects' Renderings

Photographs and renderings are useful in reports too. Have you ever tried to describe a particular building to someone who has never seen it? It is difficult to do because the words you use to describe the building may call up a different picture in the listener's mind. That is why architects' renderings are useful in reports. Another occasion for which "a picture is worth a thousand words" is in a report discussing an object such as computer hardware or a large piece of production machinery. Such equipment can best be illustrated by a photograph.

As with other kinds of figures, you must give the photo or rendering a figure number if it is not the only one in the report. You must also give it a title and label any parts that you want the reader to take particular note of. Exhibit 6–9 shows a rendering of an art gallery that an architectural firm used in a report to its client.

EXHIBIT 6–8
Sample Map from Annual Report

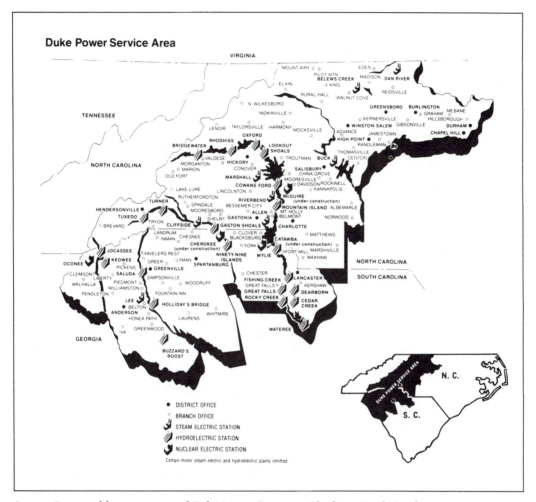

Source: Reprinted by permission of Duke Power Company, Charlotte, North Carolina.

Other visual aids to improve communication in a report include schematics, blueprints, and diagrams. As with photographs and renderings, sometimes the best way to clarify how an item is to be installed or how something functions is to include a schematic, blueprint, or diagram. Like other figures, these too need a figure number and a title unless the title appears on the blueprint or schematic (it often does). Also, these illustrations should be attached to the report and folded so they can be opened out; place them just after the page on which they are discussed.

**Schematics,
Blueprints,
and Diagrams**

EXHIBIT 6–9
Architect's Rendering

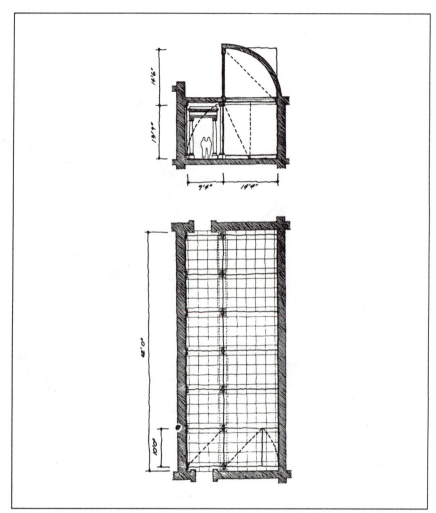

Source: Reprinted by permission of Wolf Associates Architects.

Exploded and Cutaway Drawings

These illustrations are useful in reports in which the reader has limited technical knowledge. An exploded drawing takes a diagram of an object and enlarges a particular section of it to show the reader greater detail. Exhibit 6–10 shows an exploded portion of a map (exploded drawings can also show such things as a detailed section of a piece of machinery, the molecular structure of a compound, or the number or kinds of wires that make up a strand of cable). As with any exploded drawing, the purpose of the enlarged area (large circle in this illustra-

EXHIBIT 6–10
Sample Exploded Drawing

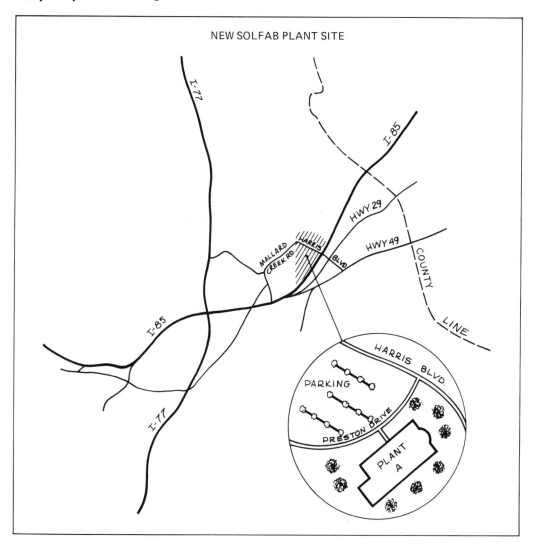

NEW SOLFAB PLANT SITE

tion) is to provide a closer look at one segment of the diagram. Similarly, a cutaway drawing removes the outer covering of an object to show the reader the interior.

Exploded and cutaway drawings are useful in showing the inner workings of a particular machine or the inner construction of a product. Exhibit 6–11 is a cutaway drawing of a swimming pool to show how a skimmer works. Both of these kinds of illustrations should have

EXHIBIT 6–11
Sample Cutaway Drawing

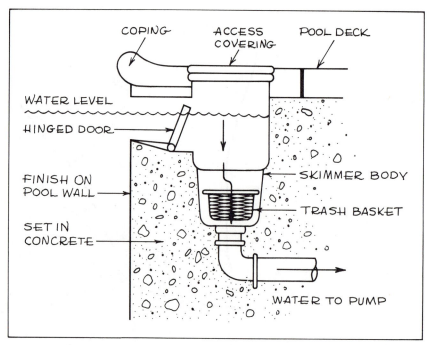

Source: Reprinted by permission of Walter C. Miles III.

figure numbers and titles, and the important parts of the illustration should be labeled clearly.

Pictographs

As the name suggests, a pictograph is part picture and part graph. Like the pie chart, it can be used to show percentages that comprise the whole of an object. Or it can show quantities. It can even show costs of a product made by your company, as Exhibit 6–12 illustrates. Pictographs should show the data accurately and have figure number, a title, and clear labels to show composition of the object. Exhibit 6–13 is an example of another type of pictograph.

Organization Charts and Flow Charts

Organization and flow charts look different from all other kinds of illustrations we have discussed so far. You have already seen an organization chart in this book (Figure 1–1 on page 7). Such a chart shows the formal status and power positions, lines of authority, titles,

EXHIBIT 6–12
Sample Pictograph

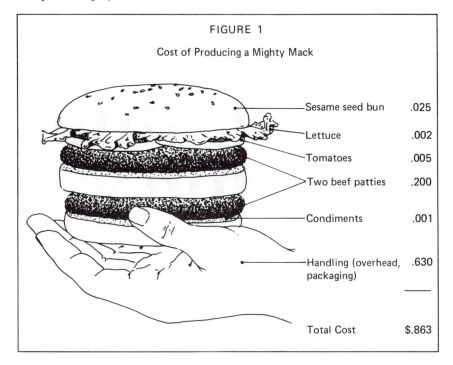

FIGURE 1

Cost of Producing a Mighty Mack

Sesame seed bun	.025
Lettuce	.002
Tomatoes	.005
Two beef patties	.200
Condiments	.001
Handling (overhead, packaging)	.630
Total Cost	$.863

and relationships among various people and jobs within an organization. These charts should be neat, clear, and accurate in showing the relationships. Give them a figure number and a clear, concise title. If you are including in your report a *copy* of a chart that has already been drawn up by your company, label it as an *exhibit* rather than as an original *figure,* as we discussed earlier.

Flow charts are used to show (1) a process or a part of a process, (2) the assignment of particular jobs in the production process, or (3) the order in which certain steps in the process occur. A flow chart can show an entire production process or a particular detailed step. Exhibit 6–14 is a flow chart for the sales order procedure for B & B, Inc.

Another type of flow chart used in the data processing field shows the steps and the logic used in writing a computer program. You may already have constructed this kind of flow chart. A very simple example is shown in Exhibit 6–15. Each of these kinds of flow charts needs a figure number, a clear, concise title, and accurate labeling of the chart itself when it is used in a report.

EXHIBIT 6–13
Sample Pictograph

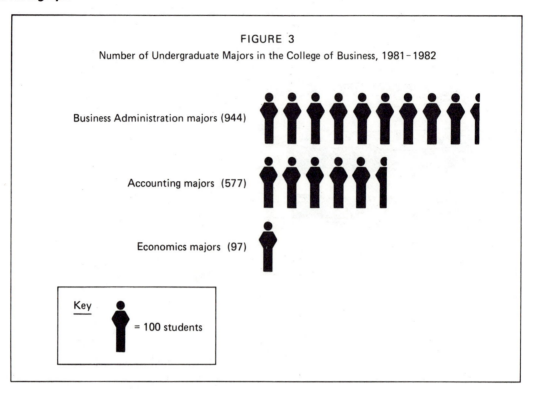

FIGURE 3
Number of Undergraduate Majors in the College of Business, 1981–1982

Business Administration majors (944)

Accounting majors (577)

Economics majors (97)

Key

= 100 students

POINTS TO REMEMBER WHEN USING ILLUSTRATIONS

Although this chapter has dealt with the most often used types of illustrations, other specialized illustrations may be useful in your work. The following guidelines should help you use any kind of illustration successfully:

1. Choose the right kind of illustration to dramatize the particular data.

2. Plan carefully; if the illustration is an original, first lay it out on graph paper and then transfer it to your report.

3. Integrate the illustration with the text for the reader's convenience. Place it just after the first reference to it, on the same page if possible. If this is impossible, put it on the next page.

4. Give the illustration a table, figure, or exhibit number unless it is the only illustration in the report.

5. Choose a clear, concise, and complete title.

6. Label clearly all the values represented.

EXHIBIT 6–14
Sample Flow Chart: Paperwork System

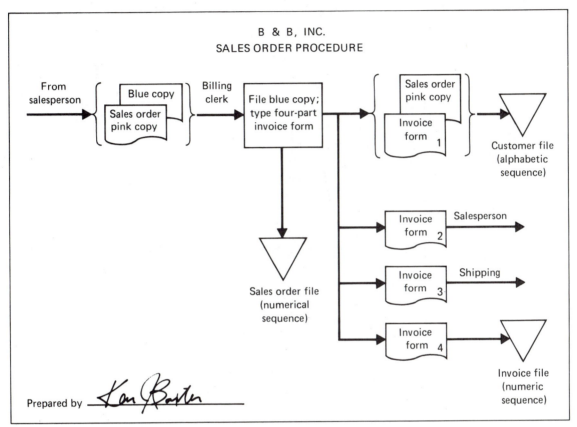

7. Give the source of the illustration if it is not your own creation.

8. Present as much information as possible in an illustration by using different shadings, colors, or types of lines to show different items, quantities, or other values.

Most large companies today have desk-top terminals that can produce computer graphics as well as process words. Report writers can key in their reports, and the words will appear on the screen of their CRTs. Misspellings can be corrected and improperly arranged material can be rearranged. Similarly, graphs can be produced to accompany the report. Again, if a graph is not perfect, adjustments can be made *before* it is put on paper. Once the report appears satisfactory on the screen, it can be put on paper in a matter of minutes by using the high-speed printer that can be purchased for most small computers.

CREATING ILLUSTRATED REPORTS WITH COMPUTER GRAPHICS AND WORD PROCESSING

EXHIBIT 6–15
Sample Flow Chart: Simple Computer Program

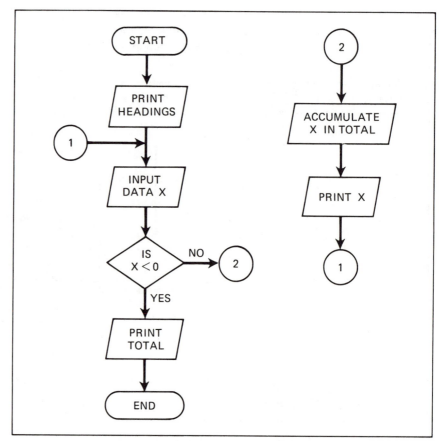

As you can see, the mechanical aspects of producing a report have changed considerably. The writer no longer has to put anything on paper; instead, everything is keyed directly into the computer. A secretary no longer spends hours typing a report; instead, the high-speed printer does it in minutes. Keep in mind, however, that even though the mechanics of producing a report have been modernized, a writer still must possess the thinking, organizing, and writing skills that this text discusses.

SUMMARY

Illustrations are useful in reports because they can show information using few words. Also, since most readers today are visually oriented, an illustration will capture their attention more quickly than words alone will. Some kinds of information — statistics, for example — are easier to read and assimilate in tabular form.

An illustration should be integrated with your report whenever feasible. Place it as near as possible to the words mentioning or describing it — on the same page if possible. If that isn't possible, place it on the next page.

There are three types of illustrations: tables, figures, or exhibits. A *table* is any set of related numbers and words grouped together in columns and/or rows for ease in reading. An *exhibit* is an actual sample, or a copy of something (of a form, contract, computer printout, or other original item) that is included in a report. A *figure* is any other kind of illustration that is not a table or an exhibit. All of these types of illustrations should have clear, concise, complete titles; they should be labeled clearly so the reader knows what the illustration represents. When there are more than one illustration in a report, they should be assigned numbers and labeled as *figures, tables,* or *exhibits* so the reader can locate them easily.

Some of the most often used illustrations are the many kinds of figures. *Pie charts* are circular illustrations used to show the *percentages* of the parts that comprise the whole — 100 percent — of anything. Each segment of the pie should show the percentage it represents as well as the item it represents.

Bar charts are used to show two variables — usually time and quantity — and have a vertical and a horizontal axis. The bars on this type of chart run horizontally. The *column chart* serves the same purpose as the bar chart, but the columns run vertically. A third type of chart that also serves this purpose is the *line chart*.

Two other useful figures in reports are the *map* and the *photograph*. Both should be labeled clearly and given a figure number. Other pictorial types of illustration are *schematics, blueprints,* and *diagrams*; these show how something functions, how it is installed, or how to construct it. If these illustrations are large, they should be folded and put on the page following the discussion; the reader should be able to unfold them easily to study them.

Exploded and cutaway drawings are useful in reports when you need to show a reader with little technical knowledge how something functions or looks. Both of these types of illustrations show an item in enlarged or detailed style.

Pictographs, as the name implies, are part picture and part graph. They can show percentage composition of an item, cost of the components that make up an item, and other such information more dramatically than other kinds of illustrations.

Organization charts show who has formal status in an organization, the relationship among departments and positions in the organization, as well as lines of authority and titles.

Flow charts can show all or part of a process, who does a particular job in a production process, or the order in which certain steps occur. Another type of flow chart is used in the data processing field to show the steps and the logic used in writing a computer program.

When using illustrations, remember to choose the right kind to show the information dramatically. Also, give your illustrations clear, concise, complete labels to make them understandable at a glance. Give your illustrations titles and table, figure, or exhibit numbers so they can be easily located in the report; integrate illustrations with the report whenever possible.

Today, many report writers will never put pen to paper. Instead, they will use desk-top computer terminals that have both word processing and graphics capabilities. The writer will key in both the words and the graphs. After any changes or corrections, the high-speed printer will print out on paper the final report in a matter of minutes. However, even with this new technology, a writer must possess good thinking, organizing, and writing skills.

LEARNING ACTIVITIES

1. Devise a pictograph that shows the composition of LifeStyle decorative paint products. Each gallon of paint contains the following ingredients in the given percentages:

Titanium Dioxide	18.4%
Silicates	9.4%
Calcium Carbonate	5.0%
Tinting Colors	1.0%
Water and Synthetic Rubber Emulsion Base	66.2%

2. Design an organization chart — for inclusion in an employee handbook — for the Buffalo Bills professional football team. Mr. Ralph C. Wilson is president. The vice-president and general manager, Robert Lustig, supervises public relations, stadium operations, the ticket department, and the marketing department. The head coach supervises the assistant coaches and works closely with the director of player personnel (scouting). The team's physician is an independent contractor who has his own medical practice independent of his services to the team. The trainers, however, are employees of the Bills.

3. Create an organization chart that shows the individuals in the department in which you work; or, if it is a small department, show its relationship to the other levels in the organization.

4. You work for a small manufacturing company that uses two basic compounds in making its product. These are purchased from a small chemical supply house; your company would benefit greatly

if it could order the compounds in larger quantity. However, your supplier will not accept orders for large quantities (at a better price) unless the entire order can be shipped all at once rather than being sent as the customer needs it. To complicate the matter, the compounds deteriorate somewhat if not used within three months of purchase. A thorough study is being made to see how this situation could be improved to save the company money. You are asked to submit a brief report showing the usage of the two compounds during the past year.

You find that compound X1319 has the following usage: January, 13,000#; February, 9500#; March, 9800#; April, 10,500#; May, 11,000#; June, 12,500#; July, 13,000#; August, 9500#; September, 9600#; October, 9700#; November, 12,500#; December, 12,400#.

Compound T1046 showed the following usage: January, 14,500#; February, 10,000#; March, 9500#; April, 10,500#; May, 11,000#; June, 12,500#; July, 13,500#; August, 9900#; September, 9800#; October, 10,000#; November, 13,000#; December, 13,500#.

Use only a few words and a good illustration to present this information.

5. You are corporate personnel manager for a large company. The following information must be conveyed to top management as part of a routine report submitted at the end of each year. You decide to use a visual aid and few words to convey the information. Prepare only the illustration, the sentence that precedes it in your report, and the sentence that follows it.

Hiring of new personnel increased in all four quarters of the year in the Atlanta region in contrast with hiring in the Houston region. In Atlanta we hired 18 salaried and 101 hourly personnel in the first quarter and 20, 28, and 30 salaried in the second, third, and fourth quarters, respectively. We added 120, 145, and 165 hourly workers in the second, third, and fourth quarters, respectively.

The Houston region, however, needed more employees than Atlanta, but could recruit only 18, 20, 20, and 21 salaried personnel in the first through fourth quarters, respectively. The record, though, was somewhat different for hourly employees in Houston. In the first quarter 200 people were added and for each of the three remaining quarters 210, 230, and 252 were hired, respectively.

6. In 1980 Porfidio and Garrett Company had sales of $10.8 billion. Broken down, the revenue came from the following product lines:

Laundry and Cleaning Products	39%
Personal Care Products	34%
Food Products	21%
Other Products	6%

The company's pretax profit totaled $1.1 billion and came from the same lines as above, but in the following percentages:

Laundry and Cleaning Products	54%
Personal Care Products	35%
Food Products	4%
Other Products	7%

a. Incorporate the data above into two side-by-side illustrations to dramatize the relationship between sales of each product line and pretax profits from the same lines.
b. Show the same data as in (a), but use a *single* illustration to do it. *Hint:* Use a different kind of illustration from those you used for (a).
c. Translate the sales and the pretax earnings percentages into dollar amounts, and construct a *single* illustration to show those amounts for each product division.

7. You are a regional sales manager for Aboud-Safra, Ltd. You must report to the district sales manager about the annual efforts of your district and of the individual efforts of your sales force. In one section of your report you decide to show the percentage of change (+, −, or no change) from last year's sales for each of your sales representatives. These are the facts you found:

Name of Representative	Percentage of Change
Will Cummins	+2.1
Phil Merritt	−3.6
Carita Ruiz	−2.1
Thom Colone	−7.1
Clifton Nethers	+15.3
Murray Hammer	+1.5
Harrison Davis	−.9
Teresa Bonanno	+7.9
Jean Abernathy	+7.3

Prepare only this section of the report; write the sentence that will precede the illustration, prepare and label the illustration, and write the sentence that will follow it.

8. Government spending has increased dramatically over the years. In a ten-year period — 1965–1975 — the percentage of increase

in spending for various functions of government more than doubled in nearly every case. Consider the following figures; then devise a single illustration that shows all four pieces of information in a dramatic way:

Function	1965 Expenditure (billions of dollars)	1975 Expenditure (billions of dollars)	Percent Increase
Education	28.5	87.8	208
Highways	12.5	23	84
Public welfare	6.3	27.1	331
Health and hospitals	5.3	18.6	251
Police and fire protection	3.9	11.9	207
Sanitation	2.5	7.8	212
Recreation and natural resources	2.9	7.8	171
Financial administration	1.4	3.9	184
General control	1.6	5.3	235
Interest on debt	2.6	9.1	253
All other	7.6	28	269

9. Devise an illustration that clearly shows the changes in enrollment in public versus private schools from 1970 to 1978. In 1970 a total of 60.4 million students — from nursery through college levels — attended school. At the nursery school level, the public schools had 0.3 million students enrolled, and private schools enrolled 0.8 million. At the kindergarten level, the public schools had 2.6 million students, and private schools had 0.5 million. At the elementary level, 30.0 million were enrolled in the public schools, and 3.9 million attended private schools. At the high school level, 13.5 million students attended public schools, and 1.2 million attended private schools. Public-supported colleges and universities enrolled 5.7 million students and private colleges and universities enrolled 1.7 million. In 1978 a total of 58.6 million students attended school. Public school enrollment showed these figures: nursery school, 0.6 million; kindergarten, 2.5 million; elementary school, 25.3 million; high school, 14.2 million; college, 7.4 million. The figures for private school enrollment in 1978 were as follows: nursery school, 1.2 million; kindergarten, 0.5 million; elementary school, 3.2 million; high school, 1.2 million; college, 2.4 million. (The source of these figures is the *Statistical Abstracts of the United States*.)

PART II

Preparing
Managerial Reports

Periodic Reports

LEARNING OBJECTIVES

After reading this chapter, you should be able to:

- Define the term *periodic report;*
- Describe the purpose of the periodic report;
- Identify what type of report it is;
- Explain what format is most often used;
- Discuss ways of ensuring good periodic reports;
- Give examples (from your own work experience) of periodic reports used by the companies you have worked for;
- Explain the process of *forms design analysis;*
- State some principles of good form design;
- Define the term *performance report;*
- Describe the purpose of the performance report;
- Discuss the types of formats used for performance reports;
- Describe some of the pitfalls to avoid when evaluating employee performance.

Of all the reports written in business, the periodic report is probably the most often used. As its name suggests, the periodic report is prepared at regular time intervals. Some are prepared daily, some weekly, some monthly, some quarterly, and some are prepared only once a year.

PURPOSE AND TYPE

The periodic report is used to present information that is needed on a regular basis for making decisions. Often both the employee who compiles the report and the superior who receives it consider it a routine report. It is routine in that the same kinds of information are reported each time; once familiar with the kind of information needed, an employee can complete the report in a short time. In fact, each report usually looks the same; only the figures change.

You will recall from reading Chapter 1 that reports are one of three types: informative, analytical, or recommendation. Periodic reports are usually informative. The employees writing them give only the pertinent facts; they are not asked to draw any conclusions or to make any recommendations based on the facts. However, the facts they present *will be analyzed by someone else* in the organization who will make decisions based on them. Therefore, writers of periodic reports must present the facts accurately, even though the report is routine — that is, like many others they have compiled.

FORMAT

The best format for any report is the one that gets the information to the reader in the most efficient and usable form. For periodic reports, that format is usually the form report. It is the most efficient for routine information because both the reader and the writer become familiar with the form and can expect to find certain items in the same place on the report each time it is submitted. This cuts down on both writing and reading time.

Form reports are often devised by someone within the organization and are printed in-house. Sometimes a business forms company may design and manufacture them to the customer's specifications. Usually the form is used, evaluated, and occasionally revised to be sure that it continues to report efficiently and gives only essential information. Form reports are usually given a form number — for reordering and filing purposes — and the date of the most recent revision. These number codes are usually located in one of the lower corners in an inconspicuous place.

Designing forms is a specialized task. In fact, many large corporations employ forms design specialists, and most office administrators spend some of their time on forms management. Simplicity is the key to designing good forms. Joseph L. Kish, Jr., a forms design authority, stresses that

FORMS DESIGN

> . . . since nearly every procedure requires, at some stage, a form be completed, processed, filed, or referenced, the cost and operational efficiency of that procedure will, to a great extent, be determined by the speed and accuracy with which the form can be processed and handled. If the form is simple and worksaving, the procedure will likely be efficient and cost-saving.[1]

Forms design specialists are needed because companies change and so do their operating procedures. These changes necessitate changes in the forms that facilitate the procedures. (Computers have caused many of these procedural changes in recent years.) The forms design specialist's job begins when a procedure changes.

The first step in forms design is *analysis* of the organization's needs. This is done in three stages: (1) studying the relationship of a particular form to others in the same series to see how they relate to each other, (2) interviewing those who use or receive the form, and (3) studying the entire path the form passes along in the organization. The first stage of the process is to take copies of every form used in a particular procedure, spread them out on a table, and study them to see if there is continuity in the system. Then the following questions should be asked to determine whether any of the forms need revision:

> Does each show where the form originated (company name if it goes outside the organization; department, division, and the like if it is used within the organization)?
>
> Does each clearly tell what kind of information it reports?
>
> Why was each form designed this way (consider size of paper, size of print, number of carbons, and so on)?
>
> Is there any duplication of information that could be eliminated?

Next, interview the people who fill out the form and those who receive it. Research the *who, what, when, where,* and *why* of each form. These people can point out the good and poor aspects of a form since they work with it regularly. You may find, for example, that a form that has to be folded perfectly to fit a window envelope is time-

---

[1] Joseph L. Kish, Jr., "Simplify Forms to Increase Productivity and Reduce Cost," *Graphic Arts Monthly* (January 1980) 52:162j–162k.

consuming for the employee and difficult for the customer to respond to easily if it has to be refolded for return.

The third stage, studying the path of the form, is best done by walking the form through the system from the place where it starts to the place where it (or copies of it) ends. You can see for yourself how it is used or misused, what becomes of it at the end of its path, and how often it is reused as a source of information. In every case, a form should adapt to the system, not vice versa.

After the analysis, you are ready to make the necessary changes. Research has shown that the following general principles should be remembered when designing any form:[2]

1. *Maximize the contrast* between the paper the form is printed on and the preprinted data on it so that the form is easy to read. The best contrast is usually black ink on a white glossy-finish paper. If carbons are used, black is preferable. The data entered on the form should also be in black ink, pencil, computer ribbon, and so on.

2. *Provide contrasting typography.* The form will be easier to read if the type face and size of the preprinted data differ from the type that will be used to enter the data.

3. *Limit line widths.* One study has shown that the human eye can read comfortably only seven or eight words in uppercase letters, so limit the number of capitalized words in headings and instructions.

4. *Use rules (solid lines) and leaders (dotted lines)* to lead the reader's eye from the preprinted matter to the space for data. Also use double rules for separating sections of a form.

5. *Use dingbats* (such symbols as *, ▲, ●) to call attention to items critical to completing the form correctly, such as an authorized signature or a deadline for submission.

6. *Keep ballot-type boxes lined up* so that the tab stops on typewriters, word processors, and the like can be used to complete them.

7. *Design source documents so that the same kinds of data appear in the same location* on the source document as on the other forms so that the transcriber can put the forms side by side and transfer the information easily and quickly.

---

[2] Kish, "Simplify Forms to Increase Productivity and Reduce Cost," pp. 162j–162k.

8. *Use terminology that anyone can understand* when composing the preprinted data. Use popular diction and as few technical terms as possible.

Now let's examine some periodic forms to see how they were designed and used. Exhibit 7–1 shows a *daily* report. Obviously, the person filing a daily report must understand the kinds of receipts taken in by the company and the account numbers as well as other information about the company.

Daily reports are needed for several reasons. In retail businesses and banks, for example, such reports can help forecast future needs, the busiest days, slumps in the economy, and many other things. Also, because of the volume of monetary transactions handled, accounting for receipts on a daily basis is easier and far more accurate. Of course, other periodic reports (weekly, monthly, quarterly) are often based on the information contained in a series of daily reports.

While the daily report is useful for some kinds of information, other kinds are reported more efficiently on a *weekly* basis. For example, in conducting company business it is easier to reimburse an employee for expenses incurred weekly rather than daily, especially if the employee is a sales representative who travels extensively and works in the office only one or two times a week. Exhibit 7–2 shows an expense report that would be used by such an employee to report business-related expenses. Even though the report is submitted weekly, some employees will record information on it at the end of each workday. Expense reports in larger companies are often designed with carbons so several copies are made at once and can be distributed to the various people who will use the information.

Many other kinds of weekly reports are submitted in business. For example, the accounting department of a regional meat processing plant sends corporate headquarters a weekly report showing financial data on each line of products (various sliced luncheon meats, for example) produced during that week. Submitted as a form report, the information consists of numerous figures that show the costs of producing and reprocessing the meat as well as whether the costs were above or below an established standard.

Although some information can be reported daily or weekly, other kinds must deal with longer periods of time. For example, Exhibit 7–3 shows a report that is submitted *monthly* (actually 15 days prior to the next fiscal month) by buyers at a regional department store to plan for the following month's business.

Long-range planning and forecasting are important in any business, and quarterly reports are useful in these activities. The informa-

EXHIBIT 7-1
Daily Report

PIEDMONT NATURAL GAS CO., INC.
DAILY CASH RECEIPTS

DISTRICT _____ FOR DATE _____

BANK DEPOSITS

BANK	TODAY	MO. TO DATE
WACHOVIA BANK & TRUST CO	$	$
NORTH CAROLINA NAT'L BANK		
MECHANICS & FARMERS BANK		
WACHOVIA BANK & TRUST CO. ASHEBORO/THOMASVILLE		
NORTH CAROLINA NAT'L BANK THOMASVILLE		
FIRST CITIZEN BANK & TRUST GIBSONVILLE		
SECURITY BANK & TRUST CO.		
BANKERS TRUST OF S.C. GREENVILLE		
SOUTH CAROLINA NAT'L BANK		
BANKERS TRUST OF S.C. SIMPSONVILLE		
FIRST NAT'L BANK OF S.C.		
PEOPLE'S BANK OF IVA		
SOUTH CAROLINA NAT'L BANK BELTON, S.C.		
CAPITAL BANK & TRUST CO. BELTON, S.C.		
CITIZENS & SOUTHERN NAT'L		
WOODRUFF STATE BANK		
FIRST NAT'L BANK CATAWBA COUNTY		
CAROLINA FIRST NAT'L BANK		
NORTHWESTERN BANK MORGANTON		
FIRST UNION NAT'L BANK OF NORTH CAROLINA		
WACHOVIA BANK & TRUST CO. MORGANTON		
TOTAL DEPOSITS	$	$

CASH RECEIPTS

	ALLOCATION BY ACCT CONTROL	NOT REPORTED TO ACCT CONTROL	TODAY	MO. TO DATE
142.11 - A/R GAS LEDGER	$	$	$	$
142.12 - A/R 30-DAY CHARGES				
142.13 - A/R MDSE. INSTALL.				
142.14 - A/R METER LPG				
142.15 - A/R BULK LPG				
142.16 - ACCOUNTS RECEIVABLE - LPG JOBBING				
142.17 - ACCOUNTS RECEIVABLE - OTHER				
143.21 - A/R EMPLOYEES *				
143.23 - A/R MISCELLANEOUS *				
144.10 - U/R - GAS LEDGER				
144.20 - U/R - MDSE. & 30 DAY				
144.30 - UNCOL. ACCTS.-LPG				
235.00 - CUSTOMERS DEPOSITS - NATURAL GAS *				
235.10 - CUSTOMERS DEPOSITS - LP GAS *				
253.10 - CASHIERS OVERAGE (SHORTAGE)				
SUNDRIES *				
TOTAL RECEIPTS			$	$

* GIVE DETAILS ON BACK

PREPARED BY _____ APPROVED BY _____ DATE _____

C-13
REV. 5/77

Source: Reprinted by permission of Piedmont Natural Gas Company, Charlotte, North Carolina.

142

EXHIBIT 7–2
Weekly Report

(EXPENSE REPORT)

Please type or print information.

NAME	EMPLOYEE NUMBER	WEEK ENDING

TRIP INFORMATION

	Monday	Tuesday	Wednesday	Thursday	Friday
From (City)					
To (City)					
Departure Date/Time					

Purpose of Trip:

TRAVEL EXPENSES

Indicate all items charged to or paid by the company. Use an (*) to show charges.

	Mon.	Tues.	Wed.	Thurs.	Fri.	Sat.	Sun.	Totals
Lodging								
Meals (include tips):								
Breakfast								
Lunch								
Dinner								
Airline/Rail Tickets								
Taxi/Limo/Bus								
Tips: Hotel/Baggage								
Telephone/Telegraph								
Laundry/Valet								
Auto Expense								
Gas/Oil/Lube								
Tires/Tubes								
Wash								
Repairs								
Tolls/Ferry								
Parking								
Auto Rental								
Mileage Allowance:								
__Miles								
Other:								
Entertainment:								
Key each amount to								
respective item on								
reverse side.								
TOTALS FOR WEEK								

Unused transportation
attached. Value $_____

Less Expense Advance (_____)
Less Credit Card Charges (_____)

Sign here_____

Balance due (Company)_____

Send check to:_____

(Employee)_____

Dept. Approval_____

ATTACH
ALL
RECEIPTS

EXHIBIT 7–3
Monthly Report

```
                              IVEY'S
                      BUYER INFORMATION SHEET
   Buyer_____
         DEPARTMENT(s)_____         MONTH_____

         PLANNED SALES_____         LAST YEAR ACTUAL_____

         Major Volume Classes

                 1.  _____

                 2.  _____

                 3.  _____

         Best Sellers

                 1.  _____    3.  _____

                 2.  _____    4.  _____

         Departmental Presentation    Layout   (Focus on Important Trends)

                     Stores to focus on the following trends in order listed below
                     for better uniformity and clarity of offering.

         1st Week:   1._____

                     2._____

                     3._____

         2nd Week:   1._____

                     2._____

                     3._____

         3rd Week:   1._____

                     2._____

                     3._____

         4th Week:   1._____

                     2._____

                     3._____

         5th Week:   1._____

                     2._____

                     3._____


                                                    9210-601-32A
```

Source: Reprinted by permission of Ivey's Carolinas, Charlotte, North Carolina.

tion in a quarterly report is often compared with that in reports from previous quarters of the same year and from the same quarter a year earlier. Also, inspection reports such as those made by the board of health or the Bureau of Standards and Measurements cover longer periods of time — usually a quarter, six months, or a year.

Some kinds of reports are used frequently but may not be submitted at regular time intervals because of the nature of the business. On some days, for example, the form may be used more than once; on other days it may not be used at all. Exhibit 7–4 shows such a report — one needed any time a buyer places an order exceeding $100,000. Large construction companies, for example, might use a form like this. A similar one might be used by a discount department store buyer who can get an exceptional price on a closeout item by ordering larger-than-usual quantities that may run over budget. Such purchases would need approval from the buyer's superior.

So far we have looked at some formats for daily, weekly, monthly, and quarterly reports. Of course, these are not the only time intervals for periodic reports. One company may need a biweekly report; another may need a bimonthly one; and yet another, a semiannual one. Remember that periodic reports are used to make everyday decisions that affect the company, so the kinds of reports generated will be based on the company's need for information.

Periodic reports are the backbone of a company. They are used to support routine decisions that must be based on day-to-day operations. Regardless of the frequency with which you or your subordinates must submit periodic reports, here are some suggestions that you should offer your employees to make routine reporting faster and easier:

POINTS TO REMEMBER

1. *Get organized* before attempting to write the report so that you will not waste unnecessary time and energy once you begin. For example, if your daily task is reporting receipts, be sure *all* are nearby; then count each category separately. If your task is taking figures from ledgers, be sure you have *all* the ones you need before starting. If you must write ideas in your own words, first write brief notes on scratch paper before transferring them to the report.

2. *Don't allow yourself to feel pressured* because this can lead to mistakes. Good organization can eliminate some kinds of pressure. For example, if your report must be submitted by a particular time, plan ahead and put aside other work so you will be free to do the report. If, however, you cannot set aside time to work on your

EXHIBIT 7–4
Periodic Report

REQUEST FOR MANAGEMENT APPROVAL TO PLACE ORDER IN EXCESS OF $100,000

Request from_____ Date_____

Contract No._____ Requisition No._____

Project Description_____

_____

Client_____

Location of Project_____

Vendor	Total Price	Delivery Date	Comments

Funds Available for Items
   in Contract Estimate

Estimate Based on Scope
   of Work Quoted

To be ordered from (company)_____

Based on_____

APPROVED BY: _____
          (Project Manager)

Management Approval_____
                (Name, Title)

COMMENTS:

M-21

report because your job involves interacting with people all day, get all your materials organized and devise a way to mark your place whenever you must stop to talk to a customer, client, or co-worker. To avoid such distractions, some people prefer to come in early to work before the crowd arrives. Others stay late to work in relative quiet. Still others take work home. Be honest with yourself; find the plan that works best for you and your job and stick with it. Once you feel in control of the situation, you will no longer feel pressured.

3. *Be accurate.* Sometimes routine information will seem boring. So when possible, work on the report when you are at your peak of performance. For some people that will be early morning; for others it will be at 10:00 A.M.; for still others it will be 4:00 P.M. Become aware of your natural rhythms and do tedious work when you are most alert. Also, don't hesitate to question your superior if you do not understand how to complete the report. Taking a small amount of time now to ask a question is better than wasting a great deal of time later to correct mistakes.

4. *Refer to previous reports* whenever possible, especially if this is your first time preparing a particular one. Usually a company uses its forms for a long time, and copies of past reports will show you how to complete the form correctly.

5. *Document your work* the first time you are asked to fill out a complicated periodic report. This means *making step-by-step notes about how you got your figures or where you found your facts.* File the notes with the office copy of the report. Accounting department employees, particularly, understand the value of documentation; often a complex process is involved in preparing figures for certain kinds of accounting reports. By writing the step-by-step process down, you can be sure of getting the proper figure — and getting it faster too — the next time you do the report. Another advantage of documentation is that if you are absent for some reason, someone else can complete the report by following the documentation.

Being well organized is a must for managers; the more responsibilities you have, the more important this element becomes. If you manage an office or a department that submits numerous periodic reports each year, it will be worth your time to establish a schedule of reports that shows which internal reports are due at what time and to whom each one goes. Also, if your office is responsible for submitting periodic

ESTABLISHING A SCHEDULE OF PERIODIC REPORTS

government reports, you may want to add these to the schedule of reports.

If your subordinates are writing reports, such a schedule is also valuable to them; they will know the deadline for filing each one and can budget their work load accordingly. You may even want to post the schedule and have the people filing reports initial the proper space when a report is finished. Or you may prefer to use the schedule for your own personal record of what has been done and what has yet to be done. Being organized will make routine reporting easier. Exhibit 7–5 is an example of a schedule of reports.

Periodic reports are relatively easy to prepare because you do not need to plan a format or organize the material; the form used does that for you. However, there are other kinds of reports that are not routine, and these will be dealt with in the next several chapters.

PERFORMANCE REPORTS

One particular kind of periodic report that is used by most companies is called the *performance report.* If you plan to to be a manager, you will probably write many performance reports about each of your subordinate's performance and development. The performance report, also called performance evaluation or performance appraisal, is a tool used by managers to assess the strengths and weaknesses of the performance of each of their employees. It must be used judiciously.

Title VII of the Civil Rights Act of 1964 prohibits discrimination in employment on the basis of race, color, religion, sex, or national origin. Over the years, court challenges have attempted to clarify the specific employment practices the act encompasses. The definition has come to include performance appraisal systems in the realm of Title VII and its enforcing agency, the Equal Employment Opportunity Commission (EEOC). Although no one has challenged the use of performance appraisals, courts have addressed issues that often relate to areas that may be influenced by performance reports: transfers, promotions, compensation, layoffs, and training programs. So most companies have been careful to see that their performance appraisals are valid. To validate the evaluation, the company must perform a formal analysis of any job and set objectives, standards, and procedures for hiring and promoting. Then the company can establish guidelines for appraising the performance of those doing the job. A company's evaluation system is not likely to be challenged if it meets the following guidelines:[3]

1. The appraisal process should be formalized, standardized, and made as objective as possible.

[3] Gary L. Lubben, et al., "Performance Appraisal: The Legal Implications of Title VII," *Personnel* (May–June 1980): 11–21.

EXHIBIT 7-5
Schedule of Reports

SCHEDULE OF REPORTS

A. Internal Reports

Report Title	Due Date	Receiver	Preparer (Please initial and write date completed)

B. External Reports

Report Title	Due Date	Receiver (Name of Agency/Organization)	Preparer (Please initial and write date completed)

2. The evaluation should be as job-related as possible.

3. A supervisor's evaluation should be only one component of the overall evaluation for promotion, training, and so on.

4. Evaluators should be trained to use appraisal techniques.

5. Evaluators should have daily contact with the employee being evaluated.

6. Employees, as well as supervisors, should be able to initiate promotion/transfer procedures.

Although these guidelines are useful to a company, you will probably not have to worry about developing an evaluation instrument unless you work in the area of personnel. What is important is to remember the legal implications of assuming responsibility for appraising an employee's performance.

Purpose and Type   The performance report is usually completed at regular intervals — quarterly, semiannually, or annually — and a copy of it is sent to the personnel department, where it is filed with the employee's other records. As we said earlier, in some companies the report is used to determine promotions, merit salary increases, terminations, and other job-related decisions. Most people, however, would agree that the best performance reports are those that serve only one of those purposes. Regardless of its specific purpose, the function of the performance appraisal is to allow both the manager and the employee to look at recent past performance. The report should praise the employee's strengths and discuss how weak areas can be improved.

Legally, employees may see the manager's evaluation of their performance. In fact, many companies require that the evaluation be shown to and discussed with the employees; likewise, the employees are to sign the evaluation and/or write comments about their perception of the manager's appraisal of their performance.

Sharp managers do not depend solely on memory to write performance reports, nor do they write without giving careful thought to the subject. Good managers are well organized. For example, they might keep a box of 4×6 cards — two or three for each employee — in their desk drawer. Every so often they spend a few minutes before or after the workday thinking about the previous day's work. If an employee did something praiseworthy, the manager writes the date and a brief note about the achievement on the employee's card. Likewise, if an employee has been negligent in some area, the manager writers a comment on the card. Of course, many days an employee will do nothing exceptionally good or exceptionally poor, so comments are not needed for every employee every day. At any rate, it is wasted mental effort to attempt to remember everything employees do; the cards will do the remembering for you.

When the time comes to write the performance report, the manager pulls out the cards and quickly and accurately evaluates the employee's work during the period under consideration. These notes also help when the manager is discussing performance with the employee. Once the report and discussion are completed, most managers destroy the old cards and begin a new set. Just a few words of caution are needed about keeping these notes:

1. *Make them brief;* a busy manager does not have time to write much.

2. *Do not be vindictive.* Sometimes a good night's sleep causes a manager to have a different perspective on a situation. That is why you should not write about the *current* day's work, but rather review the *previous* day's work. You will get a more honest feeling for your employees' accomplishments and shortcomings.

3. *Keep the notes yourself;* do not let your secretary or administrative assistant keep them for you. The secretary or assistant can put the employees' names on the cards for you each evaluation period, but *you* should make the notes and keep the cards. This assures privacy on sensitive matters that involve only you and the employee.

4. *Write your comments on the cards at the beginning or at the end of the day* when employees are not present. Otherwise, they may feel that you are constantly checking up and reporting on them. Such feelings breed resentment toward the superior.

5. *Record the employees' reactions to your discussions* about their performance so you can remember any verbal agreements made and can review them to see if they were kept.

Exhibit 7–6 shows a sample card for a new employee whose company prepares quarterly evaluations for the first year of employment. Thereafter, the company requests semiannual performance evaluations.

By now you have probably determined that performance reports are informative. They present only facts. You should not feel compelled to analyze an employee or an employee's performance for a performance report, although you may want to do so for your own personal use in working with the employee.

EXHIBIT 7–6
Sample 4×6 Card with Notes About an Employee's Performance

ERIKA BLOSSOM

1/8 Entered dept - completed 8 wk. training class

1/25 Observed E.'s sales techniques: good presentation skills, well-organized, effective close

2/1 Sales for Jan: 80% of estab. avg. for mo.

2/15 Two days unexcused absence; Called in sick Mon., took Tues. and Wed. without calling in.

3/2 Sales for Feb : 90% of estab. avg. for mo.

3/3 Exceeded expense budget by 20% for Feb. Agreed to keep

Format

As with other kinds of periodic reports, the performance appraisal is usually submitted as a form report. Of course, the kind of form varies greatly from company to company. For example, Exhibit 7–7 shows a form used only in evaluating a new employee, and Exhibit 7–8 shows another one used for other employees in the same company. Notice that both forms have a checklist section that can be completed without much writing, as well as a section requiring sentences and/or paragraphs. Some other examples of performance evaluation forms can be seen in Chapter 4 (Exhibits 4–1 and 4–2).

Special Kinds of Performance Reports

Some companies give special recognition to employees for outstanding performance on the job, the purpose being to build morale and develop company loyalty. Such recognition is often given through a written *commendation,* frequently on a form that is general enough to accommodate many kinds of recognition. Exhibit 7–9 shows a commendation for perfect attendance at work for one year, and Exhibit 7–10 shows one for outstanding performance on a skilled labor job.

Precautions

Because of the legal ramifications of putting in writing anything about an employee, many managers are afraid to be honest in evaluating subordinates who perform poorly. This attitude results in bland re-

EXHIBIT 7–7
Performance Evaluation Form

PIEDMONT NATURAL GAS COMPANY INC.

New Employee Evaluation

EMPLOYEE'S NAME _____

DEPT./DISTRICT _____ JOB TITLE _____

DATE EMPLOYED _____ SUPERVISOR'S NAME _____

REPORT FOR MONTH ENDING _____

PERFORMANCE RATING:

	EXCELLENT	GOOD	FAIR	POOR
QUALITY OF WORK	☐	☐	☐	☐
QUANTITY OF WORK	☐	☐	☐	☐
SAFETY ATTITUDE	☐	☐	☐	☐
COOPERATION	☐	☐	☐	☐
ABILITY TO GET ALONG WITH OTHERS	☐	☐	☐	☐
PUNCTUALITY	☐	☐	☐	☐
ATTITUDE	☐	☐	☐	☐
ATTENDANCE	☐	☐	☐	☐

THINGS EMPLOYEE DOES PARTICULARLY WELL: _____

_____

_____

_____

SUGGESTIONS FOR IMPROVEMENT: _____

_____

_____

SUGGESTIONS BY EMPLOYEE: _____

_____

_____

RECOMMEND FOR PERMANENT EMPLOYMENT: ☐ YES ☐ NO

FORM NO. C-130   SIGNED _____
                                                    SUPERVISOR

Source: Reprinted by permission of Piedmont Natural Gas Company, Charlotte, North Carolina.

EXHIBIT 7–8
Performance Evaluation Form

PERFORMANCE MEASUREMENT

AND REVIEW

C158

Name_____   Location_____
     (last, first, middle initial)

Job Class_____   Effective Date_____

Previous Job Class _____   Effective Date_____

SUPERVISOR'S APPRAISAL

Indicate which category below best describes the employee's job during this
review period.

Check (✔) One

☐   OUTSTANDING-exceptional accomplishments.

☐   SUPERIOR-results well above those expected.

☐   FULLY SATISFACTORY-satisfactorily accomplished all basic
                       requirements.

☐   FAIR-did not fully accomplish basic requirements.

☐   UNACCEPTABLE

_____
            Supervisor's Signature

The information on this form is <u>confidential</u> and <u>must</u> be <u>treated as such</u>.

EXHIBIT 7–9
Employee Commendation Form

PERFORMANCE AND DEVELOPMENT REPORT

SPECIAL RECOGNITION

Name of Employee___Marybeth Allison_____Date of Employment_5 May 1979_

Job Title_____Secretary III_____Date of Report_9 February 1981_

Division/Unit/Department__Electronics-Purchasing_ Employee Number___PC 361____

The purpose of this report is to recognize superior employee performance on the job. Please give reasons for making this report including facts, figures, dates and other pertinent data.

COMMENDATION: PERFECT ATTENDANCE 1980

Marybeth is commended for her perfect attendance record on the job from January to December 1980. This is an outstanding accomplishment that reflects Marybeth's dedication to her work as well as to her good attitude toward her work.

Management congratulates Marybeth on this accomplishment and wishes her continued good health and success.

Supervisor:

I have discussed this report with the employee. *Ann P. Mahoney*
                                              Supervisor's Signature

Employee:

I have read this report. *Marybeth Allison*
                         Employee's Signature

                         Approved by:___*J. W. Holsinger*___

FORM M310
REV. 3/78

EXHIBIT 7–10
Employee Commendation Form

PERFORMANCE AND DEVELOPMENT REPORT

SPECIAL RECOGNITION

Name of Employee _____ Harold Smithfield Hanley _____ Date of Employment 18 May 1974 _____

Job Title _____ Plastic Extruder Operator _____ Date of Report 30 January 1981 _____

Division/Unit/Department   Electronics--Dept. 33X   Employee Number D467 _____

The purpose of this report is to recognize superior employee performance on
the job. Please give reasons for making this report including facts, figures,
dates and other pertinent data.

COMMENDATION: OUTSTANDING PERFORMANCE

Harold was trained as a P.E. operator in February 1976 and has been an
operator since that time. He immediately accepted responsibility for his work
and gave us excellent quality wire products.

In 1978 he began training new operators on his extruder. He has done an
outstanding job of training both in teaching the technical skills and in
encouraging new operators to stay on the job once they have been trained.
He knows his job well and communicates easily with all other operators
in the department.

Harold is to be commended for his fine work. His talents have improved
both the quality of work in the department and the morale of the department
employees.

Supervisor:

I have discussed this report with the employee. *J. Miller Hayes*
                                                 Supervisor's Signature

Employee:

I have read this report. *Harold S. Hanley*
                          Employee's Signature

                          Approved by: *David D. Hammond*

FORM M310
REV. 3/78

ports couched in vague language that help neither the employee nor the manager nor the company.

Of course, managers should have *regular* discussions with employees, not just at performance evaluation time. However, managers should and can be honest in evaluating employees' performance if they remember the cardinal rule: *cover yourself!* That means you must have accurate evidence of everything you write about an employee, documented with dates, times, places, and so forth. That is why the 4×6 note cards you keep on each employee are valuable. However, here are some other guidelines to help you do a better job of evaluating employee performance:

1. *Be sure you have all the facts* and any other specific evidence, such as time cards and inspection sheets before discussing negative performance with an employee. Being emotional or hasty can earn you the reputation of being erratic, incompetent, or mean.

2. *Set aside a specific time for the review* and don't allow yourself to be interrupted. The employee needs to feel that he or she has your undivided attention during that time.

3. *Put the employee at ease* by providing a nonthreatening atmosphere. If possible, sit beside the employee rather than behind your desk so no physical barriers come between you.

4. *Discuss the employee's good points first.* If, however, the overall evaluation is poor, get to the point early in the conversation so that later on the person doesn't feel you were misleading.

5. *Discuss the employee's work, not his or her personality.* Even though you may not like the employee personally, your task is only to evaluate the person's work.

6. *Don't compare the employee to other co-workers.* You must consider talents and capabilities only in determining whether or not performance is improving as measured by past performance and by what you think the employee is capable of doing.

7. *Emphasize future improvements in performance.* Do not bring up past performance reviews; no one wants to be reminded of past mistakes that can't be remedied anyway. Good future performance can help to erase the memory of past errors.

8. *Be specific both about the things you do not like and about suggestions* to improve the negative performance. General statements such as "Work harder" are poor; the employee may be working as hard as possible and will resent your comment. In-

stead, be specific: "Mary, it's important that we get *all* orders processed and sent to the purchasing department *every day* to avoid a backlog at the end of the week, throwing production off schedule. Do you think you can do that?" If Mary flatly says no, be prepared to suggest how she might be able to meet your standards of performance. Here are some other examples of general rather than specific statements. The reporter who uses these is leaving loopholes for the employee to slip through:

a. John has missed work on many occasions, all on Fridays and Mondays. (too general)

b. During this quarter, Sarah has several absences that she did not call in about.

Those general statements could be improved by giving specific details:

a. John has missed work on the following occasions:
Friday, April 10 and Monday, April 13
Friday, April 24 and Monday, April 27
Friday, May 8 and Monday, May 11
Friday, May 22 and Monday, May 25

b. During this quarter, Sarah has been absent three times without calling in: September 22, October 21, and November 14.

9. *Be a good listener.* If a subordinate gets angry with you or breaks down in tears, be calm. *Don't* try to calm the person or put an end to the emotional outpouring; leave the room and allow the person some privacy. Once the emotion is spent, you may discover other factors, previously unknown to you, that have influenced this performance. Such a discovery can open new channels of communication with the employee.

10. *Be aware of how the employee feels about the evaluation* and what he or she intends to do about performance. Try to get an honest *verbal* commitment from the employee about his or her intentions to change or improve performance. By involving the employee in the evaluation, you are more likely to get cooperation.

The following two examples are of information from a performance report. Study the comments beside them to see how to improve them.

Example A

Be more specific; "good" is too abstract. ⟶

Positive Comments:
Ms. Blossom is a very good saleslady with good sales techniques. She is a quick

learner of company policy. In three short months, Ms. Blossom has reached the established average for her territory.

Poor word choice. *Areas Needing Improvement* **has a better connotation.**

Negative Comments:
Inexperience sometimes causes delays of projections. Her carefree attitude hurts her performance in attendance. Ms. Blossom needs to cater more to the individual customer.

Paragraph is vague and unclear. If her projections have been late, say so. Tell *what* **she is doing wrong with customers. Has she agreed to try to improve in these areas?**

Conclusion:
As Ms. Blossom gains experience and learns how to handle customers more effectively, she will become more valuable to XYZ Corporation.

Example B

Good. Specific comments about meeting her quota, positive attitude, good presentation skills; well-organized and effective close.

General Statement:
Erika Blossom has demonstrated an overall grasp of the knowledge and skills necessary to be an effective representative of XYZ Corporation. Her steady progress toward achieving established sales goals is excellent proof of her skill and improvement. Erika's attitude is positive with regard to her work and her personal ability.

Strengths:
Erika is well organized. She has good presentation skills and is effective in closing sales.

Vague and unclear. Is she checking into the office often

Weaknesses:
Erika needs to pay closer attention to detail, especially

enough? Did she fail to call in when absent? What about the needs of the customer? What advice was given?

order specifications and expense policy. She also needs to be more specific in her communications with the area office concerning her schedule.

Attitude:

Monotonous sentences; all be-⟶ gin with "Erika."

Erika has a positive attitude when it comes to herself and her sales ability. However, Erika is somewhat ambivalent about the needs of certain customers and defensive of her ability to deal with certain individuals. Erika has been counseled about those particular accounts and has consented to follow instructions and suggestions concerning them. Erika seems willing to accept constructive criticism.

Performance Rating:
Very good.

Progress:
Excellent.

Although preparing honest and useful performance appraisals is never easy, the guidelines discussed in this chapter should help you write better ones.

SUMMARY

Periodic reports are used more often than any other kind of report. They are usually submitted at regular time intervals and are used to conduct routine everyday business. Periodic reports are usually form reports. There is little need for audience analysis because the form has been carefully designed for a particular audience and for reporting specific information. Periodic reports also require fewer writing skills since only numbers, check marks, or short phrases are needed to complete them.

Report forms are usually designed by a professional, either within the company or at a business forms company where forms are commercially made. Forms design specialists study the company's needs and develop a form that will fit neatly into the existing system.

The *performance report* is a particular kind of periodic report. Its purpose is to allow managers to evaluate the job performance of each employee at regular time intervals and to recommend ways of improving performance. These reports should be supported by evidence collected in writing over the period covered by the evaluation. Managers should never write anything on a performance report that cannot be substantiated.

Sometimes a special kind of recognition is given to outstanding employees. These reports are called *commendations* and may be given to those who have good attendance records, save the company money, and so on. The purpose of the commendation is to praise good employees and to build morale among all workers.

1. You are field sales manager at XYZ Corporation. The partial organization of XYZ Corporation is shown in the following chart:

LEARNING ACTIVITIES

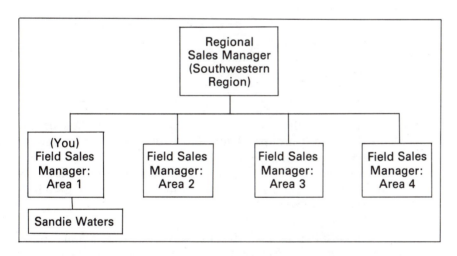

As manager, you have kept accurate typewritten notes of discussions you have had with each of your sales representatives (see "Notes on Sandie Waters," p. 162).

Two days ago, you received a letter (see p. 163) from Betty Harrington, purchasing agent at Corman, Inc., one of your company's best accounts. She discusses Sandie Waters, your company's youngest representative, who is now working the territory you once served several months ago.

```
┌─────────────────────────────────────────────────────────┐
│                  NOTES ON SANDIE WATERS                   │
│                                                           │
│  1/20   Sandie entered department after six-month         │
│         training period.                                  │
│  2/1    Observed Sandie's sales techniques — very good    │
│         presentation skills, well organized, effective    │
│         close.                                            │
│  2/15   Two-day unexcused absence. Sandie called in       │
│         sick on Monday but also took Tuesday and          │
│         Wednesday without checking in.                    │
│  3/1    Sales for February: 90% of established average    │
│         for the month.                                    │
│  3/3    Sandie did not turn in her projections on time,   │
│         causing a delay in calculating the team's         │
│         projections. Regional sales manager got after     │
│         me about that.                                    │
│  3/6    Exceeded expense budget by 10% for February.      │
│  3/18   Order processing advised me of erroneous          │
│         information on one order, which caused a          │
│         delivery delay and angered the customer. The      │
│         sale was saved.                                   │
│  4/1    Sales for March: 102% of established average      │
│         sales for the month.                              │
│  4/2    Talked to Sandie about letter from B.             │
│         Harrington.                                       │
│                                                           │
└─────────────────────────────────────────────────────────┘
```

a. Read through this entire problem first. Then the class should break up into groups of five or seven people. As a group, design a performance evaluation form specifically for the sales division to use in evaluating the sales representatives and staff. Choose the best form, mimeograph it, and give it to everyone for (c).

b. Today you must call Sandie in and discuss with her the problem mentioned in the letter. Be prepared for all eventualities because you don't know how she will react; you have counseled her several *other* times during the past three months about other matters.

c. The first quarter has ended, and you must submit a performance report to the personnel department for each of your sales representatives. Write the performance report on Sandie, as well as her response when you discussed the letter from Betty Harrington. Remember that anything you say goes on record in Sandie's official personnel file; the file may be used to support any future change in the status of the em-

---

CORMAN, INC.
246 Eastway Industrial Park
San Angelo, TX 76901

March 28, 1981

Mr. Terry Maxwell
1265 Tower Building
Fort Worth, TX 76180

Dear Terry:

We hope you are enjoying your promotion and the challenge
of the new position. We miss you. It must be hard for the new
rep. to fill your shoes in our territory.

Ms. Waters is congenial and knows the product line well.
However, she needs to be more serious about her job. Yesterday,
I waited half an hour for her presentation while my co-workers
came out to greet her, buy her coffee, and so on. I have called
their behavior to the attention of my superior, but the real
problem is the way she dresses.

Yesterday, she was wearing no upper-foundation garment,
and her dress was too tight and the fabric too clingy to be in
good taste.

We knew you would want to speak to her about her attire so
our business with your company can proceed more smoothly.
Please stop by to see us if you should be in the area on
business.

Cordially,

Betty Harrington

Betty Harrington

---

ployee. Use only *facts* available to you in writing the report;
make no assumptions that you can't support either from the
notes or the conversation with Sandie. Submit the report on
the form developed by the class earlier in (a).

2. Think about your work experiences, and bring to class blank copies of some of the forms used to report routine information by the
company you have worked for. If you have had no work experience, ask an employed friend to lend you a copy of a periodic
report form.

The instructor can divide the class into groups and give each group time to plan a brief oral presentation about the forms. One group may discuss weekly reports; another group, daily reports, and so forth. Or if the class is large, the members could be grouped by industry, such as banking, electronics, chemicals. Each group's reports would be about the periodic reports used by that industry. In giving your brief report describe:

a.   The purpose of the report;
b.   How often it is submitted;
c.   What kinds of information it reports;
d.   How it is used in the decision-making process at this company.

3.   If you have work experience, plan to share with the class your observations about performance appraisals. How often are employees evaluated, what kind of form is used, how useful are the reports, and what use does the company make of them? Bring samples of forms used to review employee performance, if possible.

4.   Recall a job you have had recently. List the important responsibilities you were instructed about when you took the job. Next assume the role of your supervisor and complete either (a) or (b) below.

a.   Write a performance evaluation on *yourself* using the format shown in Chapter 4, Exhibit 4–1. Remember to use some section headings to show important categories of performance being evaluated.
b.   Write a performance evaluation on another employee who did the same job as you did when you worked for this supervisor. Use the format shown in Exhibit 4–1, choosing some section headings to show the categories of performance being evaluated.

5.   Go to your library to read a popular (as opposed to a learned or theoretical) business magazine article on performance appraisals and give an oral report on it in class. One such article, "Employee Performance Reports," *Savvy* (November 1980): 48–50, is written by Susan Antilla, a reporter for *Dun's Review*.

6.   Read an article from a scholarly publication on employee performance appraisals and report on it to the class. Such an article is "Attitudinal Congruence and Similarity as Related to Interpersonal Evaluations in Manager-Subordinate Dyads," by K. N. Wexley, et al., in the *Academy of Management Journal* (June 1980): 320–330.

Interview Reports, Progress Reports, and Methods and Procedures Reports

LEARNING OBJECTIVES

After reading this chapter, you should be able to:

- Describe the purpose of the *interview report;*
- Identify what type of report it is;
- Explain what formats are used for this type of report;
- Discuss some techniques for writing good interview reports;
- Describe the purpose of *progress reports;*
- Identify what type of report they are;
- Explain what formats are used for this type of report;
- Discuss some techniques for writing good progress reports;
- Describe the purpose of *methods and procedures reports;*
- Tell what type of report they are;
- Explain what formats are most often used for this type of report;
- Discuss some techniques for writing good methods and procedures reports;
- Give examples from you own work experience of this kind of report.

Although periodic reports can consume much of a manager's time, many can be delegated to subordinates. Other kinds of reports can be compiled only by the manager. This chapter discusses many types of managerial reports that you will use during your career.

INTERVIEW REPORTS

An interview is a structured discussion with another person or with a small group of people. Before meeting with the interviewee, the interviewer defines the purpose of the discussion (what he or she would like to accomplish through the interview) and prepares questions that will generate the desired answers. Then, interviewer and interviewee meet at a mutually agreed-upon place and time for the purpose of asking and answering questions. Afterward, the interviewer often reports on what took place at the interview.

Interview reports can be informative, analytical, or recommendation reports, although they usually simply describe what occurred during an interview. The type of report will depend on the purpose of the interview — whether it was an employment, exit, or information interview. The *employment interview* is conducted with a prospective employee. In a report the interviewer tells what occurred at the interview and gives an evaluation of the interviewee's chances of being a productive employee with the company. Contrary to popular belief, employment interview reports are written by people other than personnel recruiters or interviewers. For example, the personnel department screens out unlikely prospects during a first interview, and those who make a favorable impression are invited back for a second interview. This time the interview is conducted not by a member of the personnel department but rather by the manager, supervisor, or department head for whom the prospect would work if hired. The manager then gives an *evaluation* of the prospective employee to the personnel department; this latter evaluation is what usually determines whether or not the person is hired.

Another type of interview is the *exit interview,* usually conducted by someone in the personnel department with an employee who is about to leave the company. The interviewer tries to learn the reasons for the employee's leaving and the employee's perceptions of the company, of the immediate supervisor, and so forth. Often a form is used to report information gleaned from an exit interview.

A third type of interview is the *information interview,* in which the interviewer is seeking answers to specific, factual questions. Later these answers may be used in preparing a report for a customer or a client. More immediately, however, the interviewer may prepare a brief report of the interview for a superior, the idea being to keep the superior abreast of the interviewer's activities.

All job candidates deserve respect; they have no way of knowing who the competition is and how you view their qualifications in comparison. Furthermore, you are "the company" to the candidates since you represent it. For that reason, you should leave all candidates with a good impression of the company even if you do not plan to hire any of them. The good interviewer will put a candidate at ease so the person relaxes and feels free to be candid. The skillful interviewer is patient, friendly, attentive, and gives no signs — verbally or nonverbally — that anything the interviewee says is unfavorable. Again, this encourages the candidate to show negative as well as positive traits. In fact, if you handle the interview well, the interviewee should leave feeling successful and sure to be invited for a second interview — only you will know differently. Experienced interviewers are able to size up a candidate within the first few minutes of talking, even though the conversation will continue for half an hour or more.

What should you look for in a candidate? First, assess the job carefully. The job description will state what skills are required, but that isn't enough. Consider, for example, whether this job is routine. If so, do not hire someone who is creative and independent; you will soon lose the person. Does the job require people skills? If it does, do not hire someone who is shy, reserved, and soft-spoken but does meticulous work; the person will be miserable trying to do something that isn't natural. By hiring such a person, you will do a disservice to the candidate and to yourself. Remember the following when you make a decision to hire an applicant:

> The candidate's salary comes out of your department's budget;
>
> The candidate's performance will reflect on yours;
>
> The candidate's objectives, goals, and needs will affect yours;
>
> You must live with your decision for a long time.

To prepare for an interview, study the applicant's resume and ask about anything that is unclear, questionable, or unusual. However, because of legal implications, interviewers must be careful not to ask personal questions that indicate a bias against an applicant regarding race, age, sex, handicaps, or other areas that would jeopardize the applicant's opportunity for a job with the company. For example, it is demeaning (and illegal) to ask a woman what kind of arrangements she will make for the care of her preschool child while she works. It is not illegal, however, to ask if she will be able to meet the work days and hours required for the job in question. Of course, men should be asked the same question. Following are some other questions that interviewers should avoid:

The Employment Interview

1. Inquiries about ancestry, descent, and national origin of spouse or parents.

2. Inquiries about marital status, sexual preferences, and so forth.

3. Inquiries about religious preference or affiliation.

4. Inquiries about arrests (you may ask questions about *convictions* that relate to performance of the job in question).

At the actual interview try these tips:

1. Start with a warm greeting and some small talk to put the applicant at ease.

2. Tell the applicant you need to refresh your memory on the resume; this tactic allows the interviewee time to relax, to size you up, and to get used to the environment (and you can actually review the resume).

3. Start with easy questions about family, background, activities, and so on so that the applicant can answer with a certain amount of confidence.

4. Ask open-ended questions to get the applicant talking; examples of some harder, open-ended questions are: "What type of work do you do least well?" or "Why should we hire you over all the other applicants for this job?" or "What is your greatest weakness?" If the applicant falters at any of the hard questions, take over the conversation as if the poor response is of no importance; then resume your line of questioning.

5. At the end of the interview, thank the applicant for coming, and tell how (letter, phone call, or other) the applicant will be informed of the hiring decision.

The interviewing process just described is the *distributive* style; the interviewer is open, friendly, relaxed, and asks open-ended questions. Most interviewers prefer this style, and applicants respond well to it. However, other styles are often used when interviewing middle- or upper-level managers. In the *reflective* style, the interviewer asks a question, and the applicant responds and waits for the next question. However, instead of asking another question, the interviewer is silent; the applicant should take that as a cue to carry the interview from that point, with the interviewer steering the conversation from time to time if he or she isn't getting the needed information. In the *stress interview*, the interviewer begins not with small talk but with an open-ended question. During the entire interview, the interviewer tries to put the applicant on the spot by using hypothetical situations, probing questions, and challenging statements in response to the applicant's answers. The purpose of such an interview is to see how the applicant can handle pressure.

To assist you in learning to ask questions that reveal the applicant's true character, here is a list of possibilities:

Easier Questions

What subjects did you like at school? (Might indicate basic personality traits.)

Describe how you spend a typical day.

What are your hobbies or spare-time interests? (Shows if interests are wide.)

Why did you choose the particular college you attended?

What determined your choice of major?

How would you describe your academic achievement?

How did you decide to become an accountant, engineer, or (whatever is applicable)?

In what types of extracurricular activities did you participate?

How did you spend your summers while in college (high school)?

Did you hold any class or club offices? Which ones?

What were your vocational plans at the time of college (high school) graduation?

In general, how would you describe yourself?

What do you regard as your outstanding qualities?

What traits or qualities do you most admire in someone who is your immediate superior?

What are some of the things in a job that are important to you?

What would you want in your next job that you are not getting now?

Do you presently belong to any social, civic, or professional clubs or organizations? Which ones? Why did you join them?

Do you hold office in any of these? Which office?

How do you spend your vacations?

If you had more time, are there any activities in which you would like to participate? Which ones? Why?

Harder Questions

What has contributed to your career success up to the present time?

What disappointments, setbacks, or failures have you had in your life?

How might you further your own business career?

What are your long-range goals and objectives?

What kinds of situations or circumstances make you feel tense or nervous?

What kind of position would you like to hold in five years? In ten years?

Why do you want to work for us? (Reveals if applicant has done any background work on the company.)

What suggestions did you make in any previous job to increase morale, cut costs, improve productivity or (whatever is appropriate)? (Helps pick out the idea person.)

What are some of the major problems you have had or decisions you have had to make?

If you had to do it all again, what changes would you make in your life and career?

In considering joining a company, what are some of the factors that you take into account?

If you joined our organization, where do you think you could make your best contribution? Why?

Looking into the future, what changes and developments do you anticipate in your particular field?

What were your reasons for leaving XYZ Company?

How would you describe your present (past) superior? What do you consider to have been his or her major strengths and limitations?

What is your greatest weakness?

As you see it, what advantages would you gain by joining our company?

In what way does the job with our company meet your career goals and objectives?

In what way has your present job prepared you for greater responsibilities?

Tell me a story.

FORMAT AND CONTENTS OF THE REPORT

Usually interview reports are used within the organization, so the memo report format is most common. However, in some cases employment interviews are evaluated on a form report.

Whether you use a form or write a memo report from scratch, the following information should be included:

1. A brief statement of the purpose of the report, including the name of the applicant and the position he or she was interviewed for.

2. Several paragraphs discussing the applicant's qualifications for the job: educational background, special training, licenses, and so on; work experience; civic and personal activities; personality characteristics and ability to fit into the organization; personal appearance; and any other qualities that are important for this particular job.

3. A recommendation to reject, to hire, or to invite the applicant back for a second interview, as well as reasons for the recommendation.

Exhibits 8–1, 8–2 and 8–3 are examples of employment interview reports. Notice that Exhibit 8–1 gives the recommendation first, while Exhibit 8–2 saves it until the end. Exhibit 8–3 mentions the recommendation in the opening statement of purpose and then states it again formally at the end, giving reasons for the recommendation. All of these methods are acceptable, but each serves a slightly different purpose. Sometimes a superior or company procedure will require that the material in any report be summarized at the beginning. The reader can get the gist of the report without reading all of it. However, the facts are found in the remainder of the report if more information is needed. With this style, a reader can tell at a glance the most important points. The style that shows the recommendation last is probably more typical, and the reader generally starts at the top and reads the entire report. The third type is a blend of the other two; the reader gets the gist of the report but at least must read the recommendation section to find out the reasons.

EXHIBIT 8–1
Employment Interview Report

MEMORANDUM

DATE: 6 March 1983
TO: DAVID BROWN, PERSONNEL MANAGER
FROM: KARYN RANSHAW, ASSOCIATE
SUBJECT: RECOMMENDATION FOR NEW EMPLOYEE

RECOMMENDATION

For the past two weeks, I have been interviewing several
potential employees to fill an opening in the Trust
Department. The opening is in the Personal Trust Business
Development area. This area works closely with individuals in
planning the handling of their estates, distribution of their
assets, tax savings after death, and so on. My recommendation
for this job is a senior at UNCC, Sylvester Hannaman.

WORK EXPERIENCE

Sy worked part–time while in high school at Zippy Mart. He had a
lot of responsibilities, including opening and closing the
store, running the cash register, and waiting on customers. He
worked this past summer at the Federal Reserve. He was
responsible for large amounts of money and keeping ledger
accounts of money transactions. He was bonded while on his job
at Federal Reserve and is still bondable. His working while
going to school shows initiative, willingness to work, and
ability to handle responsibility.

EDUCATION

Sy attended West Mecklenburg High School. His favorite subject
was English, and his favorite sport was, and still is, soccer.
He was an A/B student. He is majoring in Business
Administration, and his grade point average, 3.0 on a 4.0
scale, proves he is a diligent, intelligent worker. Sy was born
and raised in Charlotte and has two sisters. He expects to
start at the bottom and work his way up the corporate ladder
with a large company. He is interested in working with the
public and in handling accounts with our Trust Department.

CONCLUSIONS FROM INTERVIEW

Sy makes a very good first impression. He is very personable, very relaxed, and speaks clearly and concisely. All these traits would enable him to meet and talk with people easily. He is confident, but not overconfident or pushy. Since there is little supervision in this job after the six-week training program, his self-reliance and initiative will be a big plus. I think this young man will become a great asset to NANB and will be worth the money and time we spend to train him.

EXHIBIT 8–2
Employment Interview Report

MEMORANDUM

Date: February 3, 1983
To: Sheila Gray, Personnel Director
From: Sam Kosinsky, Personnel Associate
Subject: Darin Mahn Interview

On November 19, I interviewed Mr. Mahn for a position as manager in our Mr. Sport Retail Division. The interview was conducted on the UNCC campus as a result of our advertisement in the Eastland Mall store. I conducted a nondirective interview, with questions from the Personnel Evaluation Series I–7–A.

Background Data

Mr. Mahn is a senior business administration major at Davidson and will graduate in May 1983. He has taken management courses in several fields, including operations, production, finance, and human resources. He has taken several accounting courses to round out his education. He has recent work experience as a part-time clerk and summer assistant manager for Fast Fare. He is looking for a full-time job after he graduates as well as a part-time job until then.

EXHIBIT 8–2   (Continued)

<u>Interview Results</u>
Mr. Mahn impressed me from the start of the interview as a shy, intelligent person; this impression was supported during the balance of the interview. My first impression of his shyness was reinforced due to his soft speaking manner in the interview and his failure to press to learn any information about the position other than what I told him. When he was asked the standard hawk–or–goose question,* he chose the hawk but was unable to give any reasons why. When he was asked what he liked about retail sales work, he appeared to be slightly surprised, which makes me question whether he had something else in mind.

<u>Recommendations</u>
Based on his work background and education, Mr. Mahn definitely appears to have the qualifications for a manager trainee. However, I believe it would be in our best interest to request a second interview to investigate more thoroughly his goals and plans.

* The question is, "If you could be either a hawk or a goose, which would you prefer to be?" The response may tell whether the person thinks power, prestige, and so forth are important because these attributes are often associated with hawks.

EXHIBIT 8–3
Employment Interview Report

<u>MEMORANDUM REPORT</u>

17 March 1983

TO: Jack McLellan, Personnel Associate
FROM: Sara Mowry, Marketing Supervisor
SUBJECT: Report on Market Analyst Candidate, Janice Law

On March 13, I interviewed Janice Law, applicant for the position as Market Analyst. I recommend that we not consider her for the position.

EXHIBIT 8–3   (Continued)

Analysis of Applicant

Ms. Law was recommended to me by Charlotte Glidden, Advertising Coordinator. She worked for Ms. Glidden as part-time office assistant and received high ratings for her work. She has a good appearance and a pleasant personality. She is a business administration major with a concentration in marketing and sales. She will complete her education in May and would be able to begin work immediately thereafter.

Ms. Law is single with no dependents. She lives in Charlotte with her parents. When I asked her about future personal plans, she confided that she had no plans and that she ''hadn't thought much about it.'' This attitude indicates a certain instability in her personal life that may affect her job performance in the future.

Also, the applicant has no work experience in the field of marketing. Her work history includes part-time jobs held while attending college, including working at Pneumafil as an office assistant and currently as a salesperson at J. C. Penney Company.

Ms. Law was very positive about her ability to handle the job. She attributed her confidence to taking courses in marketing, yet she is an average student whose favorite course was business law.

Recommendation

Since Ms. Law does not have any experience in the field of marketing and given the relative instability of her personal life, I doubt that she would be able to coordinate the marketing functions of three divisions. I recommend that we not consider her for the position of Market Analyst.

The Exit Interview

Since companies keep records of all communications with their employees, when one leaves for another job, is terminated, or retires, the employer wants to know details about the departure. Company officials use the information from exit interviews to assess the company's strengths and weaknesses in the areas of wages and salaries, employee morale, working conditions, and the like. When interviewing the departing employee, remember that you may be the last person he or she has a business contact with in the company. For that reason, you should help the person leave with the best possible view of the company. Even if the employee has been terminated and has a negative view, provide an opportunity for the angry feelings to come out in the open. You may find out things about the company or about a particular department that you wouldn't have known otherwise.

Encourage the departing employee to talk by using some of the listening responses discussed in Chapter 3 to show that you are listening carefully. Ask open-ended follow-up questions such as, "I'd like to know more about that," or "How did you feel about that?" when you are told something negative.

Some terminated employees may be so angry that their emotions prevent a good interview. In such a situation, allow the employee to shout, cry, or sulk as long as necessary to vent the emotion; such outpourings usually last only a few minutes. Meanwhile, remain calm and don't get involved in the emotion or respond to it. Once the employee is more rational, assure the individual that the emotional outburst is understandable and common; then try to steer the person into discussing his or her feelings about the company. The employee may even admit in the end that the company was justified in its decision to terminate.

If the departing employee is leaving to take a job with another company, it is vital that you understand why. A company invests a great deal of money in training and developing their employees. When they go elsewhere, that investment goes with them. Using much the same techniques as described earlier, find out the reasons for the departure.

FORMAT AND CONTENTS OF THE REPORT

Often exit interviews are reported on a form that is filed with the employee's other personal records. However, whether you use a form or write the report from scratch, you should include the following information:

1. The type of departure (resignation, termination, retirement, and so on);

2. The specific reasons for the employee's leaving;

3. An assessment of the employee's attitude about leaving; describe specifically what the employee said or did in the interview that caused you to make the assessment.

Exhibit 8–4 is an example of an exit interview submitted as a form report.

EXHIBIT 8–4
Employment Exit Interview Report

PERFORMANCE AND DEVELOPMENT REPORT

EXIT INTERVIEW

Date of Original Employment____5 January 1979_____

Name__Joy Eileen Hassana_____   Employee Number__30671-A____

Job Title__Accountant I_____   Last Working Day_16 Jan. 1981_

Division/Unit/Department__Financial & Statistical Accounting_____

Date of Report_12 Jan. 1981_

TYPE OF REPORT:

__X__ Resignation   ____ Termination   ____ Retirement

____ Other_____

REASONS FOR LEAVING:

Joy has accepted a position with Dessler-American in Corporate Accounting,
with responsibilities for SEC reporting activities.

EMPLOYEE'S PERCEPTION OF COMPANY:

Joy feels that this company has been a good place to work and that her
superiors have given her opportunities to assume responsibility.

However, she feels that opportunities for advancement are not available
here and that she can earn more by going with a larger firm. Even though
we offered to match Dessler's salary, she felt the opportunities for
advancement outweighed salary considerations.

I have shown this report to the employee. _____
                                            Interviewer's Signature

I have read this report. _____
                          Employee's Signature

Comments:

FORM PD101
REV. 3/79

**The Information
Interview**

Information interviews are conducted to find answers to specific questions; the person interviewed should therefore be an expert. The information interview should follow the guidelines set down in Chapter 3. You may then report your information to a client or to your superior, the purpose being to keep them informed of your activities.

FORMAT AND CONTENTS OF THE REPORT

Most information interview reports will be submitted as memo reports if the facts and figures are to be used within the organization. If it is prepared for someone outside the organization, the format will be either a letter report or a long formal report. But whatever the format, you should include the following information:

1. Write a brief statement of purpose, including the interviewee's name and job title. These pieces of information are important because they establish the credibility of your source of information.

2. Give brief details about the interviewee and about the company he or she works for.

3. Use several paragraphs to present the facts that you gathered during your questioning.

4. Close the report by drawing some conclusions based on the facts discovered in the interview.

Exhibit 8–5 shows a completed information interview report, based on a telephone interview. Exhibit 8–6 shows another one, based on a face-to-face interview.

**PROGRESS
REPORTS**

When large projects are undertaken, the work load is usually distributed among a number of people. The manager who delegates the work segments is responsible for the coordination and ultimate results of each segment as well as for the total project. So to keep track of what each segment is doing, the manager may ask for *progress reports* at certain intervals to see what has been accomplished and what remains to be done.

Progress reports are generally informational reports, although some may also require an analysis of the information. Their purpose is threefold:

1. To review briefly information on a project's past activity.

EXHIBIT 8–5
Information Interview Report

MEMORANDUM REPORT

DATE: December 8, 1983
TO: Ann Kominsky
FROM: Sara Blue

On Tuesday, December 2, 1983, I conducted a telephone
interview with Mr. Lewis F. Camp, Jr., of Duke Power Co. Mr.
Camp is the Secretary and Associate General Counsel of Duke
Power. The responsibilities of his position include
registering and filing reports with the Securities and
Exchange Commission (SEC). Our discussion focused on the
various forms required by the SEC and how Duke Power handles
the filing of these documents. The interview was informative,
but Mr. Camp was extremely busy and therefore had to place a
limit on our time. He did, however, answer all my questions and
give me his opinion of the necessity of the SEC. This
memorandum reports on the information and impressions
obtained during the interview.

DUKE POWER COMPANY

Duke Power is a publicly owned corporation whose stock
shares are traded on the major stock exchanges. They have
assets totaling over $1 million and more than 500 shareholders
of record. In view of these facts, Duke Power is required to
file and register its securities with the SEC, under the
Securities Act of 1933.

LEWIS F. CAMP, SECRETARY AND ASSOCIATE GENERAL COUNSEL

As Secretary and Associate Counsel of Duke Power, Mr. Camp
must sign all reports filed with the SEC. He also handles
disputes that arise involving transactions in the securities
and financial markets. He advises Duke Power on any investment
decisions under consideration.

EXHIBIT 8–5 *(Continued)*

Page 2
Interview Memorandum

<u>REPORTS FILED WITH THE SEC</u>

All reports filed with the SEC are actually prepared in the Financial and Statistical Accounting Division of Duke Power. After this division compiles the data and presents them in report form, Mr. Camp reviews all the information before placing his signature on the report documents. The reports are then returned to Mr. Camp's secretary, who mails the forms to the SEC.

Duke Power is required to file several reports with the SEC. The following is a list of these report forms, including a brief description of the report and the period of time allowed for filing each one.

Form 3:   Report on the stock of officers and directors at any time they buy or sell shares. Must be filed within ten days after the month of sale or purchase.

Form 4:   Report on the amount of securities owned at the end of the period for a particular class of securities only if there has been a reported change in beneficial ownership of securities of such class. Must be filed within 15 days of the end of the period.

Form 10K: Comprehensive forms requiring information on salary of officers, indebtedness of firm, list of assets, property, and inventory. These forms are filed once a year at the fiscal year end.

Form 10Q: Comprehensive forms requiring information on salary of officers, indebtedness of firm, list of assets, property, and inventory. These forms are filed quarterly within 15 days after end of quarter.

Once a year the company does a mass filing on all stock purchase savings programs. These are programs that employees of Duke Power participate in.

<u>MR. CAMP'S VIEW OF THE SEC</u>

Through his various dealings with the SEC, Mr. Camp has had an opportunity to observe the work done by the commission.

EXHIBIT 8–5   (Continued)

Page 3
Interview Memorandum

His review of all reports sent to the SEC provides him with a
knowledge of just exactly what type of paperwork the
organization requires.

　　As do other regulatory agencies, the SEC requires numerous
reports to be filed with the commission in Washington. Mr. Camp
feels that although these reports are time-consuming for the
clerical staff, they are necessary for the smooth operation of
the SEC. Without these reports, the SEC would be unable to
perform efficiently. The commission was created to regulate
the financial and securities markets. This objective serves to
protect companies such as Duke Power.

　　Mr. Camp stated that ''you may get a different opinion
from the people in the Financial and Statistical Division.
They are the ones who do all the dirty work. My opinion may be
somewhat more objective.''

---

2. To give a detailed account of the current phase.

3. To preview coming phases of the project.

In short, these reports cover work done, work in progress, and work to
be done. In addition, they may discuss unforeseen problems with
manpower, materials, government regulations, and so on, which have
affected the progress of the project.

　　All kinds of organizations use progress reports to keep managers
informed about the work they have delegated to others. For example,
government service organizations require progress reports of programs and projects they fund. Look at these excerpts from the Community Services Administration Instruction #6800-9 telling grantees
how to submit progress reports:

1. **Purpose**
    The purposes of this Instruction are to set forth the proce-
    dures for monitoring and reporting program performance of
    grantees as prescribed by references (1) and (2) above and to
    communicate CSA's specific requirements in these areas.

EXHIBIT 8–6
Information Interview Report

MEMORANDUM REPORT

DATE: October 23, 1983
TO: Sam Raybourn
FROM: Tim Bellow
SUBJECT: Interview with Sales Operations Manager at Bealer
           Wholesale

On October 1, 1983, I interviewed Rob Barnett of Bealer
Wholesale in Richmond. Our discussion focused on various
periodic reports written or received within the company. The
interview was informally structured and lasted about 45
minutes. This memorandum reports on the information gathered
during the interview.

Bealer Wholesale

Bealer Wholesale distributes six brands of beer in the
Richmond market. The brands, produced by Anheuser Busch, are
Budweiser, Busch, Natural Light, Michelob, Michelob Light,
and Classic Dark. Bealer has 45 employees of which 26 are route
salesmen.

Rob Barnett, Sales Operations Manager

As Sales Operations Manager, Mr. Barnett has line authority
over all office employees, supervisors, and route salesmen.
His major responsibility is in sales forecasting and
operations planning. Mr. Barnett reports directly to the
president of Bealer Wholesale.

Report Writing––Least productive job

Mr. Barnett's attitude toward report writing was made clear in
one comment he made early in the interview: ''You don't sell a
case of beer by filling out reports.'' He feels that report
writing is the least productive but one of the most necessary
jobs performed in the company. Unfortunately, most reports
deal with ''history'' and are written ''after the fact.''

Reports Used at Bealer Wholesale

Daily   Each route salesman fills out an order form at every
           account to which he sells beer. At the end of the
           day, this report is turned in to the secretaries,

EXHIBIT 8–6 (Continued)

who type the information into a computer. The
following morning a computer printout report is
sent to Mr. Barnett with all sales figures,
inventory on hand, age of the inventory, and
month-to-date figures. He uses these to check
company progress with previous forecasts. (The
majority of all reports Mr. Barnett receives are
computer printouts based on the previous day's
activities. He receives or writes very few other
daily reports.)

<u>Weekly</u>   At the end of each week, all daily sales figures are
totaled and sent via computer telephone to the
Anheuser-Busch main office in St. Louis. The
following Monday, Mr. Barnett receives a computer
printout report indicating year-to-date trends for
each package nationwide. This information about
the inventory level and availability of all brands
nationwide can determine whether he needs to
reforecast his sales and requirement figures.

<u>Monthly</u>   Monthly figures are produced in the same manner as
are weekly reports except that they deal with a
month's worth of data.

<u>Quarterly</u> The president of Bealer Wholesale must do a census
report each quarter indicating gross sales,
inventory, valuation, number of employees, and
other company highlights.

The majority of periodic reports written or received at Bealer
deal directly with Anheuser-Busch and are in the form of a
computer printout. Anheuser-Busch uses the information to
check the effectiveness of advertising and the success of each
brand, and to determine the market segmentation and sales
trends. Feedback is then relayed to wholesalers throughout the
nation.

<u>A Complaint Regarding Periodic Reports</u>

The Anheuser-Busch Division Office in Richmond receives
30-day information regarding brand placements in on- and
off-premise accounts. This information is determined by

EXHIBIT 8–6   (Continued)

---

account reorders occurring every 30 days. However, some
accounts do not reorder every 30 days, and this can show
underestimated placement figures.

Suggestions Made for Report Writing

1. Reports should not require a lot of study.
2. Get to the point.
3. Use indicators (Barnett: ''I look for red flags . . .
   marking the important material'').
4. Make it ''short and sweet.''
5. Keep the number of reports to a minimum.

Concluding Comments

Through this interview assignment, I learned not only the
necessity of report writing but also the importance of
reporting the most relevant material. It appears that what is
said is more important than how it is reported. Each business
must employ the most effective and practical reporting methods
for its operations. What works well for one company may not be
at all suitable for another.

Grantees shall submit a performance report for each agreement that briefly presents the following information for each project, function, or activity involved as prescribed by CSA.

(1)   A comparison of actual accomplishments with the goals established for the period, the findings of the investigator, or both. If the output of programs or projects can be readily quantified, such quantitative data should be related to cost data for computation of unit costs.

(2)   Reasons why established goals were not met.

(3)   Other pertinent information including, where appropriate, analysis and explanation of cost overruns of high unit costs.

Special Reporting Requirements (Grantee)
Between the required performance reporting dates, events may occur that have significant impact upon the project or program. In such instances, the grantee shall inform the

appropriate CSA administering office by letter as soon as the following types of conditions become known.

(1) *Problems, delays of adverse conditions that will materially affect the ability to attain program objectives, prevent the meeting of time schedules and goals, or preclude the attainment of project work units by established time periods.* This disclosure shall be accompanied by a statement of the action taken, or contemplated, and any Federal assistance needed to resolve the situation.

(2) *Favorable developments or events that enable time schedules to be met sooner than anticipated.*[1]

Format

Most progress reports use the memo report format if the information is to be used within the organization. The letter report or long, formal report format is used to report progress to customers, clients, or others outside the organization. Occasionally, however, an organization will choose an unusual format, as shown, for example, in Exhibit 8–7. Although the letter format was used, it was done with creative flair; because of the nature of the organization, this format may encourage support for the group, whereas the more traditional letter format might merely have been read and tossed aside.

Even when the memo report format is used, it may not follow the standard sentence and paragraph style we have seen in most memo reports. Exhibit 8–8 shows a progress report using the technical outline to convey the information. Notice, too, that this report is very brief. The same progress report submitted to the president would contain details about each of the heads under "Progress in Current Phase." Since this report is to the board, it is concise and covers only the major accomplishments during this phase and the objectives for the coming one. From the dates in section 2.0, it would appear the progress on this project is reported on a monthly basis.

Occasionally an organization that has numerous ongoing projects may want standardized information in all its progress reports. In such cases, the organization may design a special form.

Contents

The phase of the project will determine what specific information to include in a progress report. For example, a first (or initial) report will differ from a final (or summary) report. However, certain kinds of information should be included in all progress reports, and section

---

[1] Published in the *Federal Register*, August 31, 1977.

EXHIBIT 8–7
Unusual Progress Report

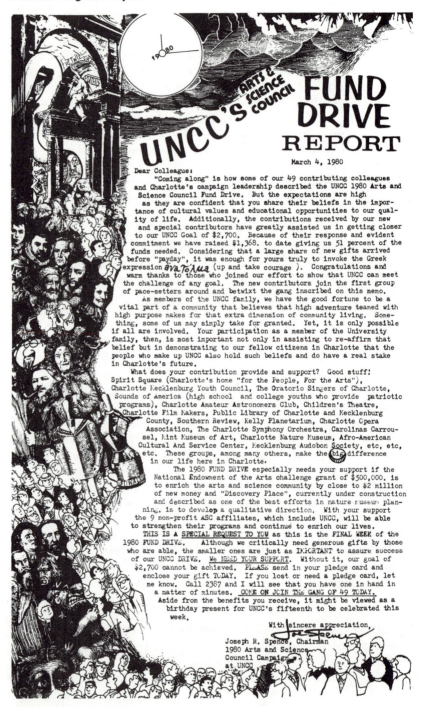

UNCC'S ARTS & SCIENCE COUNCIL FUND DRIVE REPORT

March 4, 1980

Dear Colleague:

"Coming along" is how some of our 49 contributing colleagues and Charlotte's campaign leadership described the UNCC 1980 Arts and Science Council Fund Drive. But the expectations are high as they are confident that you share their beliefs in the importance of cultural values and educational opportunities to our quality of life. Additionally, the contributions received by our new and special contributors have greatly assisted us in getting closer to our UNCC Goal of $2,700. Because of their response and evident commitment we have raised $1,368. to date giving us 51 percent of the funds needed. Considering that a large share of new gifts arrived before "payday", it was enough for yours truly to invoke the Greek expression ανατολμα (up and take courage). Congratulations and warm thanks to those who joined our effort to show that UNCC can meet the challenge of any goal. The new contributors join the first group of pace-setters around and betwixt the gang inscribed on this memo.

As members of the UNCC family, we have the good fortune to be a vital part of a community that believes that high adventure teamed with high purpose makes for that extra dimension of community living. Something, some of us may simply take for granted. Yet, it is only possible if all are involved. Your participation as a member of the University family, then, is most important not only in assisting to re-affirm that belief but in demonstrating to our fellow citizens in Charlotte that the people who make up UNCC also hold such beliefs and do have a real stake in Charlotte's future.

What does your contribution provide and support? Good stuff! Spirit Square (Charlotte's home "for the People, For the Arts"), Charlotte Mecklenburg Youth Council, The Oratorio Singers of Charlotte, Sounds of America (high school and college youths who provide patriotic programs), Charlotte Amateur Astronomers Club, Children's Theatre, Charlotte Film Makers, Public Library of Charlotte and Mecklenburg County, Southern Review, Kelly Planetarium, Charlotte Opera Association, The Charlotte Symphony Orchestra, Carolinas Carrousel, Mint Museum of Art, Charlotte Nature Museum, Afro-American Cultural And Service Center, Mecklenburg Audobon Society, etc, etc, etc. These groups, among many others, make the big difference in our life here in Charlotte.

The 1980 FUND DRIVE especially needs your support if the National Endowment of the Arts challenge grant of $500,000. is to enrich the arts and science community by close to $2 million of new money and "Discovery Place", currently under construction and described as one of the best efforts in nature museum planning. is to develop a qualitative direction. With your support the 9 non-profit ASC affiliates, which include UNCC, will be able to strengthen their programs and continue to enrich our lives.

THIS IS A SPECIAL REQUEST TO YOU as this is the FINAL WEEK of the 1980 FUND DRIVE. Although we critically need generous gifts by those who are able, the smaller ones are just as IMPORTANT to assure success of our UNCC DRIVE. We NEED YOUR SUPPORT. Without it, our goal of $2,700 cannot be achieved. PLEASE send in your pledge card and enclose your gift TODAY. If you lost or need a pledge card, let me know. Call 2387 and I will see that you have one in hand in a matter of minutes. COME ON JOIN THE GANG OF 49 TODAY.

Aside from the benefits you receive, it might be viewed as a birthday present for UNCC's fifteenth to be celebrated this week.

With sincere appreciation,

Joseph R. Spence, Chairman
1980 Arts and Science
Council Campaign
at UNCC

Source: Reprinted by permission of the Department of Creative Arts, University of North Carolina at Charlotte.

EXHIBIT 8–8
Progress Report Using Technical Outline

Environmental Research Division Progress Report

DATE: October 9, 1983   File No. 10061
TO: Mr. Russell Sage   C.C.: All other members of
                                        the Board of Directors
FROM: Martin Kapler, Manager,
           Environmental Research Division
SUBJECT: Anti–Pollution Project #3162––Air Refractor

1.0 Past Progress
    1.1 Design of the Refractor has been completed––five face
        styles are available.
    1.2 Prototype of the Refractor has passed all tests, no
        fail, and has been operational since August 10.
2.0 Progress in Current Phase––September 1––October 1
    2.1 Corporate General Counsel Jerome Misner completed
        copyright check––no problems with name of product.
    2.2 Marketing Division completed study on the impact and
        acceptability of the name––results decidedly
        positive.
    2.3 Status of production of the Refractor has improved.
        2.3.1 State Architectural Commission accepted design
              of new plant addition––September 8.
        2.3.2 Building permits were approved––September 10.
        2.3.3 Construction of addition began September 14.
        2.3.4 Confirmation of arrival of new machines on
              October 30 received by Purchasing––October 1.
3.0 Objectives for Phase IV
    3.1 Completion of plant addition––October 20.
    3.2 Completion of market surveys––October 15.
    3.3 Presentation of sales and technical information and
        demonstrations to manufacturer representatives––four
        regional locations––week of October 26–30.

headings and other devices which facilitate reading should be used also.

The following items should be included, regardless of the format:

1. *Statement of purpose.* Early in the report, make clear what it is you are reporting on. The progress report in Exhibit 8–7 uses its boldface heading as its statement of purpose:

    ### UNCC's Arts & Science Council Fund Drive Report

    Following is another example of a statement of purpose used for the heading of the report:

    SUMMARY PROGRESS REPORT
    of the
    1980–81 Graduate Studies Committee

    Since this is a summary (final) report, it presents only the final accomplishments or results of the group rather than what was done in stage one, stage two, and so on. A more conventional statement of purpose is used in the report in Exhibit 8–9.

2. *The period of time covered* or the phase of the project covered by the report. In the example above, note that the word *Summary* and the date 1980–81 tell the reader that this report covers the outcome of a year-long project. However, a heading such as the one in Exhibit 8–9 is used to show the period of time discussed in the report if it is less than a full year.

3. *A brief discussion of previous progress made.* This information is important because it brings the recipient up to date. But another reason for including it is that if for some reason the project coordinator must be replaced by a new one, the project could continue smoothly.

4. *A detailed discussion of the current phase.* Since the report is mainly about the work just finished, you must give the reader details of the accomplishments and any difficulties you encountered during this phase.

5. *A brief discussion of expected progress in the future.* This information will help the reader ascertain whether or not the project is proceeding as planned. You may use this part of the report to discuss any foreseeable problems with materials, manpower, inspections, and so on.

Exhibit 8–9 is an example of a complete progress report.

Finally, before you begin a progress report, remember to make a good outline listing past accomplishments as well as the progress

EXHIBIT 8-9
Progress Report

Oak Hill Homeowners Association
Progress Report #2
Contracting to Repair Pool

TO: Members   February 14, 1983
       Oak Hill Homeowners Association
FROM: Pool Maintenance Committee

Phase 2: Accepting Bids
This report discusses the second phase of our project, the repair of the Oak Hill pool for the coming season.

Summary of Work Done Previously
In late November the committee hired David Jymson as consultant on the repairs needed for the pool. His report indicated the pool needed to be patched, the surface repainted, and a new motor installed in the filtration system.

Work Done in Current Phase
The committee:

1. Used the consultant's report to prepare a list of specifications for the work to be done.
2. Sought the names of all companies, within a 50-mile radius, that specialized in pool repairs.
3. Sent a request for bids along with a list of specifications to each of five companies: Aquatech, Baylor Pools, Bikini Pools, Inc., FunTime, Inc., and Waterwonder, Inc.
4. Accepted sealed bids, to be received by 12:00 noon January 30.
5. Received bids from Aquatech, Bikini Pools, Inc., and Waterwonder, Inc. Low bidder was Aquatech.
6. Will hear open discussion of the bids at the scheduled meeting on Tuesday, February 17.

Work to Be Completed
After a bid is accepted, the committee will contract with the company and work will begin within a specified time. The committee will inspect the work and keep you posted on the progress of the job.

Paul Hill
_____
Committee Chairman

made in the current phase. Your report will be easier to write and will seem well organized if you first plan what you want to discuss.

METHODS AND PROCEDURES REPORTS

Methods and procedures reports detail the step-by-step process of carrying out a particular task or a general procedure. Obviously, they are informational reports that can be used to describe a number of processes such as these:

A *physical task* such as how to operate a computer.

A *mental task* with several steps, such as how to estimate the cost of a commercial construction project, how an account is analyzed, or how credit scoring is done.

A *paperwork system,* such as the steps to follow in requesting a permit to build a nuclear power generating station or details of how an information system functions in a company.

A *production process,* such as a description of how a product is manufactured, in which the activity of each department, station, or location in the process is discussed.

As you can see, methods and procedures reports can describe the fine details of a task; or they can show the broader, basic parts of a process. Your statement of purpose will define for the reader which type your report is.

Defining a Procedure

To be certain that you are including every step in a procedure, there are several methods of defining a procedure. One of these is the *process chart,* in which established symbols are used to represent the steps in a process. Following are the symbols and their meanings:

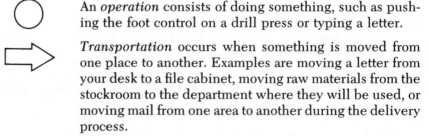

An *operation* consists of doing something, such as pushing the foot control on a drill press or typing a letter.

Transportation occurs when something is moved from one place to another. Examples are moving a letter from your desk to a file cabinet, moving raw materials from the stockroom to the department where they will be used, or moving mail from one area to another during the delivery process.

A *delay* occurs when something stops or delays what is taking place. If you are taking materials to the data processing center and you have to wait a minute for the elevator, that is a delay. Downtime for machine repairs is another example of a delay.

▽   *Storage* involves having an item out of the work area until it is needed. It includes such things as the holding of products in the warehouse while awaiting shipment, or storing stationery supplies in a cabinet until needed. Remember that storage is not a delay but a legitimate step in the operation.

☐   *Inspection* means checking on the quality of work done. It can be proofreading a report that was typed for you or checking for defective $1 bills at the Bureau of Printing and Engraving.

Exhibit 8–10 shows a partially completed process chart using the symbols just listed to show how a requisitions picker completes the job. Usually the process chart is used by industrial engineers who try to spot ways of improving the efficiency of a process by timing each part of it and looking for ways to cut down on the time spent on a particular step or on the whole process. It would be difficult for the engineer to study the process of picking requisitions since the picker does not receive requisitions from the same departments for the same items every day; the process fluctuates from day to day. However, notice that the engineer deals with a *finite* part of the path that a requisition form follows. In this example, the engineer is not concerned with the process of filling out the requisition for stationery and delivering it to the requisitions board. Nor does the engineer worry about what happens to the requisition once it is returned by the picker to the filled-requisition box. That is because those two jobs would be handled by other employees. The engineer studies only one unit of work at one time. As we learned in an earlier chapter, the forms design specialist would, on the other hand, be concerned about how the requisition form was filled out, how it was used by the picker, and what happened to it after it left the filled-requisition box; the forms design specialist studies the entire path of the requisition.

Another method of defining a procedure is with a flow chart. We saw an example in Exhibit 6–14, which showed what happened to a sales order once the sales representative received it from the customer. Let's look at another flow chart — this time one that emphasizes the person doing the work rather than what happens to the paperwork. Exhibit 8–11 is a flow chart based on the process chart in Exhibit 8–10; it shows part of the path taken by the requisition picker to deliver materials. If the process you will report on is a production that involves making the most efficient use of time, materials, man-

EXHIBIT 8–10
Process Chart

Subject Charted _____ Requisition Picker _____

Location _____ Picking Board-Stores _____

Present
Proposed
Charted by:

cjm

Page __1__ of __3__

		SUMMARY					
		Present		Proposed		Saving	
		No.	Time	No.	Time	No.	Time
Operation							
Transportation in feet							
Delay							
Storage							
Inspection							

Dist. in feet	Symbol	Description	Time	Remarks
	▽	Requisitions on board-Stores		
	⇨	Picker pulls requisitions		
	O	Picker reads requests and organizes them by department		
	⇨	Takes hand truck to Stores D		
	O	Pulls all items on each department's requisition		
	⇨	Goes to elevator		
	D	Waits for elevator		
	⇨	Travels to Engineering department		
	O	Unloads items; gives copy of requisition to clerk		
	⇨	Goes to elevator		
	D	Waits for elevator		
	⇨	Travels to Production Control department		
	O	Unloads items; gives copy of requisition to clerk		
	⇨	Goes to elevator		
	D	Waits for elevator		
	⇨	Travels back to Stores		
	O	Puts filled requisitions in box		

EXHIBIT 8–11
Flow Chart

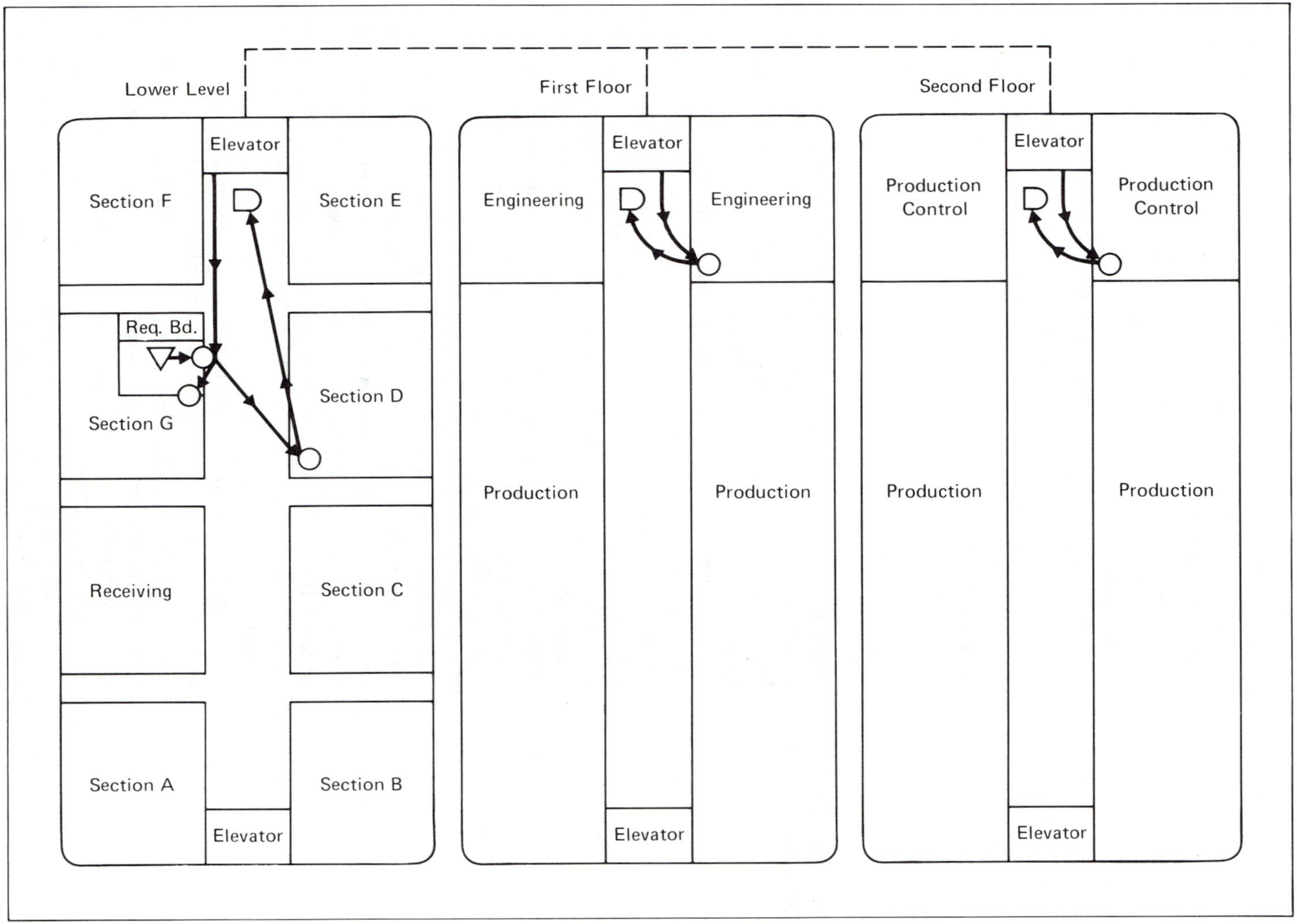

power, and machinery, someone may have used the critical path analysis method or the program evaluation and review technique (PERT) to determine the order in which certain things must be done. You may base your report on these analyses too. In cases involving complicated paperwork systems, the methods described above may not be as useful as merely outlining every step in the process. Sometimes outlining is a follow-up step to the other methods we mentioned, or it may be used alone. If you use it alone, leave plenty of space between each main head and each subhead so you can go back and fill in any steps or any precautions that you may have left out as you worked through the outline the first time.

Format and Contents

Since methods and procedures reports are used primarily within an organization, they are submitted as memo reports if the procedure is brief or as long formal reports if it is lengthy. In either case, the kind of information to include is similar.

Whether your report is a brief memo report or a long formal one, you need a *statement of purpose.* In some cases you may also need to discuss the importance of the job. For example, if your audience does not know the relationship of this job to others in the department, in the division, or in the company, a brief statement can clarify matters. The report in Exhibit 8–12 shows such a section in the second paragraph under the heading "Purpose/Importance of the Job." Notice that this report describes another step in the process of requisitioning materials that we saw earlier in this chapter.

If specific equipment or machinery or materials are needed to carry out the process, you will need a section heading such as "Equipment/materials needed." If the reader needs to understand the *theory of operation* for the process, you will need a brief section for that. The longest section of the report will of course cover the *steps in the process itself.* Some reports, especially long formal ones, may also need a conclusion; you will have to determine that point for each report.

Although the items discussed above are common in procedures reports, you may find that your particular report requires additional sections. For example, you may need to define a term or terms for some audiences before you can adequately explain the procedure. Or you may need to mention special precautions that must be taken before undertaking the task described. Exhibit 8–13 shows some unusual headings in a procedures report. Just remember to let your audience's needs and your good judgment guide you in determining what to include.

EXHIBIT 8–12
Procedures Report

PROCEDURES REPORT

Receiving Department

DATE: 29 September 1983
TO: John Schlagel, Department Head
FROM: Terri Rosenbladt, Supervisor
SUBJECT: Procedure for Sorting/Filing Requisitions to Be Sent
           to Data Processing.

This report details the procedure for sorting and filing
requisitions that our department has filled. These
requisitions show information that is used by the Data
Processing Department.

Purpose/Importance of This Job
All departments within the plant request materials from
us--manufacturing materials, stationery supplies,
housekeeping supplies, and so on.
When these requests have been filled, our department files a
copy of the requisition for future reference. Another copy is
sent to the Data Processing Department. Here the information
is entered into the computer to update inventory records and
determine what items must be purchased. Newly purchased items
are then received by our department, and the process starts
over again.

No Special Equipment Is Needed to perform this job. The
employee handles only stacks of filled requisitions and files
them in the department's metal filing system.

Procedure
The three-part requisition form consists of a white, a pink,
and a yellow copy. The top copy (white) is given to the
requesting department when the materials have been delivered.
The remaining copies are dropped into the ''filled'' box on the
sorter's desk.
      1. At 11:30 each day (the Data Processing Department
         requests we follow this schedule), pull all the filled
         requisitions out of the box.

EXHIBIT 8–12 (Continued)

2. Tear apart the two remaining copies, throwing away the carbon.
3. Make two stacks of requisitions, one for pink copies and one for yellow copies.
4. Set aside the yellow copies.
5. In the top right-hand corner of the pink copies, look for a code number.
6. Sort the pink copies as follows:
   Put all stationery items in one pile. The code for stationery is STAT.
   Put all cleaning supplies in another pile. The code is HSKSP.
   Put all X-numbered compounds in a third stack. A sample code is X1130.
   Put all T-numbered items in a fourth pile. A sample code is T2041.
   Put all crate reels into a fifth pile. A sample code is CR 39.
7. When all pink requisitions are sorted, put a rubber band around each stack. Stack all the rubber-banded piles and fasten them all together with another rubber band.
8. Deliver the sorted requisitions to the assistant manager of Data Processing (located on the second floor).
9. Return to the desk and sort the remaining yellow copies to be filed in our office.
10. Look at the lower right-hand corner of the copies to see if materials were sent to our other plants. Other plants will be listed as Franklin, Gaston, Lafayette, or Cumberland.
11. Pull out all the requisitions that list any of these plants (there are usually one or two). Set this group aside.
12. Sort all other requisitions as follows:
    Stationery supplies
    Housekeeping supplies
    X-compounds

EXHIBIT 8–12   (Continued)

```
          T-items
          Crate reels
     13.  File all requisitions for materials that went to
          another plant in the second drawer of the file. A
          separate section is set aside in the drawer for each
          plant. File the slips under the proper plant in front
          of the ones that are already there.
     14.  File all other requisitions in drawers 3 and 4. File
          the slips by code (stationery, X-compounds, etc.) and
          by date, putting the current slips in front of past
          ones.

     Conclusion
     When questions are asked about materials requisitioned by
     another department or another plant, the clerk can go to the
     file to locate the requisition in question.
```

Before you can write a good procedures report, you must know the procedure very well. If it has been a while since you performed the task you must report on, either consult someone who now does the job regularly and who can review the process for you, or actually perform the process to remind yourself of all the details. Once you know the procedure well, follow these guidelines for writing a clear report:

Guidelines for Methods and Procedures Reports

1. *Make a formal outline* so you can check for omitted details before you begin to write.

2. *List every step in the process* in a consistent format. For example, if the procedures report is general, don't go into detail about some aspects of the process and not others; if the report is specific, give the same amount of attention to each step in the process.

3. *Describe any precautions to be taken* or any unusual circumstances that would cause the reader to alter the process in any way. Usually these items should be discussed *just before* the step in the process that relates to them; however, sometimes the precautions are listed in a separate section *before* the one on the steps in the process.

EXHIBIT 8–13
Methods and Procedures Report

Methods and Procedures Report

DATE: 10 June 1983
TO: Mary Lisk, Scheduler Trainee
FROM: Katherine Ostrowski, Supervisor
SUBJECT: Preparing for Daily Morning Meeting

One of the most important jobs of a production scheduler is to
collect and organize production information for the daily
meeting with supervisors, planners, area supervisors and the
production manager. This information determines what will be
run in the afternoon, on the evening shifts, and the following
morning.

Preparing for Morning Meetings
Before the meeting, you must determine:
1. How much of the previously scheduled production has
   actually been run;
2. What is left and why;
3. How much will be run that morning;
4. What has been scheduled to run for afternoon and
   evening shifts;
5. If enough personnel are available and how many will be
   necessary for afternoon and evening runs;
6. If all needed components are available;
7. If bulk is ready, and if not, how long will it take to
   get it.

Procedure for Answering Above Questions
Questions 1, 2, 3:
a. Take three production report forms from the top
   left–hand file.
b. Take one to the foreman in liquid makeup, one to the
   foreman in pancake makeup, one to the foreman in eye
   makeup.
c. Have them fill it out—<u>WAIT FOR IT</u>—don't let them tell
   you ''later.'' THEY ARE BUSY BUT SO ARE YOU.
d. Transfer all the information from the small production
   report forms to one of the large forms titled ''Daily
   Production Report,'' in the middle left–hand file. The

EXHIBIT 8–13 (Continued)

column titles are the same on the small and large
production reports, so just copy the information in the
appropriate column.

Question 4:

Check planners' reports from the previous day. It is their
responsibility to have it on your desk no later than 7:00 a.m.
If any are not there, call the responsible planner at the
extension on the phone pad next to the phone. Remind them that
you need it immediately.

Question 5:

On the foremen's production reports is a column titled
''Available Personnel.'' Total these figures from all three
reports and put the total onto the large production report. At
the meeting it will be decided if there is enough personnel for
production planned and scheduled.

Question 6:

Go back to the planner's report. For each item planned, there
is a list of components needed. If there is a check next to the
component, the planner has been advised that it is available.
Call Stores (Receiving Dept.) and order everything with a
check next to it.

Question 7:

Go back to the planner's report again. For each item planned,
there is a bulk number listed.

    a. Call ''Bulk Manufacturing.''

    b. Order all bulk listed and have it brought to the
       manufacturing floor.

    c. If they don't have it made, find out how long it will
       take or if anything can be substituted for it.

    d. If it is made or can be substituted, put an X on the
       planner's report.

    e. If it is not made and something else can't be
       substituted, find out how long it will take and mark
       the time and/or date that it will be available on the
       planner's report.

You should now be ready to answer any question that comes up at
the meeting.

4. *Use descriptive details* such as sizes and colors of items, code numbers, locations, and so on to help the reader understand the key points in the process.

5. *Use the listing technique* for the materials needed, for the steps in the process, and in other places where it is practical. Listing makes the report easier to understand, and it also allows your readers to mentally (or physically) check off the steps as they read.

6. *Use strong verbs* (review Chapter 5) to state the steps in the process so the information is direct and concise.

7. *Keep the steps in the procedure parallel* — that is, similar in form.

Study Exhibit 8–13 as an example of a procedures report using the memo report format to see the way in which many of the above guidelines were used.

SUMMARY

This chapter discusses several kinds of managerial reports, of which *interview reports* are one type. There are three kinds of interview reports: the *employment interview* report, the *exit interview* report, and the *information interview* report. The first of these interviews is conducted with job applicants to try to hire the best person for a job. The second is conducted with an employee who is leaving the company to take another job, to retire, or because of termination; the interviewer wants to find out the employee's perception of the company, benefits, salary, and so on. The third type is conducted with someone who has expertise in some field that you would like to know more about. When writing employment interview reports, include a statement of purpose, several paragraphs discussing the applicant's strengths and weaknesses, and finally your recommendation to hire, to invite for a second interview, or to reject the applicant. The exit interview report should tell how the employee feels about the company, the particular job, and so on. The information interview report will tell the important facts learned from the expert you interviewed.

Often you will be part of a team that works on a project. In such cases, each person on the team assumes a particular responsibility and must report on the progress of that part of the job. These *progress reports* should briefly review progress in earlier stages of the project, give detailed information about the current phase, and mention objectives for the next phase.

Methods and procedures reports are used to train new employees and to keep records of procedures in a particular department, section, or division. This type of report may detail a physical task, a mental task, a production process, or a paperwork system flow. The report should make a statement of purpose and indicate the equipment/materials needed, the theory of operation (if applicable), and any precautions that should be taken. Finally, it should discuss the process step by step.

1. Probably you have had several jobs for which you were given little training when you began work. Discuss how methods and procedures reports or procedures manuals could help make new employees in such jobs more productive immediately.

2. Conduct an interview with someone in the training and development group, department, or division in a company near you. Find the answers to these questions:

   a. Is the department autonomous, or is it a part of a larger department (many are part of the personnel function)?
   b. Does the department use a procedures manual or procedures reports to train new employees?
   c. Who prepares such reports or manuals? How are they used in the training process?

3. Prepare a progress report on some activity you are involved in, such as writing a long report for a class, reaching a particular personal goal, or some other ongoing activity. Use the memo report format and submit the report to your instructor. Assume this is the second report on your progress. Include the following:

   a. A statement of purpose;
   b. A brief statement of past progress;
   c. Details of progress made to date in the current phase and problems encountered;
   d. Work yet to be done;
   e. Your deadline for completing the work.

4. Assume that you are applying for a job. Prepare and bring to class a resume to be used by a job interviewer. Members of the class will be paired and will exchange resumes. Now assume that you are the interviewer, and prepare questions based on research both of the company and of the job in question. At the next class meeting conduct a simulated interview with your classmate, then reverse roles. (The interviews may be tape-recorded or videotaped if the instructor wishes.) Write a memo report on the interview you conducted, address it to the director of personnel, and make a recommendation.

5. Arrange an interview with someone who does a job that interests you. Write an information interview report, including the following in your discussion:

   a. A brief statement of purpose;

   b. A short discussion of the company for which the interviewee works as well as information about the interviewee;

   c. A list of qualifications for obtaining this job;

   d. Details about what the interviewee does in his or her day-to-day work;

   e. The salary range for people in the geographic area who do this job;

   f. Your conclusions about this kind of work.

6. You are personnel associate for a large public school corporation. You have a position for a physical education teacher/basketball coach for the coming year in one of the senior high schools. From twenty applicants, you narrowed your choice to two. After a second interview with each of the candidates, you have decided that Boris Brown, now a college senior, is the better candidate. Send a brief hiring recommendation to your superior, the personnel director for the school system, advising that Mr. Brown be offered a three-year contract. Your report will be based on the following information you gathered from interviewing him:

   a. Mr. Brown has played college basketball at a private college for four years.

   b. During his junior and senior years the team won its conference championship.

   c. He has coached a YMCA boy's basketball team this year in addition to studying and playing on his college team.

   d. His grade point average is 3.5.

   e. During summers between college years, he went back home to work on his parents' farm and to help with summer recreation programs — especially baseball — in his hometown.

   f. You were impressed with him because he seemed sincere, honest, and somewhat idealistic about wanting to help young men learn sportsmanship and the means of making the most of their potential.

   g. When asked what he thought this position should pay him, he gave a realistic answer of $16,500.

   h. He seemed congenial and would likely fit in well with the senior faculty at the school where you want to place him.

   i. He had specific ideas about how to produce a winning team when you pointed out that this school had a record of 14 losses and 4 wins for the season.

7. It is early March. Your club wants to sponsor a Jog-A-Thon to raise money. Members of the group will participate in running and will solicit sponsors who agree (in writing) to pay a set amount for each mile completed by the member. The president of the club asks you to study the responsibilities of sponsoring such an event and to submit a brief report establishing a time-table for each responsibility, which he will pass on to various committees. The club would like to hold the event on Saturday, May 24. The following things must be done before that time:

   a. Get approval from the director of student affairs to hold the event on campus.
   b. Arrange with the security department to use one of the campus parking lots as the starting and finishing point of the event.
   c. Arrange with the student health service to have one person on duty to treat any injuries.
   d. Obtain permission and support from county law enforcement officers to run along a portion of a county highway.
   e. Obtain commitments from members to participate in the event.
   f. Solicit sponsors for the members.
   g. Plan for refreshment stations at three-mile points along the route.
   h. Obtain spotters and judges from outside the group to assist in measuring the distance covered by members.
   i. Get publicity in the college and local papers about the event.
   j. Collect money from sponsors after the Jog-A-Thon.
   k. Submit final report (treasurer) to the club on the proceeds of the event.

   In your report set specific deadlines (dates) by which each item should be completed; make a brief comment about each so that committee members understand what their responsibilities will entail. Address this memo report to the president of the club.

8. Using your work experience as the basis for a topic, write a methods and procedures report about some aspect of a job. Use these guidelines to prepare the one-to-two page report:

   a. Prepare a formal outline;
   b. Use the memo report format;
   c. Write a brief introductory statement that tells both the purpose of the report and the relationship of this job to others in the department, division, or company;
   d. Use section headings to break up the report;
   e. Use lists whenever possible.

9.   You are the regional manager for the Do-Nut Shoppe chain, and you supervise 12 baker supervisors, who come from the ranks of the best manager/bakers who operate individual shops throughout the area. Four months ago it was suggested that you move Tom Schlotterbeck, manager/baker at one shop, into training for a position as baker supervisor. He looked promising because his shop showed a high profit margin, and he seemed aggressive and eager to move up the corporate ladder. He also did well in the two-week training session. However, you have not been pleased with what has happened in his area since he assumed his new duties. In the past three months profits are down 20 percent in his area, and five manager/bakers have quit. You have had numerous complaints from other managers who have threatened to quit. Among the complaints are the following:

a.   Tom has not visited one manager's store except on the day when he knows the manager is not on duty.
b.   He has made no personal visits to another store; instead, he has called the manager to say he wanted several things changed.
c.   He threatened to fire a manager for not having a neat store; the manager felt his store was as neat as it had always been.
d.   Another manager said that Tom expected him to do things that were not in the job description given him when he was hired.
e.   Another complained that Tom got him out of bed at 3:00 a.m. on his night off to say that he needed a substitute for a manager/baker at another shop who couldn't work the next evening.
f.   Every manager has mentioned that Tom is a "know-it-all" and that he won't even listen to their point of view.

After the first few complaints, you talked to Tom about the situation, and he explained that he was new on the job but was learning and that things would improve. Now, three months into the job, things have not improved. You decide to give him the option of going back to a shop as a manager/baker or to resign from the current position. Send a memo report to the company's personnel manager explaining why you are taking this action.

10.   For three years you have worked for a man who owns several "quick print" shops in various locations in your state. Your job is to establish, open, and manage a new shop until the president is ready to establish another. Most recently, you have been sent to set up a new shop in Oakdale. You have completed many of the preliminary tasks and must submit a *progress report* to the presi-

dent telling him what you have done. Since he is in another city, submit the report to him in letter format. Following are some of the tasks you have done:

a. Leased space in a small but busy mall that your superior had recommended to you.
b. Negotiated with the mall manager about redecorating your space; she agreed to repaint, clean the carpet, and build a counter to your specifications.
c. Purchased these items for the office:
   (1) four chairs for the small lobby area
   (2) three plants to decorate the lobby area
   (3) desk and chair for your work
   (4) desk, chair, and typewriter for the part-time clerical workers
   (5) coatrack for employee use
d. Ordered:
   (1) the standard initial quantity of paper for printing from the supplier
   (2) a telephone for the office
e. Placed an advertisement in the local paper announcing the grand opening, January 25; signed a contract for an advertisement in the Thursday paper for the next three months.
f. Hired:
   (1) two part-time clerical workers from twenty-five applicants; they will report to work January 23 for training
   (2) one full-time press operator from three applicants; she will report to work January 22 for training.

CHAPTER

9

Suggestion Reports, Recommendation Reports, Feasibility Reports, and Proposals

LEARNING OBJECTIVES

After reading this chapter, you should be able to:

- Describe what elements these three types of reports have in common: *suggestion reports, recommendation reports, feasibility reports;*
- Describe how these three types of reports differ from each other;
- Write each of these kinds of reports;
- Define the term *proposal* and tell how it differs from other kinds of reports in this chapter;
- Describe the kinds of information to include in a proposal.

The four types of reports discussed in this chapter are similar in that they require an *analysis* of a problem or situation and they *suggest some kind of action* be taken, based on the analysis. Analyzing means breaking down the situation into its parts, scrutinizing them, and presenting the facts you have discovered. In your business you may need to analyze trends, causes and effects, results, processes, ideas, conditions, or numerous other factors. One of the most important things in all these reports is the *interpretation* of the facts for your reader. For some readers you will need to make careful explanations of the meaning of the facts; for others the explanations can be brief.

DIFFERENCES AMONG THESE REPORTS

Although many textbooks make little or no distinction among the types of reports discussed in this chapter, there are some differences. For example, the content of suggestion and recommendation reports is similar: both give facts about a single situation and both tell how and why that situation should be changed. However, the authority and responsibility for these two kinds of reports differ.

First, consider suggestion reports. Many companies have instituted suggestion systems whereby employees can submit ideas about improvements in a process, work layout, or other aspects of the work place. Top management solicits suggestions from employees at all levels since the employees know a great deal about the jobs they do. The most important distinction, then, between suggestion and recommendation reports is that *suggestion reports* are voluntary and may be accepted or rejected by management. An employee has no responsibility to submit them, and management has no obligation to accept them.

Recommendation reports, on the other hand, are a part of the responsibility of managers who want to advance in their organizations. Business situations change constantly, and managers may need to recommend changes in such areas as these:

promotions/salary increases

new purchases

procedural changes

strategies (marketing, production, and so on)

Recommendation reports may also be prepared for customers or clients if a company hopes to sell them a product or service to meet a particular need. We saw in Chapter 2 an example of the need for such a report when a sales representative called on a company to sell it a temperature control system for a new building.

Usually, both suggestion and recommendation reports deal with a *single* topic; they suggest or support only one thing. *Feasibility reports*, on the other hand, usually deal with *alternatives*. This type of report presents evidence about two or more situations; it may compare or contrast them and allow the facts to speak for themselves. In such cases, the recommendation will seem obvious to the reader after considering all the facts. The following are examples of situations that call for feasibility reports:

a new or better way of doing a task

the choice of one product or service over another

Occasionally, a feasibility study will deal with only one topic; the study may be conducted to determine if a single situation is viable. For example, an entrepreneur may do a feasibility study to determine if a new product should be added to the current line. The report will end with a specific recommendation: that it is or is not feasible to follow the plan that was studied.

Proposals seek a yes or no response from a superior or from a funding source, and the facts can be studied at length before any commitment is made. In some cases, proposals attempt to be more persuasive than recommendation and feasibility reports because they strive to *obtain immediate approval* to conduct a more extensive study or to *obtain authorization* for a particular course of action. On the other hand, recommendation and feasibility reports can be implemented at any time — now or later.

SUGGESTION REPORTS: FORMAT AND CONTENTS

Usually companies devise special forms on which employees make suggestions for changing things in the organization; the form gives instructions for submitting the report. The most important things to remember when submitting a suggestion are to (1) state your ideas clearly, concisely, and completely and (2) tell how your suggestion will benefit the company. Exhibit 9–1 shows a form used to submit suggestions.

If the form report format is not used, the writer should submit the report using the memo report format and the heading "Suggestion Memorandum" or "Suggestion Report." The body of the report should include the following:

1. *A brief statement of the suggestion.* For example:

   I suggest that all department work for our three secretaries be placed in a single in-basket and that a secretary do a job as it comes up in the basket.

EXHIBIT 9–1
Suggestion Report Using the Form Report Format

Employee Suggestion Form

Name_____ Date_____

Job Title/Grade_____

Department/Division_____

Social Security Number_____

Please write your suggestion in simple, clear language. Include all
important information such as quantities, code numbers, sizes, colors, and
so on. Complete the form, sign it, and have your supervisor sign it.
Return the top copy to the Personnel department, and keep the second copy
for your records.

_____
(Employee's Signature)

_____
(Supervisor's Signature)

Form ESF 101
Rev 7/82

2. *A brief explanation of the current situation.* For example:

> Currently each secretary handles work for two particular buyers. Some days one secretary may be very busy while the others are idle.

3. *An explanation of how the new suggestion will benefit the company* (save time and money, increase productivity, improve morale, and so forth), and facts and figures that support the change. Be sure to anticipate any questions your superior might have or any potential problems that the new plan would cause, and try to answer these objections in your report.

Exhibit 9–2 shows a complete suggestion report in the memorandum format.

RECOMMENDATION REPORTS: FORMAT AND CONTENTS

Recommendation reports are usually submitted to one's superiors. The format is the memo report, unless it is a lengthy report requiring much detail or unless it goes to top management, in which cases the long formal report is usually used. But whatever the format, the following information should be included:

1. A brief statement of purpose (to recommend . . .) and a list of the criteria by which you judged the soundness of the recommendation.

2. A detailed discussion (use section headings) of the criteria mentioned in the introductory statement. Give specific facts in this section (sizes, costs, time consideration, personnel needs, and so on).

3. A specific recommendation based on the facts presented.

Study the marginal comments in Exhibit 9–3 to see how the criteria were used to organize this recommendation report.

FEASIBILITY REPORTS: FORMAT AND CONTENTS

Feasibility reports that will be used within the organization are submitted as memo reports or as long formal reports; those done for customers or clients are written as letter reports or as long formal reports. Feasibility reports that present two or more alternatives should include the following information:

1. A brief statement of purpose (to study the feasibility of . . .), the alternatives under consideration, and the criteria for each alternative (the same criteria must be applied to each alternative).

EXHIBIT 9–2
Suggestion Report Using the Memo Report Format

SUGGESTION REPORT

Date: January 30, 1983
From: Jessica Ledford, Supervisor
To: Ben Velasco, Purchasing Manager
Subject: Proposed Change in Secretarial Responsibilities

Ben, I suggest that all department work for our three
secretaries be placed in a single large in-basket and that each
secretary do a job as it comes up in the basket. This change may
alleviate some of the ill will that has been growing among the
secretaries.

Current Situation

Currently, each secretary handles work for two specific
buyers. On some occasions one secretary may be overloaded with
work while the other two are idle. This situation has caused
some ''hard feelings'' among the secretaries.

How the New Plan Would Work

With the new plan, buyers would place all secretarial work in a
single in-basket rather than taking it to ''their secretary.''
Secretaries would be instructed to work through a job, then
begin work on the next job in the in-basket. Since all the
buyers do similar work, the secretaries already know how to
handle all the paperwork.

Benefits of the New Plan

This plan should improve the morale among the secretaries
because all will share equally in the work of the department.
This will also eliminate their feelings of having two bosses
(buyer as well as supervisor). In addition, since each
secretary's work carries his/her initials, it would be
possible to determine how productive each secretary is. Merit
pay increases could later be tied to the level of productivity.

Possible Problems and Solutions

If the work is carried over into the next day, there could be a
problem in determining who would take the first job out of the
in-basket. We can eliminate that in one of two ways:

EXHIBIT 9–2   (Continued)

```
   1. Seniority--Each morning Jane would take the first job
      from the basket since she has most seniority; Sally
      would take the second job since she has second-highest
      seniority; Bill would take the third job.
   2. Rotation--Each day of the first week Jane would take
      the first job; Sally, the second; Bill, the third. The
      second week Sally would take the first; Bill, the
      second; Jane, the third; and so on.
```

2. A detailed discussion (use section headings) of the criteria for each alternative.

3. A conclusion reached after weighing the alternatives.

Study the marginal comments in Exhibit 9–4 to see how to organize a feasibility report. Notice that specific costs are shown in tables.

When doing a lengthy feasibility study for a customer or client, again consider all the criteria needed to make a valid evaluation; discuss all of these in the reports. Exhibit 9–5 is an outline for a long feasibility report for a client who wanted to find out if it would be wise to invest in a grocery store in a particular location. Notice that the consultants evaluated the project on three main criteria (first-degree heads) and that each of these was broken down into many subcriteria (second- and third-degree heads). The conclusion of the report included a recommendation to invest in the business, based on the facts discussed.

PROPOSALS: FORMAT AND CONTENTS

Proposals that go to your superior will be submitted as memo reports or in some cases as long formal reports. Proposals to organizations outside your company may be in any format — a form report, a letter report, or a long formal report — depending on the situation. Outside sources offering funding for projects usually have specific guidelines for writing proposals. If you are seeking funds for a project, follow the guidelines to the letter since failure to do so is reason for rejecting the proposal.

EXHIBIT 9–3
Recommendation Report Using the Memo Report Format

MEMORANDUM REPORT

TO: Al Tyson, Regional Manager
FROM: Tom Horrigan, Branch Manager,
                           Charleston
DATE: February 12, 1983
SUBJECT: Handwritten vs.
                           Dictated/Transcribed Correspondence

Within this company all
correspondence addressed to
noncompany recipients is supposed to
Alternatives under ———→ be <u>dictated and transcribed</u> via
   consideration   electronic word processing
                          equipment. Some individuals prefer
                          to use <u>longhand</u> in all
                          correspondence, regardless of
                          whether the recipients are company or
Brief statement of ———→ noncompany personnel. These two
   purpose   approaches to written correspondence
Criteria for ———→ will be evaluated according to three
   evaluation   criteria: (1) time/service, (2)
                          resources used, and (3) product
                          quality.

Section heading: ————————→ <u>TIME/SERVICE</u>
   criterion 1

Subsection heading ———→ <u>HANDWRITTEN</u>
                          Whenever written correspondence is
                          necessary, an individual simply
                          pulls a three-page snap-out memo out
                          of the desk drawer and writes. It
                          will take a few minutes or possibly a
                          few hours to complete the memo. This
                          act of writing involves only one
                          person and single handling.
                          Telephone conversations can be
                          confirmed immediately and mailed the

EXHIBIT 9–3 (Continued)

same day--an aspect of the insurance
industry that is most important due
to the heavy dependence on the
telephone. Service often means the
difference in a sale or no sale when
comparable products are sold.

DICTATED/TRANSCRIBED

Two people are needed to generate
written correspondence--one to
dictate and one to transcribe.
Sometimes it takes the same amount of
time to dictate correspondence as it
does to write it in longhand. When a
situation involves double handling,
additional time is always expended.
Additional time can mean delayed
reaction and service to a customer's
needs.

Criterion 2 ———————————————→ RESOURCES USED

HANDWRITTEN

Only paper, pen, and time are needed.
The only energy used is the energy of
the writer.

DICTATED/TRANSCRIBED

Paper, recording tapes, and
electronic equipment--recorder,
transcriber, and typewriter--are
needed. With the use of these pieces
of electronic equipment, there is an
additional outlay in use of
electricity. Occasionally, the
electronic equipment can
malfunction, thus prolonging the
time to complete the simplest
correspondence. When there is a

EXHIBIT 9–3 (Continued)

```
                          malfunction of equipment, added
                          costs are incurred for maintenance
                          and repair. The work time of two
                          people is tied up in handling a
                          single piece of correspondence.

  Criterion 3 ─────────────────→ PRODUCT QUALITY

                          The quality is not standard and
                          varies from poor to excellent, with
                          most being average. The longhand form
                          is less formal in style and form.

                          DICTATED/TRANSCRIBED
                          The quality is standard and
                          excellent, and very formal in style
                          and form.

                              RECOMMENDATION

                          Except for only specifically
                          designated formal reports, as
                          required occasionally by the
                          company, all written correspondence
                          should be done in longhand to realize
                          better service to our agents and less
                          cost to the company.
```

If there are no guidelines, you should include the following information in your report:

1. A brief statement of purpose (to propose . . .); be concise, yet as specific as possible about your ideas. This statement should give background information on the situation such as organizational relationships (who in the organization is affected by the proposal), the specific problem you are addressing, and why it merits consideration (your purpose in proposing it).

2. A statement of your objectives or the ultimate goal of the project. Be specific; tell the audience what you believe the outcome of the project will be and how it can benefit them.

EXHIBIT 9–4
Feasibility Report Using the Memo Report Format

MEMORANDUM REPORT

TO: Harry Smith, Chief Engineer
FROM: John Cancione
DATE: 12 February 1983
SUBJECT: PLASTIC–LINED PIPE VS. STAINLESS STEEL PIPE

The acid solution produced by the Harrisonburg Plant will corrode unprotected carbon steel pipe. To avoid this problem

Alternatives ——————————→ either <u>stainless steel</u> or <u>plastic–lined</u>

Statement of ——————————→ <u>carbon steel</u> pipe can be used. This report
    purpose and   will show that stainless steel pipe is more
    recommendation   cost-effective for this project.

Criterion 1 ——————————————————→ <u>INITIAL COSTS</u>

A 20–ft. straight length of plastic–lined pipe costs roughly 25 percent less than stainless steel (see Table 1).

TABLE 1: Comparison of Purchase Cost

| Pipe Sizes | Cost per Foot (in 20–ft. lengths) | |
	Plastic–Lined	Stainless Steel
2 in.	$ 5.90	$ 7.75
4 in.	12.40	16.50
6 in.	28.55	38.00
8 in.	53.95	69.25

However, straight lengths of plastic–lined pipe less than 20 ft. long must be custom made. Labor charges to make these lengths add 15 percent to the cost of the pipe. Two flanges and a Teflon gasket per length add an additional 5 percent. Stainless steel pipe can be cut to length in the field and is normally welded, eliminating the need for flanges and gaskets. Table 2 shows the comparative prices per foot ready for field installation.

EXHIBIT 9–4   (Continued)

TABLE 2: Comparison of Costs Ready for
         Installation

| | Price per Foot | |
Pipe Sizes	Plastic–Lined	Stainless Steel
2 in.	$ 6.79	$ 7.75
4 in.	14.26	16.50
6 in.	32.83	38.00
8 in.	60.89	69.25

Criterion 2 ⟶ INSTALLATION COSTS

Stainless steel pipe must be cut, fitted, and welded in the field. A welder, pipefitter, and helper are required. Experience shows installation labor operations add $15.00 per foot to the cost of the pipe.

Plastic–lined pipe is pre–cut and requires no welding; therefore, no welder is needed, and the pipefitter and helper spend no time measuring and cutting. Installation adds only $7.50 per foot to the cost of the pipe. Table 3 shows the comparative installed costs.

TABLE 3: Installed Costs

| | Cost per Foot | |
Pipe Sizes	Plastic–Lined	Stainless Steel
2 in.	$14.29	$22.75
4 in.	21.76	31.50
6 in.	40.53	53.00
8 in.	68.39	84.25

Criterion 3 ⟶ MAINTENANCE COSTS

The expected useful life of the plant is fifteen years. During that time the outside of the plastic–lined pipe will have to be repainted every three years at a cost of $4.75 per foot each time.

EXHIBIT 9–4 (Continued)

There are no maintenance costs for stainless steel pipe. Table 4 shows the total comparative costs of the two systems.

TABLE 4: Comparative Costs Installed and Maintained

	Cost per Foot	
Pipe Sizes	Plastic–Lined	Stainless Steel
2 in.	$33.29	$22.75
4 in.	40.76	32.50
6 in.	59.53	53.00
8 in.	87.39	84.25

Conclusion and recommendation based on the facts presented ⟶ CONCLUSION/RECOMMENDATION

Over the useful life of the plant, the cost of stainless steel pipe is less than that of plastic–lined pipe. We should use it on the Harrisonburg project.

3. A lengthy section detailing how you will achieve the goals or objectives. Discuss your *research procedures* or how you will carry out your plan. Include a *timetable* showing when certain parts of the plan will be completed or how much time you will need to do certain things. In addition, present a *proposed budget* or cost schedule and a list of *other items,* such as extra personnel or special materials, that you will need to complete the project.

4. A request for approval of your proposal. Some people like to see this in the opening paragraph; others prefer it at the end after the facts have been presented.

5. Attachments of any supporting information that might help the reader see the merit of your proposal.

Proposals call for persuasive writing. Logical statements supported by strong evidence are usually most persuasive to business people; always remember to show them what benefit they can derive from your proposal. (See also "Persuasion in Government Reports," Chapter 12.) Exhibit 9–6 is a proposal submitted by a consultant.

EXHIBIT 9–5
Outline for a Long Feasibility Report

A MARKET SURVEY TO DETERMINE THE SALES POTENTIAL FOR A
SO FINE GROCERY IN ALLENTOWN, INDIANA

I. Introduction
   A. Market survey
      1. To determine sales potential
      2. Feasibility of success
   B. Sources of information
      1. Titles of publications
      2. Dates of publications
   C. Definitions of terminology

II. Trade Area Characteristics
   A. Location
      1. Region of state
      2. Distance from major cities
   B. Social and economic characteristics
      1. State of economic characteristics
      2. Bass County
      3. Allentown
   C. Population
      1. Surrounding area
      2. Allentown
   D. General sales trends
      1. United States
      2. Indiana
      3. Bass County
      4. Allentown

III. Characteristics of Competition
   A. Name of competitor
   B. Location
   C. Store size
   D. Parking facilities
      1. Own parking
      2. Adjacent parking
   E. Operating hours
   F. Services offered
      1. Deli
      2. Bakery

EXHIBIT 9–5 (Continued)

```
              3. Wine department
              4. Stamps
              5. Check-cashing policy
         IV. Site Evaluation
             A. Accessibility of site
                1. Ingress
                2. Egress
                3. Traffic flow
                4. Traffic controls
             B. Visibility of site
             C. Lot
                1. Grade
                2. Topography
             D. Other business in immediate area
                1. Proposed
                   a. Family steak house
                   b. Apartment complex
                   c. Mall cinemas
                2. Existing
                   a. Allentown Mall
                   b. Restaurants
                   c. Others

          V. Conclusion
             A. Average weekly sales potential
                1. Based on months
                2. Based on years
             B. The market share
             C. Recommendations
```

Notice that it has section headings showing similar points to those suggested in the guidelines above.

This chapter has shown you several kinds of managerial reports. All of them require that you analyze your audience and that you tell that audience what they need to know or how your information can benefit them.

EXHIBIT 9–6
Sample Proposal

PROPOSAL:

In–House Technical Writing Seminar
for Pro–Tech, Inc.

Submitted by:

Ned Schifano

Acme Business Consultants
Tampa, Florida

Objectives:
    The technical writing seminar will help the individual
learn to write in a simple, direct, and concise manner. The
course will provide specific models of technical writing and
will provide participants with opportunities to practice good
writing techniques.

Scope:
    The seminar will consist of ten weekly two–hour meetings
to begin at your convenience. The first 75 minutes will be
devoted to discussing general principles and techniques of
good writing; the remaining 45 minutes will be set aside for
individual instruction. During the individual time, I will
meet with those who wish to consult privately about various
writing problems encountered in their current work
assignments.

    Throughout the seminar, I will ask participants to submit
samples of their work for group discussion. Also, after the
third or fourth meeting, weekly writing projects will be
assigned to give practice in writing effective technical
descriptions, definitions, process explanations, outlines,
and abstracts. These assignments will be tailored to each
individual's specialty and will be written for the intelligent
lay reader. (If during the seminar participants feel they need
practice in other kinds of technical writing, substitutions
can be made.)

    To provide the best possible preparation for such writing
assignments, the course will cover:

EXHIBIT 9–6   (Continued)

1.0 Words (jargon, abstract–concrete, active–passive
    verbs, and wordiness)
2.0 Primary structural problems (including grammar and
    punctuation)
    2.1 Phrases
    2.2 Clauses
    2.3 Sentences
3.0 Secondary structural problems
    3.1 Paragraphs
    3.2 Sections

The last session or two, depending on group progress, will
analyze effective informational memos and letters, stressing
organization, reader identification, and tone.

Course Materials:

    I will provide handouts as needed and gather material from
a wide range of sources and from ongoing projects at Pro–Tech.
I do recommend, however, that participants order the Brusaw
Handbook of Technical Writing (St. Martin's Press, 1976),
which discusses many of the problems commonly encountered in
technical writing.

Facilities:

    Because the seminar will be run primarily as a workshop, I
will need a classroom with the following facilities:
blackboard, screen, overhead projector, and tables or chair
desks for in–class writing. In addition, photocopying (or
mimeograph) and transparency–making equipment will be needed
to reproduce materials for class discussion.

Cost:

1. $60 per hour for seminar
2. $60 per hour for individual conferences
3. $10 per hour for writing analysis
4. Travel allowance (total round–trip distance from home to
   Pro–Tech: 50 miles)
5. Any materials and support not supplied directly by Pro–Tech

SUMMARY   This chapter deals with several kinds of managerial reports. These
                     include suggestion, recommendation, and feasibility reports, and pro-

posals. *Suggestion reports* recommend some kind of change and are distinguished by the fact that they are voluntary. An employee has no obligation to submit them, and management may accept or reject them.

Recommendation reports also suggest changes, but managers are expected to submit them whenever a better way of doing something is found. These reports should make a statement of purpose, describe the current situation, and explain the new recommendation and how it will benefit the company.

Feasibility reports often deal with two alternatives; the report explores the alternatives and tries to determine which is better. This kind of report should include a statement of purpose, a description of the alternatives under consideration, the criteria to be applied to them, and finally the recommendation of one of the alternatives.

A *proposal* is a suggested plan for which the writer seeks approval either to implement it or to study it further. The proposal should include the statement of purpose, the goals or objectives and a detailed plan for achieving them, a timetable, a budget or estimate of costs, and an indication of any additional supplies or personnel required.

1. The dean of your college wants to determine what courses in each department are most valuable to students. She asks you to study the situation and to submit a proposal to her (you may poll current students as well as alumni) for finding out this information. Submit the report in memo format and include in the report the following:

    a. A statement of purpose;
    b. An explanation of the procedure for gathering the needed information, including details on how and when to do each step and the anticipated cost of obtaining the information;
    c. An indication of any anticipated problems and how they can be handled;
    d. A recommendation for a date to begin the task.

2. Write a feasibility report showing that one thing is better than another. Use your work experience or your participation in clubs or organizations as the basis for the report. You may decide to use one of these as a topic: (1) a new or better way of doing a task or of using a paperwork system, (2) a comparison of two products or services (buying vs. leasing an airplane or computer, for example), or (3) the selection of one hotel or mode of travel over an-

LEARNING ACTIVITIES

other for a group excursion. Use the memo report format and include the following:

a. A brief statement of purpose and any background information that is needed;
b. The criteria by which you will evaluate each alternative (for example, initial cost, operational cost, time involved, energy involved, personnel involved, return on investment, payback period, service provided, and so on);
c. A presentation of the facts for each criterion;
d. A conclusion (one alternative is preferable to another).

3. Prepare a proposal in which you request authorization for a detailed study of your proposed action. Draw on either your work experience or your participation in clubs or organizations for the report. You may choose to be a member of the group or a consultant to it (base the format for the report on your choice). Include the following in your proposal:

a. A statement of purpose, including background to the problem and who is affected by it;
b. A description of the problem you will address, the goals, and the anticipated outcome of the project;
c. A discussion of costs, timetables, research methods, personnel needs, or any other appropriate items;
d. A request for authorization to do the detailed study;
e. Attachments of any kind to support your proposal.

4. You are manager of the Candlelight Supper Club in Lafayette, Louisiana. The Candlelight is a "tablecloth" restaurant specializing in steaks and has a seating capacity of 200. Since entertainment and dancing are available on Friday and Saturday, these are the busiest evenings.

Each table is covered first with a white cloth, then with a red one placed diagonally on top. Fresh red cloths are used daily, but the white ones are changed only after Saturday night diners have left and on Thursday before diners arrive. Larger tables (seating four to six couples) have only white cloths, which are changed when they become soiled.

The Candlelight opened a year and a half ago and has been renting its table and kitchen linens (laundry service included). The Candlelight's owners are looking for ways to cut costs and/or generate more profit from the business and have asked you to see if it would be more profitable to *purchase* linens and pay only for laundry services. Based on the following facts, present in letter format a *brief recommendation report to the owners*, Harry and Ruth Gentry, who live in Sarasota, Florida:

a. In an average week the Candlelight uses 200 white table-cloths, 200 red tablecloths, 800 white napkins, 45 waitress tunics, 30 chef's coats, and 100 dish towels.

b. Current rental costs are $0.25 per tablecloth, $6 per 100 napkins, $0.50 per chef's coat, $0.40 per waitress tunic, and $5 per 100 dish towels (laundry service included).

c. You have talked to two restaurant supply houses, and they advised you that you could *purchase* the average weekly quantity of linens for $2,500 if all were bought on a single contract. Linens have a useful life of approximately two years.

d. If the restaurant buys its own linen, the linen supply service it now uses will contract to pick up and deliver twice a week (Thursday afternoon and Monday afternoon) at a cost of $125 per week.

e. The present storage area is large enough to accommodate about half a week's supply of linen since present deliveries are on Monday and Thursday and only part of the week's supply is ever in storage.

Suggestions: (1) Consider the initial cost, life of the linens, tax advantages, and so on when deciding which course of action to recommend to the Gentrys. (2) Use an illustration to help present the *figures* to the Gentrys.

5. Pat Holmes is a staff resident who supervises a group of resident advisers who live and work in the dorms on campus. Because of a crowded school calendar this semester, the school will begin final exams on Sunday afternoon rather than on Monday so students can be home for Christmas Eve. Ordinarily the food service serves evening meals Monday through Friday only. However, at a recent meeting, the advisers felt that an evening meal should be provided for students on the Sunday that exams begin. Many students either have exams or will be studying on that day and dislike the inconvenience of going elsewhere for their Sunday evening meal. The advisers' arguments convince Pat to suggest this change to the director of residence life. Write the proposal — giving the arguments for the change — that Pat should submit.

6. A young woman who worked for your company last summer has asked if you could recommend her to the Business and Professional Women's Society as a candidate for a $1,000 scholarship the group will award in June for the coming academic year. You feel she is a qualified candidate and agree to write a short report recommending that she be considered for the scholarship and explaining her responsibilities when she worked for you and how she handled them.

These are the qualifications candidates must meet:

a. Be a female student preparing for a career in business or a profession.
b. Be a rising senior at an accredited university.
c. Have a 3.5 or higher grade point average.
d. Be active in extracurricular activities.
e. Have some work experience.

You know that she meets the first four criteria, which you will mention briefly. In the rest of the report, you will deal specifically with her work for you last summer. This brief recommendation report should follow the letter format and be addressed to:

> Ms. Florence Gaither, Chairwoman
> Scholarship Committee
> Business and Professional Women's Society
> P.O. Box 10022
> Rapid City, IA 52404

7. You are program planner for a local TV station. Submit a report to your superior, John Villani, suggesting a new, once-a-month feature for the evening news. Since the public is concerned about inflation and the food dollar, you believe that a "Monthly Market Basket" feature would be successful. Your plan would include sending a reporter each month to three or four of the most popular stores in the area (use names of stores) to purchase 30 items, of the same brand name whenever possible (you make up the "grocery list," using staples and other items most people probably purchase). The reporter will then comment on these costs and the probable causes of any increases or decreases from month to month.

8. For this exercise, reread problem 7 in Chapter 8. Develop a proposal for Joan LeGrande, Director of Student Affairs, indicating that your club seeks approval to sponsor the Jog-A-Thon. Present the persuasive arguments as well as the details involved in your club's sponsoring the project. Include in the report the same kinds of information listed for problem 3 in this chapter.

Long Formal Reports

LEARNING OBJECTIVES

After reading this chapter, you should be able to:

- Identify the three ways of receiving *long report* assignments;
- Explain when to use the long formal report format;
- Identify all the possible parts of a long formal report and describe their purpose;
- Prepare a long report for a course project.

In earlier chapters we discussed several kinds of short reports. Often, though, business people must prepare longer reports for customers, clients, or top management in their own firm. Long reports are usually more formal for two reasons. First, because they take longer to prepare and because they usually contain more sophisticated information, they are often read by several people in the organization. The decision maker who receives a long report often passes it along to other managers to read — either for general information or because a particular segment relates to another manager's area of expertise. Therefore, a long report must be more durable to withstand handling by several people. Second, since long formal reports usually relate to weighty decisions made by people with much power, the writer wants to create the best possible impression on the reader. The formality of the report does just that.

DEFINING THE PROBLEM

Even when a problem is clear to the writer, assembling a long report is a hard task. If the problem does not present itself clearly, the task is even more difficult. Reports are based on the organization's needs. One type of need is to solve a problem that grows out of the routine transaction of business — we need another machine; what company should we purchase it from? Other problems arise as the functions within an organization interact to achieve an objective. Usually when you have to write a long report, you will receive the assignment for one of three reasons. First, your superior (or someone else in the organization) may ask for specific information. This request may be made orally or in writing. A second need for reports comes from the standard operating procedures followed by your company. Some kind of information needs to be transmitted so the organization can continue to function. The third type is the report that is generated by the reporter. You may see a need for a change and want to report how it can be done. Or you may have an idea that could save time, effort, or money, and you want to explore it further in a report — usually to your superior. (The main differences between this report and the suggestion report discussed in the last chapter are length and audience; if written for the company's president, it should be more formal than if written for one's immediate superiors.) Once the topic has been assigned or chosen, you need to define through the following steps how you will approach it:

1. Brainstorm for ideas; jot them down on cards or check out your thoughts with others in the company. Or you can look in a card catalogue or an index for materials related to your problem. At any rate, some thinking about the problem is a prerequisite to any writing.

2. Clearly define the purpose of the report; make a clear statement of what you want to cover (review Chapter 2 for more information on this step).

3. Write an outline of the ideas you will use to support your statement of purpose. Out of these main headings will come other subheads or subideas (again, review Chapter 2).

4. Begin your research, whether it be primary or secondary (review Chapter 3). Probably your plan before researching the topic will include a statement of the problem, its scope, and any background the reader needs. It will include a description of what method(s) of research you will use, and finally it will include a detailed outline that you expect will satisfy the statement of the problem.

Long formal reports may be informational, analytical, or recommendation reports, but most often they analyze some problem and recommend a solution to it. The *purpose* of the report will determine its *content,* but *not* the basic format. All long formal reports — whether they convey information, analyze a problem, or make a recommendation — follow a similar format. Although not all firms include in their formal reports all of the prefatory and end parts discussed in this chapter, we have described here every part that might *possibly* be included. For example, some companies may not include an authorization or transmittal; others may not include appendix material. By the same token, some reports will not *require* certain parts, such as a bibliography, particularly if only primary research was the basis for the report. Other companies prefer that source notes appear in the body of the report rather than at the end.

PURPOSE

    The long formal report consists of three divisions: the prefatory parts, the body of the report, and the end parts.

Prefatory parts are all those items that precede the body or primary information in the report. These pages are not numbered with Arabic numerals as is the body of the report. Instead, lowercase Roman numerals (i, ii, iii, iv, and so on) are used.

PREFATORY PARTS

As we said earlier, long formal reports must be durable because several people usually read them. A paper or plastic binder will protect the report from soil and damage while it is being read. In addition, the binder offers a company the opportunity to promote its name, logo, or other information (a name remembered generates additional busi-

Binder or Cover

ness). Binders may be very simple or quite elaborate, depending on the image the company wishes to promote. Usually the title of the report and the name and title of the person for whom it was prepared will appear on the binder or cover.

Title Page

The *title page* repeats the title of the report and the name and title of the person for whom the report was prepared. It will also give the writer's name and title, and the date. Sometimes, final approval of a report is given by one's superior, in which case the title page may have a space for the superior's signature. Exhibit 10–1 shows such a title page.

Table of Contents

Based on the formal outline used to plan the report, the table of contents will show all of the sections of the report that follow it. It will list these items and the page number on which each *begins*. Note that a *single* page number, rather than inclusive page numbers, is listed. Each new item in the table of contents signals the end of the previous one, so the single page number is sufficient. The table of contents should reflect the main headings in the report as well as the important secondary headings so that the reader can quickly assess what the report will cover.

Any *illustrations* used are *listed separately* at the bottom of the table of contents, even though they are integrated with the report. This separate listing should give the table, figure, or exhibit number, the title, and the page on which the illustration appears. Study the table of contents pages in Exhibits 10–1 and 10–2.

Letter or Memo of Authorization

Few long formal reports are written without a special request to do so. This can come in several forms. For example, if a company wants to sell a sophisticated computer system to an interested customer, the account representative usually will prepare a special report analyzing the customer's needs, the cost of the system, the payback period, tax implications, and so on. The authorization for such a report may be only a verbal agreement made in person or by telephone. On the other hand, the customer may request such a report in a letter. This is a *letter of authorization*. At other times, reports going to customers or clients or top management must be authorized by the reporter's superior. Often this kind of written authorization will be made on a form or in a brief memo; this is a *memo of authorization*. If a written authorization is made, a photocopy of it will often be included in the report. See Exhibits 10–1 and 10–2 for examples of a letter and a memo of authorization.

The *transmittal* is the formal written statement that turns the report over to the person for whom it was written. If the report is prepared for a customer, client, or someone else outside the organization, the writer will prepare a *letter of transmittal*. If it is to go to top management within the organization, the writer will prepare a *memo of transmittal*. The essential message of a transmittal is, "Here is the report you asked for." It may also indicate the outcome of the research (in a single sentence), the sources used, any difficulties encountered (physical or monetary), and an offer to do further research if necessary. See the transmittals in Exhibits 10–1 and 10–2.

Letter or Memo of Transmittal

Although this part of the report is referred to by different names, it has one purpose: to summarize briefly the important information. The abstract or synopsis is used primarily by those who have limited time but need to understand the gist of the report. This introductory summary is written *after* the report proper has been completed, and usually is 5 to 10 percent of the length of the body. See Exhibits 10–1 and 10–2 for examples of an abstract.

Abstract, Synopsis, Executive Summary, or Introductory Summary

The *body* is the main part of the report in which information is presented, facts are analyzed, and/or recommendations are made. Two items distinguish the *first page* of the body from other pages.

First, the information is begun two or three inches from the top of the page. Second, the title of the report — usually in capital letters — is used to officially signal the body of the report. No page number appears on this first page, but it is in fact page 1, and remaining pages, beginning with page 2, are numbered using Arabic numerals either at the top or bottom.

THE BODY OF THE REPORT

The *introduction* defines the purpose and scope of the problem under discussion and provides background information so the reader can better understand the report. The introduction often is broken down

Introduction

by subheadings such as "Purpose of the Report," "Statement of the Problem," "Background," "Definitions," and so forth. Regardless of the organization of the material in the introduction, it must clearly prepare the reader to understand the facts, analyses, arguments, and so on that follow. See Exhibits 10–1 and 10–2 for examples of good introductions.

Other Section Headings in the Body

After the introduction, the writer will present the pertinent facts about the topic. When planning the long report, you will write a detailed outline (see Chapter 2) to be sure you cover all the important facts. Usually the first-degree heads in your outline will become the section headings in the report. Second-degree heads in the outline usually become subsection headings. These headings are important because they break up the material into meaningful parts that can be read easily. In the body of the report, if you are borrowing material from either a primary or secondary source, you will need a source note (the numbers used to mark source notes are raised slightly above the regular lines and are numbered consecutively through the report). We will discuss documentation of sources in greater detail later in this chapter.

Conclusions and Recommendations

After you have presented all the facts, you will either draw some *conclusions* from them or you will make *recommendations* based on the facts and your analysis of them. The conclusions or recommendations may be presented in regular sentence and paragraph form, or they may be listed. The listing technique is best if you have several separate and distinct recommendations that might be overlooked if expressed in paragraphed form. Although the conclusion/recommendation section is usually placed at the end of the report, some companies prefer to have it at the beginning of the body. Certainly, the conclusion/recommendation will be stated in the abstract for the report.

END PARTS

The *end parts* are those that follow the body of a report.

Source Notes (End Notes)

Source notes are needed when you must give credit for information in the body of the report that was borrowed from some source. Footnotes (placed at the bottom of the page on which they are mentioned) are almost never used in business reports today. Rather, the notes are accumulated and listed on a single page at the end of the report and headed with the title "Notes" or "End Notes." This trend has come about for reasons of practicality and efficiency; it is easier and less time-consuming in both planning and typing the notes if all of them can be put on a single page. It is, however, more difficult for the reader to refer to them.

Sometimes report writers have difficulty knowing when to use a source note; perhaps the following guidelines will help.

A source note is needed:

1. When you *quote* either a primary or a secondary source. Use quotation marks around the exact words used by the source. At the end of the quotation, insert the number — slightly raised above the line — that you will use in the end notes to refer to this source.

2. When you *paraphrase* an idea that is uniquely the property of the source. That means that any idea that is not common knowledge must be noted.

A source note is *not* needed:

1. When you use material that is considered common knowledge — even if you obtained it from some source. For example, it is considered common knowledge that Frederick Taylor is called "the father of scientific management," that critical path analysis is used in planning construction projects, that the House Ways and Means Committee writes federal tax laws, and so on.

2. When you give all the pertinent information about a source *within* the sentence that refers to it. Here is such an example:

   In my interview on November 29, 1981 with Mr. Rob Jinks, Vice-President of Operations at Hiebold, Inc., I learned that 45 percent of the company's personnel have degrees in the engineering field.

When preparing your end notes page, use the following guidelines to record information the *first time* a particular source is used:

1. Number the notes on the notes page with Arabic numerals typed on the same line (not raised, as in the body of the report) as the source information. Follow the numeral with a period.

2. First, list the name of the author or source — first name first, then last name. Use this format for both primary and secondary sources. Add a comma.

3. Next present the source of the information. For example, if it is a primary source such as an interview or company records, list that information. If it is an article from a periodical or a chapter from a book, list the article or chapter title, using quotation marks around it. Place a comma after the title, within the quotation marks.

4. List the remaining information about the name of the publication if it is a secondary source. For example, list the title of the periodical or book and underline it. If it is a book, include in parentheses the location of the publishing company, the company's name, and the date of publication; add a comma. If it is a periodical, list (without parentheses) the day, month, and year of publication, using commas to separate them. If it is a primary source such as an interview or company records, list the person's job title, company, and the date of the interview or the date found on the records, again using commas to separate the items.

5. Finally, list the page number of the borrowed material and place a period at the end of the note.

6. If you need to refer to a source a second or third time in the notes, you may merely use a key word — the author's last name, for example — and cite the new page number.

Look at these examples to see how the rules above apply:

1. James S. Sells, "Packaging for Profit," *Plastics World*, April 1980, p. 21.

2. Sells, p. 23.

3. Jay Jacobson, purchasing agent, Clymer Co., Interview, 16 December 1982.

4. M. Allan Jones, *Packaging with a Flair* (Easton, NJ: Easton Publishing Company, 1981), pp. 200–201.

5. Sells, p. 23.

6. Jacobson, 16 December 1982.

7. "Inventory on Hand," Computer Printout, Clymer Co., 19 December 1982.

Bibliography

The *bibliography* page lists *all* the sources you consulted, even if you do not actually refer to some of them in the report. While the term *bibliography* refers specifically to secondary (published) sources, we often use other sources of information for business reports. Therefore, many people separate the bibliography page into two sections, one labeled "Bibliography," under which they list all secondary sources, the other labeled "Other Sources," under which they include all primary sources. Other people prefer to head the bibliography page with the title "Sources" and list all sources, whether primary or secondary, in alphabetical order. Here are some guidelines for compiling the bibliography:

1. List sources alphabetically by author's last name. If there is no author, list the source alphabetically by title along with the authored sources. If it is a publication of an organization, list it alphabetically by the organization's name. If it is an interview, list it alphabetically by the interviewee's last name.

2. Give the place of publication, name of the publisher, and date of publication if it is a book. You do not need to list this information about periodicals.

3. The name of the author or of the organization is followed by a period. For a book, the title is underlined and followed by a period; the place of publication is followed by a colon, the publisher's name by a comma, and the date by a period. For an article, the title is enclosed in quotation marks; a period (placed inside the quotation marks) follows the title. The name of the periodical (underlined) and the date are each followed by a comma, and the page number by a period.

4. Single-space the lines of the information about each source, but double-space between sources.

5. Indent five spaces for the second, third, and additional lines of an entry.

Study this sample bibliography to see how the above guidelines apply:

Bibliography

American Bankers Association. *Faces of a Bank, 1979*. First Union Corporation. *First Union Corporation 1979 Annual Report.*
First Union Corporation. *Personable, Innovative Bankers*, 1981.
Heyel, Carl. *Computers, Office Machines, and the New Information Technology*. New York: The Macmillan Company, 1972.
NCNB Corporation. *NCNB Corporation Annual Report 1979.*
NCNB Corporation. *Your Success Makes NCNB the Best in Neighborhoods Around the World*, 1981.
"The New Jet Setters." *Time*, 19 June 1975.
"Takeover Battles in the Banking Industry." *American Business*, December 1980.

Wachovia Bank and Trust Company. *1979 Annual Report.*
Wachovia Bank and Trust Company. *Your Career in Banking,* 1979.

Other Sources

Questionnaire distributed to employees at NCNB and Wachovia, November 10, 1982.
Solzenski, R. Joseph, Personnel Associate, Cobar Corporation. Interview, November 25, 1982.

Appendix

Appendix material is supplementary information. It is not vital to the reader's understanding of the report; thus if it is not read, the report will still be meaningful. For example, long complicated tables or charts may be placed in the appendix. Such materials are included so that a reader who has an intense interest in the subject may find additional information. Many other kinds of material may be placed in the appendix — for example, pamphlets; photocopies of contracts, letters, questionnaires; original illustrations; photographs; flat samples of items; and so forth.

To separate appendix material from the rest of the report, many people place a sheet of paper — with the single word "Appendix" written on it — between the bibliography and the appendix material itself. See the appendix material in Exhibit 10–1.

EXAMPLES OF LONG FORMAL REPORTS

On the following pages you will find two examples of long formal reports. Exhibit 10–1 is an analytical report; Exhibit 10–2 is an informational report.

EXHIBIT 10–1
Long Formal Analytical Report

wei-mar
 commercial
  consultants

WAREHOUSE/OFFICE SPACE FOR LEASE
IN CHARLOTTE, N.C.

Source: Reprinted by permission of Suzanne Welsch.

EXHIBIT 10–1 (Continued)

WAREHOUSE/OFFICE SPACE FOR LEASE
IN CHARLOTTE, N.C.

PREPARED FOR

A P S C O
JACKSON POLLARD
VICE–PRESIDENT OF MARKETING

BY
SUZANNE WELSCH

13 NOVEMBER 1978

APPROVED BY: _____

EXHIBIT 10–1 (Continued)

<u>INTEROFFICE CORRESPONDENCE</u>

2 December 1978

To: Suzanne Welsch
From: Carol McFarland
Subject: Request for Report on Available Warehouse/Office
         Space

Suzanne, I just talked to Jackson Pollard of APSCO in Chicago.
They are interested in a short–term lease on space in the
Charlotte area for a sales and distribution center.

Mr. Pollard would like a report on our analysis of available
facilities and our recommendation on sites by December 15.

Following are their requirements:
1. Office space—800–1,000 sq. ft. to include a reception
   area, one private office, one conference room/display
   area.
2. Warehouse space—minimum of 2,000 sq. ft. of heated
   space, 18–ft. ceilings, fully sprinklered.
3. Location—Near airport and trucking terminals and main
   thoroughfares; zoned light industry.
4. Lease agreement—length of lease (prefer two years
   plus renewal), rate, restrictions, amenities, and so
   forth.
5. Image—must be impressive and modern; successful
   executive appearance.

If you think you will need a research assistant due to the short
time to work on this project, let me know. Since this is an
important client, I am making all our resources available to
you for this project. If I can help in any other way, please let
me know.

EXHIBIT 10–1 (Continued)

WEI-MAR
COMMERCIAL CONSULTANTS

2893 St. Albans   Phone: 704 336-4949   Charlotte, N.C. 28215

12 December 1978

Mr. Jackson Pollard
Vice President—Marketing
APSCO
2489 Brandle Drive
Oakview, IL

Dear Mr. Pollard:

Thank you for the opportunity to provide you with the needed
information on the availability of warehouse/office space for
lease in the Charlotte, N.C. area.

Attached is my report on the space presently available.
Although Charlotte abounds with warehouse space, you will see
that there are few spaces vacant, and the market changes daily.

I will, therefore, keep you posted on any additions or
deletions to this report.

Sincerely,

Suzanne Welsch

EXHIBIT 10–1 (Continued)

Contents

Introductory Summary i
Introduction 1
    Statement of the Problem 1
    Purpose of the Research 1
    Research Plan 1
Available Warehouse/Office Space 2
    Free-Standing Buildings 2
    Industrial Parks 2
    Executive Parks 5
Proposed Sites 6
    Free-Standing Buildings 6
    Industrial Parks 6
    Executive Parks 7
Conclusions 7
Recommendations 8
Notes 10
Bibliography 10
Other Sources 10
Appendix 11

Illustrations

Figure 1. Industrial Parks Map 3
Table 1.   Comparison of Square Footage to
           Lease Rates 8
Table 2.   Comparison of Features 9

EXHIBIT 10–1 (Continued)

Introductory Summary

It is our recommendation that your company locate its Charlotte sales and distribution center at Corporate Center, I–85 and Freedom Drive. This recommendation is based on the fulfillment of the requisites of location, ratio of office to warehouse space, amenities, and most importantly, image.

Most of the warehouse space available is located in industrial parks or inner–city redevelopment areas not readily accessible. Corporate Center, however, is adjacent to I–85, is surrounded by a variety of commercial businesses and other distribution centers like yours, and is also conveniently located to major trucking terminals and Douglas Airport.

Whether you select the 3,000– or the 4,000–sq. ft. unit, you will have the necessary office space with the option of adding offices on the mezzanine level as they are needed. With one exception, this feature is solely available at Corporate Center.

The interiors are finished (painted and carpeted) and will require only minimal decorating expenses. In addition, the offices are heated and air–conditioned; the warehouse is heated separately. Safety features include well–lit exteriors and a complete sprinkler system.

Finally, Corporate Center has the image you require. While providing you with a complete distribution facility in the rear, the exterior reflects an image of a modern office park: efficient, modern, and well landscaped.

i

EXHIBIT 10-1 (Continued)

WAREHOUSE/OFFICE SPACE FOR LEASE
IN CHARLOTTE, N.C.

Introduction

Statement of the Problem
      Your company has indicated a need for a sales and
distribution center in the Charlotte, N.C., area. It was,
therefore, necessary to investigate the availability of
combined warehouse/office space and then select only those
that met your fundamental requisites and then investigate
those more thoroughly.
      The requisites you outlined were as follows:
1. Office Space--800-1,000 sq. ft. to include reception
    area, one private office, and one conference/display
    area.
2. Warehouse Space--minimum of 2,000 sq. ft. of heated
    space, 18-ft. ceilings, fully sprinklered.
3. Location--close to airport and trucking terminals and
    main thoroughfares; zoned light industry.
4. Lease Agreement--length of lease (preferably two year
    and renewal); rate, restrictions, amenities, and so
    forth.
5. Image--must be impressive and modern; successful
    executive appearance.

Purpose of the Research
      The purpose of this report is to provide recommended sites
for a sales and distribution center or, if necessary, to
recommend postponement on opening such a center due to a lack
of suitable locations.

Research Plan
      To find a suitable location for such a sales and
distribution center, I surveyed some 20 warehouse complexes
and industrial parks as well as 10 or more single,
free-standing buildings in varying locations.

1

EXHIBIT 10–1 (Continued)

The information was provided by a variety of publications and interviews, including those from the Greater Charlotte Chamber of Commerce, local newspapers, and data sheets provided by local real estate management firms.

Available Warehouse/Office Space

At the present time, vacancies in warehouse/office space in the greater Charlotte area are rare. The market changes daily, and even the proposals made here could, by morning, be obsolete.

Those few that are available fall into three general classifications: Free-Standing Buildings, Industrial Parks, and Executive Parks.

Free-Standing Buildings

These buildings are the least suitable for your purpose; therefore, I will not detail their individual features but rather discuss them as a whole.

Although these buildings tend to be the least expensive as well as the most flexible in lease agreements, you get just what you pay for.

The three vacancies I found were:

1115 Commercial Avenue (Figure 1, Industrial Parks Map, Location 1)

1132 Commercial Avenue (Map, Location 2)

Old Pineville/Nations Ford Road (Map, Location 3)

These are located in areas that because of zoning changes are a mixture of residential, commercial, and industrial properties. The result is a hodgepodge of confusion.

While the overall square footage of the buildings fits your needs, the interiors were apparently altered several times. As a result they would require extensive redesigning and decorating before they would suit your purpose.

Industrial Parks

Industrial Parks are by definition ''. . . planned areas, properly zoned, subdivided and under control of a

2

EXHIBIT 10–1 (Continued)

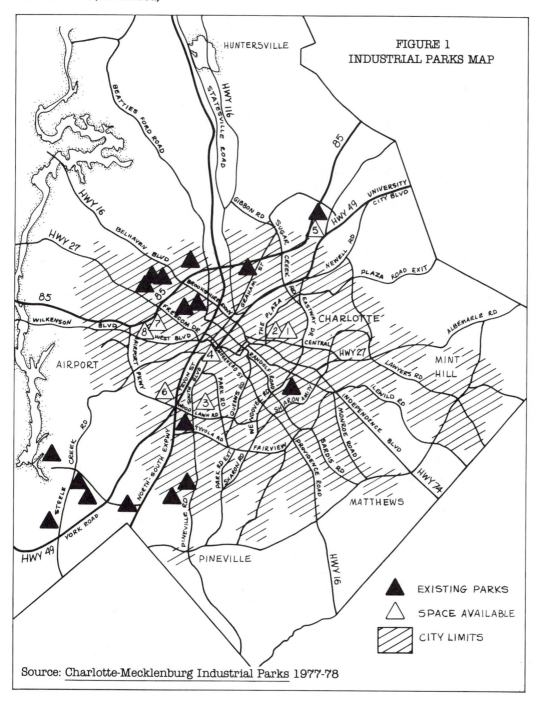

FIGURE 1
INDUSTRIAL PARKS MAP

▲ EXISTING PARKS

△ SPACE AVAILABLE

▨ CITY LIMITS

Source: Charlotte-Mecklenburg Industrial Parks 1977-78

EXHIBIT 10–1 (Continued)

developer responsible for planning, common area maintenance and street dedication.''[1] In this category I found two possible locations.

Tremont Industrial Park (Map, Location 4) is located in the South Boulevard area, a section classified as inner city[2] and zoned for distribution and light manufacturing.

The building is brick, simple in exterior design, and has both the office and shipping entrances at the front. Offices are heated and air-conditioned. The warehouse area is heated separately and is fully sprinklered.

In the completed 2,450-sq. ft. unit, 300 sq. ft. are offices, and 2,150 sq. ft. are warehouse. The leasing agent, however, feels some alterations are still possible.[3] The 4,900-sq. ft. units are still in early stages of construction, allowing for major alterations at this point. They are designed to have 600 sq. ft. of office at completion.

At present only the smaller unit is available at a rate of $600 per month, with either short- or long-term leases. Completion of the larger units is scheduled for mid-January at a projected lease rate of approximately double that of the smaller unit.

The greatest detraction is image. Because loading docks are located at the front entrance, customers are continuously faced with the hazards of trucks making pick-ups and deliveries. The noise and congestion give an industrial appearance rather than that of a sales office.

Spangler-North 29 Industrial Park (Map, Location 5), built by the same company as Tremont, has the same physical features as North 29. The major difference is location. Located on N. Tryon where I-85 and University Boulevard merge, North 29 has a distinct advantage--accessibility. It is only minutes from I-77 and major trucking terminals.

The only unit presently available has 2,450 sq. ft. and leases at the same rate as Tremont Park, $600/month. Twenty-seven of the 29 firms leasing at North 29 are

4

EXHIBIT 10–1 (Continued)

distribution centers,[4] resulting in the same problem——truck congestion.

Executive Parks

Although executive parks fall under the same general definition as industrial parks, the difference is one of perspective. Industrial parks are designed with distribution as their prime feature. Executive parks give equal but separate attention to sales and distribution by keeping the front clear and attractive for customer traffic and all shipping and receiving in the rear.

Pressley Park (Map, Location 6) is located one-quarter mile from the intersection of I–77 and South Tryon on Pressley Road, convenient to both air and truck terminals.

Both 3000 sq. ft. and 6000 sq. ft. units are available with approximately 15% as office space and the remainder as warehouse. Leasing rates are $565 per month and $1,350 per month, respectively, with a minimum lease length of one year.

Shipping, receiving, and truck parking are restricted to the rear of the building, allowing for ample auto parking in front of the offices. The exterior is an attractive, well-landscaped office park designed ''for companies that care about their image.''[5]

Corporate Center (Map, Location 7) is located on the frontage road in the southwest quadrant of the intersection of I–85 and Freedom Drive. It is equally accessible to air and trucking terminals. Its easy visibility from I–85 also makes it easy for customers to locate.

Presently there are both a 3000 sq. ft. and a 4000 sq. ft. unit available. The smaller unit has approximately 600 sq. ft. in office space, while the larger unit has a proportionate 800 sq. ft. of office space. Additional offices can be added on the mezzanine level as they are needed, resulting in double the office space.

Leasing rates are $550 per month and $700 per month, respectively, with a two-year minimum lease preferred.

EXHIBIT 10–1 (Continued)

Again, office and shipping areas are completely separate.
Offices have one heating and air conditioning system separate
from the warehouse system. The warehouse area is very well
lighted and fully sprinklered, with 18 ft. ceilings.

The office interiors are carpeted, painted, and have
either draperies or sun screens at the windows. Only minor
decorating is necessary to reflect your company's image.

Finally, the exterior image is one of a modern, efficient,
beautifully landscaped office park; but at the same time
companies have all the advantages of a complete distribution
center in the rear. It is truly the most compatible combination
for your needs.

<u>Proposed Sites</u>

Several of the builders and real estate developers have
indicated plans for either expansion of present sites or
development of new warehouse/office space.

<u>Free-Standing Buildings</u>

Southern Realty is offering for an expected occupancy date
of May 1979, an ultramodern, single building, one-quarter mile
west of Corporate Center in what will be known as Interstate
Park. (Map, Location 8)

It will feature 20,160 sq. ft. of total space with 1,000
sq. ft. in offices. Complete landscaping, paved parking, and
rear shipping/receiving docks will add to the overall
executive appearance. Offices will be heated and
air-conditioned with a separate heating system provided for
the warehouse area. The lease rate has been set at $4,200 per
month with the lease conditions as yet undetermined.

Although this building far exceeds your immediate needs,
it does have future potential.

<u>Industrial Parks</u>

Spangler Construction Company, the developers of Tremont
and North 29 Industrial Parks, is planning additional

6

EXHIBIT 10–1 (Continued)

expansion at both locations. The same features and comparable lease rate will prevail. Expected occupancy dates were not available. (Map, Location 9 and Location 10).

Many other locations are available for individual development. Land prices range from $8,000 per acre to over $55,000 per acre.

Executive Parks

Mr. Charles Floyd of Prudential Insurance's Real Estate and Investment Division announced plans of an as-yet-unnamed executive park to be located in the I-77 South-Westinghouse Blvd. area. (Map, Location 11)

The proposed building will have a total of 40,000 sq. ft., divided into individual warehouse/office combinations ranging from 5,000 sq. ft. and up. Complete details are not yet available, although Mr. Floyd termed the new site as ''. . . even more impressive than Corporate Center.''[6] Prudential financed that park as well.

Conclusions

This study of available warehouse/office space, based on the information provided by chamber of commerce publications, classified ads from the Charlotte Observer, and data provided by developers and property management firms, finds that Corporate Center is the best location for your purposes.

Based on the comparison of the information presented in Table 1, Corporate Center has the best ratio of office space to warehouse space, with the additional capacity to double that amount of office space when and if necessary.

Further comparison reveals that Corporate Center is by far the best bargain. The lease rate per square footage ratio for either the 3,000- or the 4,000-sq. ft. unit is far lower than any of the other locations. Yet Corporate Center has, as Table 2 reveals, a far greater offering in features and amenities.

Corporate Center has the best location in relation to the airport, major trucking terminals, and major highways. In

7

EXHIBIT 10–1 (Continued)

addition, it has the easiest accessibility for customers as well.

In the area of safety features, Corporate Center excels. Sprinkler systems and exterior lighting are designed to increase security for both people and property and to lower insurance rates.

In addition, Corporate Center is conveniently located to other necessary facilities such as the post office, restaurants, hotels, and convention facilities.

Finally, it has the image that your company wants--an image that reflects your executives, your product, and your company name.

Recommendations

Based on these findings, I recommend that you come to a decision as quickly as possible to lease space for your new sales and distribution center at Corporate Center. I further recommend that if the larger space (4,000 sq. ft.) is still available, you should lease it, thus allowing yourselves

Table 1
Comparison of Square Footage to Lease Rates

Location	Total Square Feet	Office Square Feet	Ware- house Square Feet	Rate/ Month	Lease Length
1115 Commercial	3,000	1,500	1,500	$ 640.	2–3 years
1132 Commercial	6,400	2,000	4,400	1,440.	2 yrs. pref.
Old Pineville/ Nations Ford	2,220	520	1,700	575.	1 yr. min.
Fremont Park	2,450	300	2,150	600.	1 yr. min.
	4,900	600	4,300	1,200.	
Spangler N. 29	2,450	300	2,150	600.	1 yr. min.
Pressley Park	3,000	450	2,550	565.	1 yr. min.
	6,000	900	5,100	1,350.	
Corporate Center	3,000	600+	2,400	550.	2 yrs. pref.
	4,000	800+	3,200	700.	

EXHIBIT 10–1 (Continued)

Table 2
COMPARISON OF FEATURES

Address	18-Foot Ceiling	Sprinkler	Front Office Entrance	Rear Shipping Entrance	Comb. Front	Land-scaping	Parking/ Loading Facility	Access to Airport	Access to Truck	Rail	Type of Industry Desired*
1115 Commercial	X	–	X	X	–	fair	poor	poor	fair	–	All
1132 Commercial	X	X	X	X	–	good	good	poor	fair	–	All
Pineville/ Nations Ford	–	–	X	X	–	none	fair	good	good	–	LM,O,S,D,R
Tremont Park	X	X	–	–	X	none	fair	good	good	some	LM,S,D,R
Spangler N. 29	X	X	–	–	X	none	fair	good	exc.	–	LM,S,D,R
Pressley Park	X	X	X	X	–	good	v. good	exc.	exc.	–	LM,O,S,D,R
Corporate Center	X	X	X	X	–	exc.	exc.	exc.	exc.	–	LM,O,S,D,R

* **LM**: light manufacturing; O: office; S: sales; D: distribution; R: research.

9

EXHIBIT 10–1 (Continued)

growing room for the duration of a two–year lease period. If only the 3,000–sq.–ft. space is available, then I would recommend that you request a one–year lease with the option of a second year in larger quarters.

Notes

1. Charlotte–Mecklenburg Chamber of Commerce, <u>Charlotte–Mecklenburg Industrial Parks 1977–78</u>, June 1977, p. ii.
2. Charlotte–Mecklenburg Planning Commission, <u>Comprehensive Plan 1995</u>, August 1976, p. 41.
3. Bill Cornwell, Spangler Construction Company, Interview, November 6, 1978.
4. <u>Industrial Parks</u>, p. 56.
5. <u>Industrial Parks</u>, p. 45.
6. Charles Floyd, Prudential Insurance Company, Real Estate and Investment Division, Telephone interview, Thursday, November 2, 1978.

Bibliography

Charlotte Mecklenburg Chamber of Commerce, <u>Charlotte–Mecklenburg Industrial Parks 1977–78</u>, June 1977.
Charlotte–Mecklenburg Planning Commission, <u>Comprehensive Plan 1995</u>, August, 1976.
''Classified Ads.'' <u>Charlotte Observer</u>, 1 October 1978, 8 October 1978, and 10 November 1978.

Other Sources

Bill Cornwell, Sales and Leasing Agent, Spangler Construction Company, Charlotte, N.C. Interview, 6 November 1978.
Charles Floyd, Prudential Insurance Company, Real Estate and Investment Division, Charlotte, N.C. Telephone interviews, 5 October 1978 and 2 November 1978.
Joe Logan, Sales and Leasing Agent, McGuire Properties, Incorporated, Charlotte, N.C. Interviews, 10 October 1978 and 3 November 1978.

10

EXHIBIT 10–1 (Continued)

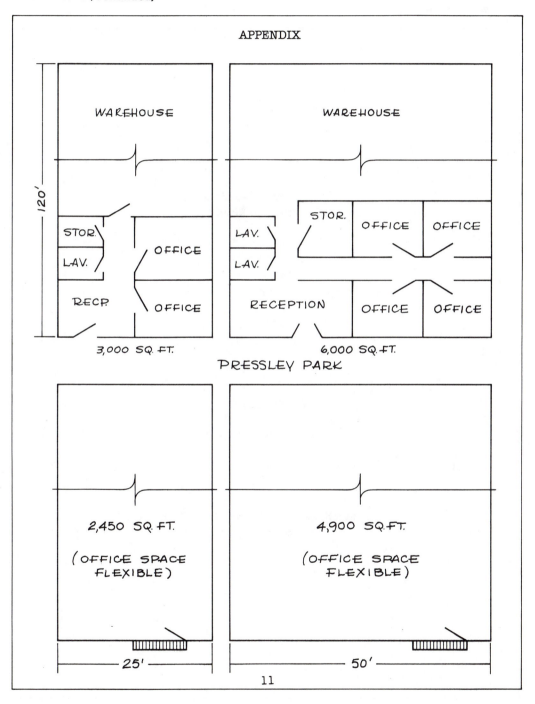

APPENDIX

WAREHOUSE

WAREHOUSE

120'

STOR.

LAV.

OFFICE

RECP.

OFFICE

LAV.

LAV.

STOR.

OFFICE

OFFICE

RECEPTION

OFFICE

OFFICE

3,000 SQ. FT.

6,000 SQ. FT.

PRESSLEY PARK

2,450 SQ. FT.

(OFFICE SPACE FLEXIBLE)

4,900 SQ. FT.

(OFFICE SPACE FLEXIBLE)

25'

50'

11

EXHIBIT 10–2
Long Formal Informational Report

```
                    RETAIL MERCHANDISING:
                     INTERVIEW REPORT
                           WITH


                       JANET SMITH
                       HEAD BUYER
                         FOR:


                   J. B. IVEY & COMPANY
                     CHARLOTTE, N.C.




                      PREPARED BY:


                  JANE ELIZABETH SPRY


                         FOR


            JANE BRYANT, PERSONNEL DIRECTOR
                  DECEMBER 12, 1982
```

Source: Reprinted by permission of Jane Elizabeth Spry.

EXHIBIT 10–2 (Continued)

TABLE OF CONTENTS

Interoffice Correspondence (Memo of Authorization) i

Memo of Transmittal ii

Synopsis iii

Introduction.. 1

    Overview 1

    Background 1

Buyer 1

Assistant Buyer 2

    Hiring and Training 2

    Responsibilities 2

    Salary 3

    Benefits 3

    Advancement Opportunities 3

    Education 4

Job Market 5

Conclusion 5

End Notes 6

Bibliography.. 7

ILLUSTRATIONS

Figure 1: Order of Potential Advancement in Retail

              Merchandising 4

Figure 2: Projected Employment 1990 by Industry 6

EXHIBIT 10–2 (Continued)

DEXTRON INC.

Interoffice Correspondence

DATE: 15 November 1982
TO: Jane Spry
FROM: Jane Bryant, Personnel Director
SUBJECT: Request for Report — Careers

I have been asked to participate in a career seminar for
students at the University of North Carolina at Charlotte in
January.

Since you have special interest and expertise in the field of
Retail Merchandising, may I ask you to present a report to me on
the latest job information in your field.

Please direct your attention to two areas:
1. The current job market in general in our area;
2. The nature and availability of jobs in your field.

I need the report by December 14, so I can assimilate the
material before the first of January. Thanks for your help.

i

EXHIBIT 10–2 (Continued)

MEMO OF TRANSMITTAL

DATE: December 11, 1982
TO: Jane Bryant, Personnel Director
FROM: Jane Spry
SUBJECT: Informational Report about Retail Merchandising

Here is the report you requested on November 15. In the report
you will find information on retail merchandising locally and
in general. There is also information on the availability of
work in this field.

It has been a pleasure to provide this report for you. I would
enjoy doing such work again. Good luck on your seminar at UNCC.

ii

EXHIBIT 10–2 (Continued)

SYNOPSIS

I recommend that students who feel they have an aptitude for retailing and who are willing to work hard consider retail merchandising as a career.

Retailing is a highly competitive business, and buyers operate under considerable pressure. However, many successful buyers feel that the stimulation and excitement that the job provides more than make up for any emotional strain.

Buyers should be good at planning and decision making and have an interest in merchandising. They need leadership ability and communication skills to supervise sales workers and assistant buyers and to deal effectively with manufacturers' representatives and store executives. Because of the fast pace and constant pressure of their work, buyers need physical stamina and emotional stability. A buyer has many responsibilities, but ultimately he or she will be judged on whether or not the merchandise that was bought sells well.

Because of the tremendous turnover in retail merchandising, there is great opportunity for advancement. The buyer who is quick and efficient can move up the corporate ladder.

The unemployment rate in the Charlotte area was 6.9% in June 1982. Since the state unemployment rate was 9.2%, the Charlotte area appears to be a relatively good place to look for employment. New businesses are opening every day in this area.

I conclude that a career in retail merchandising would be fascinating, stimulating and very exciting. This job would be interesting each and every day.

iii

EXHIBIT 10–2 (Continued)

RETAIL MERCHANDISING
INTRODUCTION

The purpose of this report is to familiarize the reader
with retail merchandising. This topic will be discussed in two
areas: (1) the nature and availability of retail buyers at
J. B. Ivey & Company and (2) the current job market in the
Charlotte area.

OVERVIEW

Retail merchandising is a fascinating business. It is fast
paced, stimulating, pressurized, and highly competitive. In
retailing, each day is different; days may be similar but no
two days are exactly alike. Some of the desirable personal
attributes for a successful career in retail merchandising
are:

- Drive and
  determination
- Ability to communicate
- Willingness to travel
- Executive potential

- A pleasing personality
- Flexibility
- Poise
- Ability to handle many
  responsibilities

This field encompasses salespeople, buyers, fashion
coordinators, and many others.

BACKGROUND

Ivey's has 13 stores in 8 cities in North Carolina.
Corporate headquarters is located in the downtown Charlotte
store. Two hundred assistant buyers and 50 buyers work at
company headquarters.

BUYER

Successful buyers have good taste, fashion knowledge, an
awareness of fashion trends, and a sound knowledge of the
quality of merchandise they buy. The buyer's job calls for
resourcefulness and good judgment, as well as self-confidence
to make decisions and take risks. In order to purchase the best
selection of goods for their stores, buyers must be familiar
with the manufacturers and distributors who handle the

1

EXHIBIT 10-2 (Continued)

merchandise they need. To learn about merchandise, buyers attend fashion and trade shows and visit manufacturers' showrooms. The amount of traveling varies for each buyer. Some travel about once or twice a month. Before ordering a particular line of merchandise, buyers study market research reports and analyze past sales records to determine what products are currently in demand. Ultimately, buyers are judged by whether the merchandise they buy sells well.

ASSISTANT BUYER

Usually the assistant buyer is delegated the responsibility of keeping records, supervising orders received, doing clerical work, and acting as liaison between the buyer and the sales force.

HIRING AND TRAINING

Ivey's, at the present time, is not hiring new employees. The next training program begins in May 1983. The training program consists of one to two years working as an assistant buyer for Ivey's Central Organization. During this phase, trainees work under a buyer and learn what the job is all about. They do bookwork, go on some buying trips, and get to know the manufacturers that they will be dealing with. The second phase of the training program is a two-year job as a department manager at one of Ivey's 13 branch stores. During this period, the trainee learns a different aspect of the business. The training does not have to be in this order, but it is suggested because management feels that if trainees first work as assistant buyers, they will acquire a better knowledge of the business and all the things that go on ''behind the scenes.'' Diane Slovensky, assistant buyer for Ivey's, went through her training program backward. However, she feels that her way is working out the best. Now, if a buyer's position opens up, she is already there at Central Organization and will have a good chance at the job.

RESPONSIBILITIES

The responsibilities of buyers are many. First, they must target the market. This entails knowing who the customers are,

2

EXHIBIT 10–2 (Continued)

what the customers want, and what motivates them to buy.
Second, buyers must know how to shop the market. Shopping the
market means going to several manufacturers and figuring out
what styles are best suited for what customers at which stores.
Buyers must know how much of everything they should buy. Third,
buyers must see that all merchandise gets into the stores at
the right time. They decide when the time is right for a
markdown and how much the merchandise should be marked down.
Fourth, and finally, all of the above must be done within a
budget and at a profit.

SALARY

The salaries vary greatly with experience and education.
Assistant buyers can begin at approximately $12,500 to $15,000
per year, and buyers can earn from $18,000 to $50,000,
depending on the company and their experience. Divisional
managers earn from the high 30's to low 60's, and general
merchandise managers earn $60,000 or more, depending on the
company.

BENEFITS

Ivey's has several benefits available for its employees,
including a 20 percent discount on all purchases. Ivey's also
has a group insurance program, contributory insurance
coverage (a medical plan), a profit-sharing program, and a
retirement plan.

ADVANCEMENT OPPORTUNITIES

A college degree can help applicants get their foot in the
door at a higher salary. Degrees are a definite plus from a pay
standpoint, but what happens from then on is all up to the
individual. The key is having an aptitude for retailing.
Prospects are likely to be best for qualified applicants who
enjoy the competitive nature of retailing and work best in a
demanding, fast-paced job.[1] If one is quick and efficient,
there is a great chance for moving up the ladder in a company.
Most retailing businesses have a tremendous turnover due
mostly to the amount of stress involved in the job. Buyers who
can handle the pressure and are good at the job have a great
chance for advancement. The typical path for advancement in
retail merchandising is shown in Figure 1.

3

EXHIBIT 10–2 (Continued)

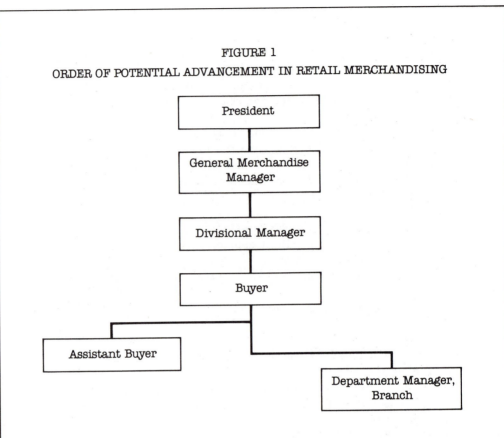

FIGURE 1

ORDER OF POTENTIAL ADVANCEMENT IN RETAIL MERCHANDISING

EDUCATION

A formal education is not required for a career in merchandising, but is highly suggested if one wants to eventually move into management positions. One college that offers a degree in fashion merchandising is American Business and Fashion Institute, located in Charlotte, North Carolina. AB & F has a four–quarter program. Included in this program are basic classes––English, math, and so on––fashion background courses, and two fashion trips. One trip is to New York; the other is a London–Paris–Rome excursion. William H. Hummel, Director of Admissions, states that 97 percent of the people who graduate from AB & F get jobs in their related fields.

4

EXHIBIT 10–2 (Continued)

JOB MARKET

The unemployment rate in the Charlotte–Gastonia Standard Metropolitan Statistical Area (SMSA) for June 1982 was 6.9 percent. The state unemployment rate was 9.2 percent. From these figures, you can see that the area economy continued to fare relatively well compared to the national economy.[2] The positions most available were in the field of clerical work and other service occupations. The largest number of placements were made in these fields also. It is likely that both population (between ages 20 and 64) and employment in the SMSA will increase at greater rates than population and employment in North Carolina as a whole.

The job market for buyers in this area of the country and in the national market as well is very good. Nationally, employment of buyers is expected to grow about as fast as the average for all occupations through the 1980s, and the employment of managers and administrators (including bank officers, buyers, credit managers, and self–employed business operations, etc.) is expected to grow from 10.1 to 12.2 million, or 21 percent.[3] Figure 2 shows projected employment in retailing compared to projected employment in other areas by 1990.[4]

CONCLUSION

This report has dealt with retail merchandising with an emphasis on buyers. J. B. Ivey and Company's buyer positions have been discussed in detail. Through this report one can see that retailing is a highly competitive business, and buyers operate under considerable pressure. However, many successful buyers feel that the stimulation and excitement that the job provides more than make up for any emotional strain. Because of the fast pace and constant pressure of their work, buyers need physical stamina and emotional stability.

The job of a buyer often brings to mind high fashion. It is true that some buyers do have this glamorous position, but the reader must keep in mind that there are many different types of buyers, not just buyers of fashion merchandise. One

5

EXHIBIT 10–2 (Continued)

FIGURE 2

PROJECTED EMPLOYMENT 1990 BY INDUSTRY

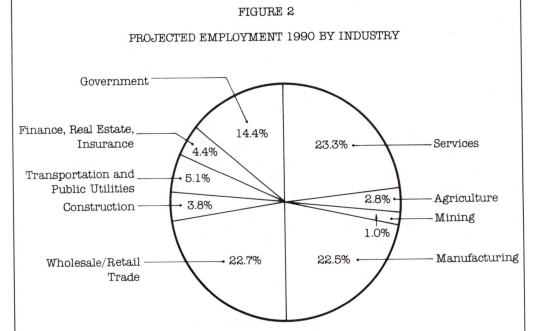

generalization safely made about all buyers is that they must work hard. The job is not easy, but it can certainly be fascinating.

END NOTES

1. Occupational Outlook Handbook, 1981–82, ''Buyers,'' (U.S. Department of Labor, Bureau of Labor Statistics), March 1982, p. 117.
2. Labor Area Summary for the Charlotte–Gastonia SMSA, (Employment Security Commission of N.C., Bureau of Labor Statistics, U.S. Department of Labor), June 1982.
3. Projections to 1982 in the Charlotte–Gastonia SMSA, ''Employment and Job Needs,'' (Employment Security Commission of N.C., Bureau of Employment Security Research), p. 4.
4. Occupational Outlook Handbook, p. 21.

6

EXHIBIT 10–2 (Continued)

BIBLIOGRAPHY

Labor Area Summary for the Charlotte–Gastonia SMSA.
   Employment Security Commission of NC, Bureau of Labor
   Statistics, U.S. Department of Labor, June 1982.

Occupational Outlook Handout, 1981–82. ''Buyers.'' U.S.
   Department of Labor, Bureau of Labor Statistics, March 1982.

Projections to 1982 in the Charlotte–Gastonia SMSA.
   ''Employment and Job Needs.'' Employment Security
   Commission of N.C., Bureau of Employment Security Research.
   1978.

OTHER SOURCES

Janet Smith, Buyer, J. B. Ivey & Company. Interview, November
   26, 1982.
William H. Hummel, Director of Admissions, American Business
   and Fashion Institute. Interview, December 1, 1982.

7

SUMMARY

Long formal reports usually take longer to compile because they contain sophisticated information derived from the writer's research. Usually they are read by several people in the organization since they contain valuable information on which decisions are based.

The purpose of long formal reports may be to inform, to analyze, or to recommend. Regardless of the purpose, the format for all long reports is similar. While some companies choose not to include all the prefatory and end parts discussed in this chapter, most companies use many of the parts. Long reports are presented in *binders,* usually printed with the company name and logo; the binder protects the report and promotes the company's image.

The prefatory parts of a long report are the title page, table of contents, letter or memo of authorization, letter or memo of transmittal, and abstract. The *title page* gives the title of the report, the name of the person who prepared it, and the name of the person for whom it was prepared. The *table of contents* shows the parts of the report and the page numbers on which the parts begin. All illustrations are listed separately at the bottom of the table of contents page. The *authorization* is the official document, usually a letter or memo, that delegates the responsibility for the report to the writer. The *transmittal* is the official letter or memo from the writer notifying the receiver that the report is attached. The *abstract* or *synopsis* is a brief summary of the report; it is useful to anyone who must understand the gist of the report but does not have time to read the entire report.

The *body* of the report is the large segment that presents the facts about the situation reported. An *introduction* is used to orient the reader to the problem. The rest of the body of the report should have *section headings* that reflect the information found in the table of contents. The *conclusions* and/or *recommendations* describe briefly the outcome of the report, what the writer discovered — based on the facts — and suggestions for a course of action.

The end parts of a long formal report are the notes, bibliography, and appendix. The *notes* are references to sources mentioned. They are numbered consecutively in the body of the report, and all are listed on this single page with the heading "End Notes," "Source Notes," or simply "Notes." The *bibliography* is the page that lists *all* sources — primary and secondary — used in compiling the report. Some writers separate this page into two parts, one labeled "Bibliography," under which all secondary sources are listed, and a second labeled "Other Sources," under which all primary sources are listed. *Appendix* material is anything included to supplement the facts stated in the report. This material is not vital to understanding the report; it just provides additional information for the interested reader.

LEARNING ACTIVITIES

1. Because of numerous suspected thefts by employees at the 15 convenience stores owned by the company, the president has asked you to do extensive research on the possibility of using polygraph tests to assist in hiring more trustworthy employees and to question any employee suspected by the president. Address the following issues in preparing a report:

    a. Can the company legally use the tests as a means of determining whom it will hire?

    b. How would such tests be conducted? Should the company contract with a consultant in this field to administer and interpret such tests, or can someone from the company be trained? What would it cost?

    c. How reliable are such tests in determining an employee's guilt?

d. What is the likelihood that the company could be sued for basing a termination decision on such tests?

e. Are any companies in the area using such tests successfully?

Use at least one primary and one secondary source to gather information for this report.

2. Your company is going to purchase a new fleet of cars for its sales representatives. You have been assigned to determine which cars offer the best value and to recommend a make and model to purchase. The company has established the following criteria for making its decision:

a. Must by American-made.

b. Must get at least 35 mpg. on the highway.

c. Must be able to carry four passengers comfortably and/or provide enough rear seat space to carry six sample cases and many catalogs.

d. Must not cost over $8,200 per vehicle with a fleet discount (company will purchase six cars).

Since several makes and models meet these criteria, you must research the field to determine which ones can be considered. Then you will submit a long report in which you recommend to your superior which car — according to your best research — the company should buy. Suggestions: Use the four criteria above as the four main ideas for your outline and for the four parts of your report. Use illustrations whenever you can.

3. You are an investment counselor. Recently, Mrs. Rose Granfort, a 50-year old woman, came to you for help with investments. Her husband, owner of a small machine shop, was killed in an auto accident six months ago. Mrs. Granfort is afraid she can't invest her money wisely enough to be able to live on it until she can draw Social Security. She is also concerned about supporting herself in old age because she has no children. Her personal property includes (all paid for):

a. 1983 Cadillac Seville

b. 1983 Datsun B210

c. 20′ Century outboard motorboat (1982)

d. $3000 in a savings account at a savings and loan association

e. Two $10,000 certificates of deposit at a savings and loan association

Since her husband did not have credit life insurance, she also has a $15,000 mortgage on her home, valued at $125,000. Her monthly mortgage payment is $225. Her home is furnished with antiques valued at $15,000. Her husband *did* have a life insurance policy that paid her $100,000, and she sold the machine shop for $250,000. Currently, she spends $95 per month (average) for electricity, $75 per month (average) for phone service, and $1,200 per year for real estate and personal property taxes. She is also accustomed to spending $500 a month for clothes and beauty items and $400 a month for groceries and dining out. Mrs. Granfort has no job skills that qualify her to earn a living, but she is not opposed to working at a job that is "not beneath her dignity."

Study Mrs. Granfort's situation, research investments she *could* make, and prepare a report for her advising her how you would invest her money and showing her the possible return from your investment suggestions.

4. Use your work experience to define an imaginary company for which you will prepare this report. This year the company will celebrate its 25th anniversary in business. Your task is to plan how the company will celebrate this occasion — with an "open house," sale days, tours of the facility, prize drawings, or other activities. Submit the recommended plan of proposed activities to your client or to your superior. Include the following in your report:

   a. Background information
      (1) Name of the company and the goods/service it provides.
      (2) Size and/or organizational structure (examples: small proprietorship with ten employees; a corporation with franchises all over the United States; a large corporation celebrating the anniversary of its oldest manufacturing facility, employing 3,000 people).
      (3) Your position and/or title (examples: director of public relations for the company; account executive for XYZ firm, which is handling this celebration; manager of the operation, reporting to the president of the company).
   b. Goal of the project — establish a goal(s) that the company hopes to achieve through this celebration.
   c. Strategy for achieving the above objective(s).
      (1) How do you plan to achieve the objective(s)?
      (2) What special problems should the company anticipate?
      (3) How do you plan to handle those problems?
   d. Budget — how much has been allotted, or how much will your proposed plan cost?
   e. The plan itself
      (1) Establish the duration of the celebration.
      (2) Give specific details about what will take place at what time and the cost of each particular event.

(3) Include any promotional items you would suggest and their estimated cost.

Remember, this is a *plan*. You alone would not be expected to carry it out. Rather, if it is accepted, certain departments, shifts, or individuals would be assigned to carry out certain parts of it to create a successful team effort. You may suggest that certain portions be handled by certain units, departments, or individuals, if you wish.

5. You are administrative assistant to the personnel manager of a small company that employs about 700 people. Your boss asks you to study the kinds of Christmas gifts that the company can give to its employees in December. The company offers no cash Christmas bonus to its employees but has set aside $12,000 to be used to purchase a gift for each employee this year. Not all your employees belong to Christian religions — a fact to consider when choosing gifts. The budget is to be spent on employees working at three levels in the organization. The first level includes 680 employees comprised of maintenance, production and clerical workers, as well as first line supervisors, and so on. The second level is comprised of engineers and heads of 14 departments for a total of 30 people; and the third level is comprised of the president, vice presidents, treasurer, plant manager, and so on and includes eight people. Although no one has said that those in higher positions should get larger or more expensive gifts, you might want to consider that as a possibility.

   Study various kinds of gifts you might give, talk to some companies about prices on the items, and prepare a report for your boss showing the numbers and kinds of gifts in each category, the cost, and finally the justification for each type of gift you suggest. Provide at least two possible gifts for each group, so your superior will have a hand in making the final choice.

6. You manage a lumber yard for a large lumber company chain. Your operation has one large sales/display building where such things as storm windows and doors, shingles, and so on are stored. Two other buildings on the site house lumber such as 2 × 4's, 4 × 4's, particle board, sheathing, siding, and so on. Recently, the Occupational Safety and Health Administration (OSHA) inspected your operation and declared that the fire extinguishers were not suitable. They gave you 90 days to comply with their regulations. You call A-1 Fire Equipment Sales (for this report interview someone who works for or owns a local fire equipment sales company and obtain pamphlets or brochures about fire extinguishers) and ask them to suggest the kind of extinguishers that will bring your

yard up to OSHA specifications. Submit a report to your regional manager telling of the OSHA inspection and requesting approval to install the proper equipment. In the report discuss the types of fire extinguishers available and A-1's particular recommendation for your operation. Be sure to include estimated costs, when the extinguishers can be installed once approval is given, how often they need to be serviced, and the cost of a service contract.

7. Choose your topic for a long formal report on the basis of your work experience or interests. If you are an employee, you may work on a problem related to your work or to a specific problem you have observed at your company. Or if you plan to start your own business someday, you may want to do a market study or a feasibility study. Here are some sample topics:

   a. Recommendations for a new filing system in the engineering department at XYZ Corporation
   b. Pork promotion: problems and possible solutions
   c. An investment study: small engine repair
   d. A study of structural versus bar shearing at ABC Plant
   e. A feasibility study of installing radiator repair equipment at D's Auto Repair, Inc.
   f. A study of scrap and rework expenses in Department 35 at LMN, Inc.

   Write a detailed formal outline showing how you will approach the topic or what you hope to find out about it. Then proceed to find the answers to those questions.

8. You have been asked by a client to set up an accounting system for her small business, which has been in operation for six months. The shop needs a good manual system since it is not large enough or successful enough yet to justify buying a computer. The owner, Ms. Zamboli, operates, manages, and keeps the books for the shop, which takes handmade gift items on consignment from local crafts people. She also carries a line of craft supplies. This shop is located in a small town that has 25 antique shops and other quaint shops, so many of her customers are out-of-town antique buyers and other visitors. Every customer gets a handwritten receipt that describes the purchase, and she keeps a copy of each receipt for her records.

   Currently, Ms. Zamboli uses a contract that she negotiates with each consignee. It describes the item and states the quantity, the price the consignee expects, the 20 percent fee Ms. Zamboli charges for selling the item, and the price the retail customer will pay; slow-moving items may be removed from the shop after 30 days. In a ledger she keeps a list of all consigned items sold, the name of the consignee, and the amount due them. At the end of each month she mails out checks for items sold that month. In another ledger she lists total receipts for each day and total receipts for the month. In a second section of this ledger she records all inventory purchases. In a third section she records all business expenses such as utilities, rent, insurance, salary for one employee, and so forth. You can see that this system requires much paperwork and makes no provision for inventory control. Submit a report to Ms. Zamboli showing her sample ledger sheets and/or other materials to help her establish and use your system.

9. Businesses are not the only organizations that use the long formal report format. Local city governments regularly publish various reports and make them available to the public. Other long reports are published by special presidential commissions and other such bodies. Go to your library's government documents section and locate the *Report of the President's Commission on the Accident at Three Mile Island* (the Kemeny report), released in October 1979. Look at the report and answer these questions:

   a. What does the table of contents contain?
   b. Who chaired the commission? Who were the members of the commission?
   c. Describe the letter of transmittal.
   d. What does the preface contain?
   e. What percentage of the total number of pages is devoted to the abstract (called "Overview")?
   f. How many pages are devoted to the recommendations?
   g. What item, found in the appendix, is essentially the authorization for the report?
   h. What else is found in the appendixes?

PART III

Special Reports and Other Kinds of Business Writing

The Corporate Annual Report

LEARNING OBJECTIVES

After reading this chapter, you should be able to:

- State the purposes of a *corporate annual report;*
- Identify who receives the report and why;
- Assess the nonverbal elements in a corporate annual report;
- Analyze the content of the report;
- Explain why the report is compiled;
- Discuss trends in corporate annual reports.

While no one person prepares a corporate annual report alone, many people in the organization work "behind the scenes" to develop a polished, professional report. Because the annual report is such an important document in publicly held corporations, we will devote this chapter to its function and how it is compiled.

PURPOSE

The primary purpose of the *corporate annual report* is to discuss the financial activities of the company during the previous year; it may also cover the company's performance, its long-range plans, current objectives, pending litigation, and so on. Since it deals largely with accounting records and because it takes many months to compile, it is of necessity one year behind the year in which it appears. Although the corporate annual report is written primarily for stockholders, it is sent to numerous other readers who have an interest in the company — for example, customers, suppliers, libraries, community leaders, and educators.

Because the corporate annual report is a promotional tool as well as a practical report, the facts are compiled in-house; however, the report is usually designed and printed professionally by an outside firm. Great care is given to choosing the right paper, cover design, layout, and so on to create the desired image of the company, and the facts chosen to be highlighted are given close scrutiny for possible public reaction.

Since the corporate annual report is a final report of yearlong activities, its impact is one of utmost professionalism. Many private and not-for-profit corporations have recognized the importance of this public relations tool and have published their own annual reports — although not, of course, for stockholders. The annual reports of these organizations contain some of the same kinds of information as the corporate annual report, but they are briefer and less expensively designed. Exhibit 11–1 shows such a report. Its original shape was a simple one-page foldout pamphlet; it was printed on tasteful gray paper in red and black ink. Although it gives information about the group's programs and activities — and even a bit of financial information — the main purpose of this report is to portray the organization as a business run by professionals who can use the contributor's dollar wisely for worthwhile projects that will benefit the entire community.

Other organizations may submit an annual report that looks like the long reports discussed in Chapter 10. These are usually printed in black ink on inexpensive white paper and illustrated only with tables and charts that require little cost to reproduce. The purpose of such reports is primarily to let members know of the activities — social, political, or professional — of various committees and of the group, as

EXHIBIT 11-1
Annual Report: Not-for-Profit Organization

TAKING IT TO THE PEOPLE

Reaching the public is the key link in the fight against cancer. People must know the latest developments in research, the environmental aspects of cancer, the incidence rate of cancer among Americans, the support systems available to cancer patients, the importance of education, and the need for funds to continue the ACS programs.

Mass media efforts were highlighted by a special half hour television special featuring local members of the Task Force On Cancer Awareness For Black Americans and LaSalle D. Leffall, Jr., M.D., immediate past National President of the ACS. The ACS committed itself, through a national push, to reaching more minority communities. Cancer sometimes strikes there more often because those communities have been hardest to reach with life saving educational programs.

The annual Great American Smokeout, a one day national campaign to get smokers to stop smoking for a day, received strong local media coverage. Betty Chafin, Mecklenburg's Great American Smokeout Chairman, and the Smokeout Rabbit mascot appeared on local radio and television broadcasts and in newspaper articles as a reminder of the importance and advantages of "kicking the habit".

Locally developed and produced series of radio Public Service Announcements also provided important educational messages for the area.

Outdoor advertising billboards carried messages on the need for funds to continue the ACS programs of Research, Service and Education. Space for these special messages was donated by local companies and businessmen.

The Unit Newsletter provided an additional source of information for the public, the Board of Directors and volunteers. Plans and schedules for screening clinics, patient services available, and educational seminars available are covered in the publication, as well as special volunteer accomplishments and awards.

Public Information efforts will continue through committee sponsored activities and campaigns to increase public awareness of cancer's warning signals and the importance of early detection. Lives will continue to be saved through the combined efforts of the ACS and the media.

FINANCIAL REPORT

1979-80 Expenditures*

Amount Budgeted	$62,806.00
Disbursements:	
Professional & Public Education,	26,430.00
Public Information	19,325.00
Service & Rehabilitation	8,970.00
Administration	8,211.00
Fund Raising	8,211.00
	$62,806.00

*Based on 1979-80 audit at N.C. Division for year ending August 31, 1980

You Do Make a Difference

AMERICAN CANCER SOCIETY
MECKLENBURG UNIT

Source: Reprinted by permission of the American Cancer Society, Charlotte, North Carolina.

277

well as its financial condition. Business and professional organizations often publish this kind of report, primarily to give members in diverse locations a feeling of belonging by knowing the details about their organization, its activities, and its concerns. Although we have seen that organizations other than corporations publish an annual report, we will devote the rest of this chapter to the corporate annual report to stockholders.

CONTENT

The first thing the recipient is likely to notice about the corporate annual report is the *cover*. Although some annual report covers are bare, many companies use the cover space to advantage by showing some important aspect of their operation — a new facility, new technological developments, or other eye-catching or attention-getting devices. Color is an important consideration, both on the cover and inside. In addition, often a company will choose a particular theme and play on it throughout the report. Reference is made to the date of the annual stockholders meeting, at which time shareholders select members of the board of directors and discuss corporate policy and other general business.

Usually the first page inside the front cover will show a brief summary of the year's financial activity (called "Financial Highlights," "Summary of the Year," "Financial Briefs," and the like) and the *table of contents*. Study the following tables of contents from three annual reports to see how the nature of the business determines what appears in the report. The first table of contents is from a modest but impressive annual report published by a small bank in a community of 50,000 people:[1]

CONTENTS

Summary   1

To Our Shareholders   2

SNB's Operations Center   3

Notes   9

Accountants' Report   10

Financial Review   11

Ready for the Future   18

A Growing Wayne County   20

[1] *Second National Bank Annual Report 1975* (Richmond, Ind.).

Community Responsibility   22

SNB People   24

Directors   26

Official Organization   28

The second table of contents is from the report of a much larger corporation that had acquired another large firm during the year;[2] notice that this report is much longer than the preceding one (see page numbers) so it can discuss the new acquisition:

CONTENTS   PAGE

Report from the Chairman   2

RJR 1979: A Photo Review   12

Products and Services Review   20

Financial Information   23

Special Report: Del Monte Corporation   61

Board of Directors   68

Management Director   70

Shareholder Information   71

Update: Government Regulation   72

The third table of contents is from a report of a very large company that has subsidiaries in the United States as well as abroad.[3] Note that this report is shorter than the one in the second example. Since this one is a multinational corporation with many large divisions, it gives shareholders a brief view of operations in each division rather than highlighting any specific activity.

CONTENTS

3   Message from Your Management

5   Description of Business

6   Transportation

8   Food

[2] *R. J. Reynolds Industries 1979 Annual Report* (Winston-Salem, N.C.).
[3] *The Greyhound Corporation 1975 Annual Report* (Phoenix, Ariz.).

10   Consumer Products and Pharmaceuticals

12   Leasing, Financial, and Computers

14   Services

16   Food Service

18   Key Subsidiaries

20   Board of Directors

22   Executives

27   1975 Financial Information

The *letter to stockholders* is usually found near the front of the report. The company's president discusses the firm's financial performance and how it was affected by social, environmental, and economic factors. Often, too, the chief executive will discuss the future outlook for the company.

The report also includes a section on the *financial highlights* of the year, special achievements, and a comparison with the previous year's activity. Included in this part are net sales, net earnings (income), total stockholders' equity, and capital expenditures.

One of the more interesting nonfinancial parts of the annual report is the *year in review*. This part tells about the company's operations, divisions, programs, activities, and so on.

The *financial statements* are of particular interest to the shareholders, who are concerned with the financial management of the company since it determines their dividends. This section shows the assets, liabilities, and stockholders' equity of the parent company and the subsidiaries, and consolidates this information. Here also are explanations of how the company obtained its operating funds and what it did with them, comparing them with previous years' activities. Finally, this section discusses how the company's inventory is valued, what notes or bonds are outstanding, and any litigation that took place during the year. It ends with the *letter from the certified public accounting firm* that audited the company's records. This letter contains an assessment of the company's financial health.

Often the annual report will also contain a *summary* of changes that have taken place in the company's financial condition over the past five to ten years.

Usually the *directors and officers* of the corporation are pictured in the report, either at the beginning or near the end. *Other data* may include a list of subsidiaries, the stock exchange symbol of the company, the name of the transfer agents, and so on. For more detailed information on the parts discussed here, consult "A Quick and Simple Guide to Understanding Annual Reports," by Robert W. Rasberry (*ABCA Bulletin* 41, no. 2 [June 1978]:34–36).

Earlier in this chapter, we said that the corporate annual report is a promotional tool. The image created is often based more on suggestion than on reason. Humans are suggestible animals, and the designers of corporate annual reports take advantage of that fact. The suggestible elements are nonlogical; if properly used, they remove many of the barriers that, consciously or unconsciously, stand in the way of a favorable reception to ideas, recommendations, and so forth. Consider the following examples of suggestion as a means of creating an image.

THE USE OF SUGGESTION IN ANNUAL REPORTS

Nonverbal techniques are those that communicate without using words or language. One of the most important of these is the photograph: out of ten reports, nine will likely have a photograph on the cover. The cover photo is usually described on the inside back or front cover. Whatever is pictured — products, operations, facilities, proposed building sites, or people — it will be dramatic. For example, one report cover shows its consumer products in the foreground, a container ship and an oil rig in the near left-hand background, and a large portion of the globe in the background. The items and their arrangement depict the company's lines as well as the implication that they are known and used throughout the world.

Nonverbal Techniques

The 1979 General Motors report also uses a photo on its cover. The background is dominated by a large stone mansion, and the shadows show us that it is a sunny day. Parked in the driveway is a new Cadillac Seville Elegante. These items are intended to suggest wealth and class. But to give the photo the proper human touch, two smiling people stand by the door of the home looking at the car, and a cat strolls by — also looking at the car!

Another dramatic photo appears on the cover of the 1979 report of Air Products and Chemicals, Inc. It shows the LaPorte, Texas, oxygen facility at dusk, just as the lights on the plant are turned on. A color filter on the camera produces large green-toned buildings against an apricot-colored sky. The unfocused lights look like diamond-shaped flashes. The suggestion is sophisticated, up-to-the-minute technology.

Photos are not limited to the cover of reports; they are also used inside. Usually the more dramatic ones show the company's product/service lines. For example, the 1977 Engraph, Inc. corporate annual report has a neutral tan and white cover, but the photos inside are unusual. On the inside cover is a brown-toned photo of an old-fashioned general store/pharmacy. This sets the theme for the entire report. Engraph plants make many kinds of packaging products, so a brief explanation with the picture contrasts consumer buying in the past with the advantages of modern packaging: less spoilage, greater and faster distribution, efficient merchandising, and so on. In the other descriptive parts of the report, more full-page brown-toned photos are used as the background for displaying the colorful types of packaging materials made by Engraph. For example, the background of the soft-goods line shows a woman at a spinning wheel, the one for the health care line shows a marble-topped counter with old-fashioned pharmaceutical tools and utensils, and so on. Photographs of people in the company are not usually dramatic; rather they suggest friendliness and businesslike customer service. Pictures of members of the board of directors usually suggest conservatism, dignity, and wisdom.

Color, another method of suggesting an image to the reader, is often used on the cover of the corporate annual report. Instead of the eye-catching red and yellow combinations associated with advertising and packaging, we often find subdued, rich colors — richer and deeper than those we normally see in nature. Since many people like blue, it is often the dominant or the secondary color on the cover of reports. For several years the trend in decor for offices as well as homes has been to use earth tones to create a sophisticated look; sometimes this look is carried over to the annual report. Color is also used — to a lesser degree — on the inside of the report to highlight graphs and charts, to outline photos, and to draw attention to special headings.

The paper the report is printed on is another suggestive element; it is usually heavy and suggests quality. The finish may be either smooth or slightly textured, depending on the other suggestive elements of the report, on the desired image, and on the kind of ink to be used. A final nonverbal element is the size and style of the print. Variation in type sizes tells which headings are main heads and which are secondary ones. Occasionally, headings will be printed in a color, such as blue or green, but usually the body of the report is printed in black. Black ink is preferred because it is easy to read and it is cheaper than colored inks, which must be custom-mixed to the desired color. Color also costs more because two-, four-, or five-color presses are expensive capital investments in the printing industry, not to mention the cost of hiring skilled operators to run them. Sometimes for variety white printing will be used on a black background, but again this is a more costly process than black on white.

Verbal Techniques

The skillful use of words is also important in corporate annual reports. You will notice that the word "profits" is never used; instead, you find "earnings," "statement of income," "changes in financial position," and other accounting terms with a softer or more positive connotation. Another interesting fact is that most companies no longer use the word "stockholder"; instead they use "shareholder." The suggestion is that one does not simply hold stock in the company, but that one's holdings truly make it possible to participate or share in decision making as well as profit taking. Since the annual report is a public relations tool, its readers must be able to understand it clearly; thus some companies try to use simple language. For example, General Motors has, for several years, tried to do just that. On the inside cover of the 1979 report, the financial highlights are discussed, and a line chart is used to show what happened from 1965 to 1979. This is labeled simply, "What Happened to the Revenue GM Received."

Another verbal element that suggests something to the reader is the trademark, logo, or slogan. Anyone in the field of advertising will tell you that name or product recognition is important in acquiring and maintaining market share. Most companies have developed a trademark, logo, or slogan to help consumers and purchasing agents remember the company's name. All of these are designed and developed by professionals to suggest something to the reader. We are all familiar, for example, with the logo or trademark of Coca Cola, Campbell soups, General Electric, FTD Florists, Kodak, and Adidas sportswear. Often these special symbols are used in the annual report. For example, the Del Monte food label is well known. When R. J. Reynolds Industries acquired the company, cans with the Del Monte label were featured on the cover of the annual report, and inside a full-page Del Monte symbol was used to introduce the section devoted to the new acquisition. Look for this method of suggestion in other annual reports.

HOW AN ANNUAL REPORT IS COMPILED

As we said earlier, no one person compiles an annual report. Nevertheless, one person *does* assume the responsibility for the end result. That individual gathers the information and acts as liaison between printer and top management in choosing cover design, layout of the report, and so forth. In addition, this person must have a good rapport with the members of the accounting department who provide the figures for the report.

The person who handles this major responsibility varies from company to company, but usually it is the director of corporate communications. The following is a sample timetable that the director of corporate communications in a medium-sized regional bank followed to prepare his firm's annual report.

Since the bank's shareholders' meeting is scheduled for April 26, the annual report must be completed and sent out to shareholders along with a proxy statement long before the meeting. In fact, since the proxy must be received by the shareholders at least 20 days before the meeting, the effective deadline for having the annual report in the mail is around March 20.

In late November, Sam Grogan, Director of Corporate Communications, sets up an appointment with Mel Garrett, who owns a design firm. Before meeting with Mel to discuss the design of the annual report, Sam studies the bank's significant achievements of the year, talks to the people who make financial analyses in the management accounting department, and solicits ideas about the corporation's financial health, the community's perception of the company as a corporate citizen, and so forth. When he has two or three themes in mind for the report, he meets with the president and vice-presidents to discuss them. Together they decide that a special event will be featured this year: earlier in the year the corporation acquired a small hometown bank in the western part of the state, opening this new territory for the first time to any larger bank. After this decision is made, Sam is responsible for seeing that the report is carefully planned, printed, and sent to the stockholders.

In his meeting with Mel Garrett, Sam presents the idea that the bank wants to emphasize. After several questions and lengthy discussions, Mel makes suggestions for getting the report under way.

Sam assigns some of the preliminary planning and writing to two of his subordinates, Jerry Cielinski, a writer, and Vicki Lamb, who handles investor relations. In early December, Sam meets with Judy Singleton, Director of Advertising. He explains this year's theme and asks her to send one of her photographers to take pictures of the bank that was acquired and its employees. Another employee is sent to photograph operations and employees at the bank's many other locations and at the main branch. Judy will make preliminary decisions on which shots to use in the report.

Also during the month of December, Sam reviews the financial statements in last year's annual report. His secretary types up the heads for all the financial statements, tables, and so on, leaving blank spaces for the new figures that will be available at year-end. All those who have been assigned work on the report are finishing up their tasks in December. In early January, Mel advises Sam on the preliminary layout.

The accounting department closes the books for the year in late January, and the figures are added to the financial statements typed earlier by Sam's secretary. In mid-February the certified public accounting firm that audits the bank's statements prepares the independent auditor's statement that must be included in the annual report.

Several days are spent proofreading everything before the report goes to the printers. Later, the printers send back page proofs to be proofread and corrected before the report goes to press. Sam's subordinates handle this important detail too. After these final corrections are made, the pages go back to the printer for final publication. On March 12, the finished reports are delivered to the bank, and the prodigious task of preparing them for mailing begins.

CURRENT TRENDS

Corporate annual reports used to be structured solely for investors; now they are geared to a more diverse audience that includes such groups as employees, civic action groups, and even regulatory agencies. Another trend is that the annual report today often deals with issues — social, political, or economic — that affect the company's long-range plans. Such things as inflation, government regulation, energy, and so on are often discussed.

Since the Securities and Exchange Commission (SEC) keeps close watch on public corporations, and since this agency has required more and more disclosures by corporations in the annual report, many companies keep one step ahead by giving background information on members of the board and their various activities. Another change in annual reports is toward a discussion of how the industry as a whole is faring, what trends are in store, and the economic picture for the industry internationally as well as nationally.

The cost of publishing annual reports is rising, partly because the reports are longer. A survey of 100 top corporations done by Ronald Goodman & Co., a Des Moines, Iowa, corporate communications firm, found that the average per copy cost for large firms was as follows:[4]

Under 100,000 copies	$2.51
100,000–200,000 copies	$1.41
Over 200,000 copies	$0.74

Of course, many companies spend as much as $3–$4 per copy, so the company expects to get a lot of good publicity from the report. And the stockholders and others want an easy to understand yet comprehensive picture of the company's activities.

[4] "Annual Report Survey Results," *Public Relations Journal*, August 1980, p. 18.

SUMMARY

The corporate annual report is a team effort by many people within and outside the organization. Although the primary purpose of the report is to present the financial activities of the company for the past year to its stockholders, other people, such as community leaders, educators, customers, and suppliers also receive copies.

The corporate annual report is a promotional tool as well as a practical report of company activities, and so the company may choose to highlight a particular theme for each annual report. The information is compiled in-house, but it is published professionally. Careful attention is given to the choice of paper, the use of color and photos, the style of print, and the general layout of the report.

Since the image of the annual report is a very professional one — and a good public relations tool — many private and not-for-profit organizations also publish an annual report, though not for stockholders. Their aim is to give information about the organization as well as present a professional image. Many business and professional organizations compile such annual reports for their members.

Even the covers of a corporate annual report are important because of the image they convey, but the information inside is even more important. Just inside the front cover are *financial highlights* and the *table of contents;* their purpose is to give the reader a preview of the main points.

The *letter to stockholders,* written by the president, describes the firm's performance and the factors that influenced it. One of the most interesting sections of the report is the *year in review,* which is a summary of the company's operations, divisions, activities, and so forth. Of course, several pages are devoted to the *financial statements,* including information on the company's subsidiaries as well as the consolidated statements. This section also contains the *letter from the certified public accounting firm* that audited the company's records and gave its opinion of the company's financial state. Sometimes the report will also contain a *summary* of changes that have occurred in the company's financial position over the past five or more years. Usually the *directors* and *officers* of the corporation are pictured near either the front or the back of the report.

Five to six months before the annual stockholders' meeting (often held in April), work on the report begins. Often the director of corporate communications is responsible for this important piece of promotion, and he or she begins by assessing the company's major achievements during the year to determine possible themes. Top management discusses the suggested themes and makes the final selection. Next a professional designer is called in to help produce the image and design that the company will be proud to display. Throughout the process the designer works closely with the person who coordinates the efforts of all the departments concerned. Usually late in

January the accounting department will close the books for the year's financial activity, and later the firm that audits the corporation's records will write the independent auditor's statement. All of the tasks that have been delegated are assembled, proofread, and sent to the printers. The company later receives the page proofs and corrects them, and the report goes to press. Usually by mid-March, the finished reports are shipped to the company, and they are prepared for mailing.

Current trends in annual reports make them more readable and interesting. Today's report often deals with issues — social, political, or economic — that affect the company's long-range plans. Very often it will discuss the entire industry and what is happening to it nationally and internationally. A final trend is that companies are spending more and more time and money on the corporate annual report.

1. Select two other people to perform this activity with you. Each of the three members of the group should obtain a copy of the most recent annual report of one particular company. The group will analyze the report and present an oral report to the class in which answers to the following questions should be discussed:

    a. What particular theme does the company emphasize this year?
    b. Evaluate the covers of the report. Is the space used effectively? How is it used?
    c. How is color used? Is it effective?
    d. How does the company incorporate its logo, trademark, or name in the report?
    e. What do the nonverbal elements — kind of type, quality of paper, photography, and so on — communicate to you?
    f. Analyze the letter to shareholders. What is significant about it?
    g. Does the report say anything about the following: international business, corporate social responsibility, problems facing the company (or the industry), legal problems, and so on?
    h. If the company is a conglomerate, identify its products/services. Analyze why the company has acquired its present lines.
    i. Who serves on the board of directors? What are their full-time occupations? Are there any women on the board? Do any of the directors serve on the boards of other companies (any conflicts of interest)?
    j. Using financial ratio analysis, comment on the financial health of the company.

LEARNING ACTIVITIES

    k. What method of inventory valuation and what depreciation method are used by the company? (Look in the notes to the financial statements.)

    l. Name the certified public accounting firm that audits the company's records.

    m. What unusual or interesting features did you observe in the report?

    n. Do you believe there is any correlation between a company's financial health or its response to poor economic times and the quality or size of its annual report?

2. For a humorous look at the language used in annual reports, read "Annual Reports Take Some Translating," by Saul M. Loeb in the *Public Relations Journal,* August 1979, page 19.

3. Make a comparison of the annual report from the same company in two different years. Then make an oral report to the class, comparing and contrasting the two on the points listed in activity 1 above.

4. Use *Standard and Poor's Directory of Corporations, Directors, and Executives* to find the address of corporate headquarters for a company you would like to learn more about. Write to the company (address it to the Director of Corporate Communications unless another public relations officer is listed in Standard and Poor's), asking for a copy of their most recent annual report for use in a class project, and use it for one of the other activities listed here.

5. Make a study of all the kinds of suggestions used in five corporate annual reports. Submit your findings in a memo report to your instructor. Review the format for the memo report if needed.

6. Make a study of the use of photographs and what they suggest in ten different corporate annual reports. Report to the class on your findings, using the photos in the reports to illustrate your presentation.

7. Go to the file of annual reports in your library. Select a company that has been in the business news because of a weakening financial position and make a study of its annual reports for the past several years. In addition to the financial statements, are there any other clues that the company is not as healthy as it once was?

8. Use the *Business Periodicals Index* and the *Wall Street Journal Index* to locate current articles about a particular company. After reading several of these articles, obtain a copy of the company's

most recent annual report. Analyze how the report reflects what business sources say about the company.

9. Do a study of the financial statements in the annual report of a company you are interested in. As a potential investor, analyze these statements and explain to the class why stock in the company would or would not be a wise investment.

10. Using the file of annual reports in your library, randomly select 50 different reports from the same year and list the companies. Next, analyze the cover of each report and list the two dominant colors. From your data, discuss what two colors were most often used in your sample, what others are currently in vogue, and what image each of these colors tries to suggest to the reader.

11. Analyze the annual reports of ten well-known companies to see how they use their trademark, logo, or slogan to advantage. What does each one suggest to the reader?

12. Read "28 Trends in Annual Reports" by William P. Dunk in the *Public Relations Journal*, August 1980, pp. 10–13. Discuss these trends in a memo report to your instructor.

Reporting to Government Regulatory Agencies

LEARNING OBJECTIVES

After reading this chapter, you should be able to:

- Describe the organizational structure of the *federal regulatory agencies;*
- Discuss the general purpose of some regulatory agencies;
- Explain where to find the number and kinds of reports a particular industry must file with government regulatory agencies.

This chapter will give you an overview of the organizational structure of federal regulatory agencies and how private business interacts with government agencies. It will *not* show you how to prepare actual reports because the number of agencies and the kinds of reports are too numerous to discuss in a book of this scope. We will, however, look at *sources* that can give you information on filing reports with specific agencies.

ORGANIZATIONAL STRUCTURE OF GOVERNMENT AGENCIES

You already know how departments and divisions in private enterprise interact, and you know that decisions are never made in a vacuum and that the effect of any decision is never confined to one department or division. The more we understand about the organizational structure of a company, the better we can see the function of each area and how these are interrelated. We can also see who wields the power in the company so we can gear our communications to make the best impression on those in control. Similarly, the more we understand about the organizational structure of the federal government and the structure of the regulatory agencies and their function, the easier it will be to prepare reports for them.

Just as the private sector uses reports to collect information on which to base decisions, so too does the federal government. We accept the fact that the major organizational functions of a private business are broken down into smaller units and that portions of the total responsibility are delegated to various subordinates within that function. Similarly, since it would be impossible for federal governmental departments and agencies to handle all the responsibilities from one office, the departments and agencies are broken down into smaller units. Figure 12–1 is a simplified partial organization chart that shows how the executive branch of the federal government delegates its responsibilities. There is a move toward less government regulation, so by the time you read this some of these agencies may have been disbanded.

Most regulatory agencies delegate some of their responsibilities to regional and then to state offices. Figure 12–2 shows how one agency (Bureau of Alcohol, Tobacco, and Firearms) of the Department of Treasury does this.

Usually, just as the original reports of first-line supervisors in the private sector never reach top management, so too the original reports of businesses to governmental regulatory agencies never reach top management. Instead, as in the private sector, government reports are often submitted to a state office, which condenses them and adds them to others in compiling one long report to the regional office, which in turn reports to the headquarters of the agency. In other cases, the

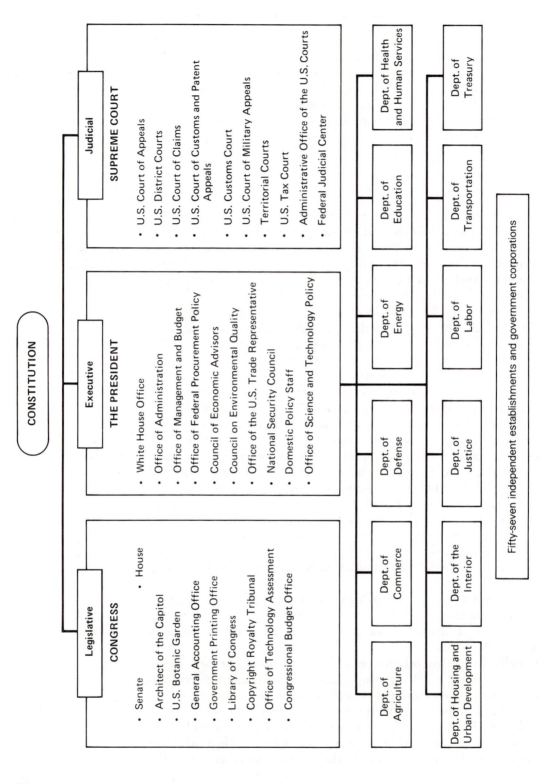

Figure 12–1 Government of the United States—How the Executive Branch Delegates Responsibility to Executive Agencies

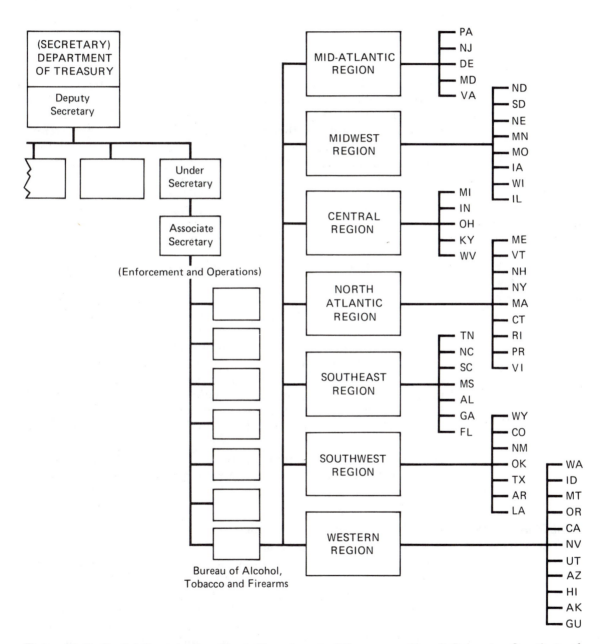

Figure 12–2 Partial Organization Chart: Department of Treasury — How It Delegates One Area of Responsibility

individual company report may be sent directly to a regional office or even to agency headquarters.

Furthermore, just as high-level decisions are made in the private sector and are passed down through the hierarchy, so too with government agencies and departments. For example, the Department of Labor requires businesses to submit statistical information about the makeup of their labor force. When the results reach the national level, they are tabulated and analyzed. Predictions are made about the employment outlook nationally, the unemployment rate, and many other things, based on the figures submitted by businesses. The results are then made available to other agencies, to various levels of the agency itself, such as the local branch of the Employment Security Commission, and to the businesses that originally reported the information. And of course, the figures are available to the general public at libraries that have a government documents section (for example, the *Labor Area Summary* compiled by the Department of Labor).

THE PURPOSE OF GOVERNMENT REGULATORY AGENCIES

Of course, different regulatory agencies perform different specific functions, but some of the basic purposes of regulatory agencies are (1) to ensure the continuation of the free enterprise system by preventing monopolies, (2) to protect the nation's citizens from unscrupulous business schemes, (3) to ensure safe, healthful working places, and (4) to guarantee equal job opportunities for all who wish to work.

Because the population is so large, many of these responsibilities must be delegated. Table 12–1 shows some of the departments mentioned in Figure 12–1, the agencies within them, and some of the 57 independent government establishments and corporations, as well as their function in the interaction between the government and private enterprise. As we said earlier, some of the responsibilities of these agencies may have been reduced by the time you read this book due to an effort to cut down on government regulation of business.

PERSONNEL WHO FILE REPORTS

Often government reports are filed by middle managers, but statistics that are used in such reports are gathered by those at lower levels who maintain the records. If you work for an organization for a long period, you may eventually become a specialist in filing reports with a particular agency since many such reports are quite complex. For example, you might become the specialist who files all reports with the Securities and Exchange Commission (SEC), or you may handle reports to the Federal Deposit Insurance Corporation (FDIC). Sometimes special consultants offer seminars to train people to file the more complicated regulatory agency reports, especially if noncompliance could

Table 12–1　Some Government Regulatory Agencies to Which Businesses Report

Regulatory Agency	Executive Department Overseeing This Agency	Duties of the Agency
Agricultural Marketing Service (AMS)	Department of Agriculture	Provides standards for grades and classifications of cotton, wool, tobacco, livestock, agricultural seed, and so on.
Federal Grain Inspection Service (FGIS)	Department of Agriculture	Regulates the inspection, weighing, and handling of American grain, such as dry beans and peas, lentils, rice, wheat, corn, and the like.
Animal and Plant Health Inspection Service (APHIS)	Department of Agriculture	Regulates the inspection of plants and animals for disease and pests; includes interstate sale of dogs, cats, circus, zoo, and laboratory research animals.
Food Safety and Quality Service (FSQS)	Department of Agriculture	Sets standards for building processing plants; inspects and grades eggs and egg products, meat, and poultry at time of slaughter.
Commodities Futures Trading Commission (CFTC)	None — An independent government establishment	Regulates all commodities — agricultural, lumber, metals, and so on — that are traded on the commodities exchange; prevents price manipulation/cornering of markets; protects consumer against fraud.
Consumer Product Safety Commission	None — An independent government establishment	Protects the public against unreasonable risk or injury from consumer goods; develops standards for similar products manufactured in different states.
Environmental Protection Agency (EPA)	None — An independent government establishment	Protects the environment against all kinds of pollutants: air, water, solid wastes, noise, radiation, and toxic substances.
Equal Employment Opportunity Commission (EEOC)	None — An independent government establishment	Attempts to eliminate discrimination based on race, color, age, re-

Table 12–1 (Continued)

Regulatory Agency	Executive Department Overseeing This Agency	Duties of the Agency
		ligion, sex, national origin, or handicap in the areas of hiring, promotion, firing, wages, testing, apprenticeships.
Federal Communications Commission (FCC)	None — An independent government establishment	Regulates foreign and interstate communications by radio, TV, wire, cable, telephone, telegraph, cable TV, 2-way radio, satellite communications.
Federal Trade Commission (FTC)	None — An independent government establishment	Maintains competitive enterprise by preventing monopolies, restraints on trade, unfair advertising practices, price fixing; enforces credit cost disclosures (Truth in Lending Act).
Food and Drug Administration (FDA)	Department of Health and Human Services	Protects consumers' health against unsafe or impure food, drugs, cosmetics, and medical devices; includes drugs used by veterinarians for treating animals.
Occupational Safety and Health Administration (OSHA)	Department of Labor	Sets and enforces health and safety regulations for the nation's workers in all kinds of work except mining.
Federal Deposit Insurance Corporation (FDIC)	None — An independent government establishment	Administers regulations and reporting procedures for bank securities as established by the SEC; insures deposits in many banks; examines such banks to determine their insurability; requires reports on condition, income, and so on from member banks; approves additions or changes in banks' locations.
Federal Energy Regulatory Commission (FERC)	Department of Energy	Sets rates and charges for transporting and selling gas and oil by pipeline and transmitting electricity; licenses hydroelectric power projects.

Table 12–1 (Continued)

Regulatory Agency	Executive Department Overseeing This Agency	Duties of the Agency
Nuclear Regulatory Commission (NRC)	None — An independent government establishment	Licenses and regulates the use of nuclear energy; sets safety standards; issues licenses to build and operate nuclear reactors and handle radioactive material.
Bureau of Alcohol, Tobacco, and Firearms (ARF)	Treasury Department	Enforces and administers firearms and explosives laws; regulates the production, use, and distribution of alcohol and tobacco products.
U.S. Customs Service	Treasury Department	Collects duties, excise taxes, and fees from imported merchandise; performs other duties in conjunction with other agencies; collects and compiles U.S. trade statistics.
Federal Maritime Commission	None — An independent government establishment	Regulates foreign and domestic offshore business; establishes fair rates for common carriers by water; enforces carrying enough insurance to cover lawsuits by passengers or accidents such as oil spills.
Interstate Commerce Commission	None — An independent government establishment	Regulates interstate surface transportation: trains, trucks, buses, and inland water transportation; establishes fair and reasonable rates for consumers.
Internal Revenue Service (IRS)	Treasury Department	Administers and enforces laws that pertain to taxes due the government.
Mine Safety and Health Administration	Department of Labor	Sets and enforces health and safety regulations for the nation's miners.
Securities and Exchange Commission (SEC)	None — An independent government establishment	Provides for disclosure to the investing public; protects against malpractice in the securities and financial markets; regulates com-

Table 12–1 (Continued)

Regulatory Agency	Executive Department Overseeing This Agency	Duties of the Agency
		panies controlling electric and gas utilities; regulates sales of securities and mutual funds; registers all investment counselors.
Economic Regulatory Administration (ERA)	Department of Energy	Administers regulatory programs on pricing, allocation, importation of crude oil, petroleum products, and natural gas among domestic users.
Federal Aviation Administration (FAA)	Department of Transportation	Regulates air commerce: safety, air traffic control; and the manufacture, operation, and maintenance of aircraft.
U.S. Coast Guard	Department of Transportation	Enforces laws, treaties on the high seas; establishes safety standards for design, equipment, construction, and maintenance of commercial ships; regulates pilotage service on the Great Lakes; sets standards for construction, operation, maintenance of bridges across navigable waterways.

result in law suits. Usually, though, the employee can file most reports after a few opportunities to practice, because most government reports are form reports. It is very important, however, to maintain detailed records so the reports can be filled out accurately. This task is often one of the most time-consuming aspects of government reporting. Occasionally, the employer must file one portion of a report and post another part for employees to see — for example, the Occupational Safety and Health Administration (OSHA) report shown in Exhibit 12–1. The note in the left-hand corner of the form clearly states the posting requirements, and the instruction beside it explains what cases must be reported. More detailed instructions take up the entire back side of the report (not shown here).

If you are new in your company and want to check the number of government agencies your company reports to, use the government publication, *Catalog of Federal Paperwork Requirements — By In-*

dustry Group. This publication uses the SIC numbers to group industries and shows the name of the report, the agency to which it goes, the form number, how often it is filed, what specific industry group is required to file it, and other information. You can begin to see the time and money expended by a business to comply with government regulations. Many companies must train employees to do almost nothing except report to specific agencies to be certain that the company is in compliance with all the agencies' rules.

The cost of complying with governmental regulatory agencies is high. For example, R. J. Reynolds Industries estimates its cost of compliance in 1978 was $34.3 million and that approximately $22 million of that total was for employees' salaries. It estimated that 738,000 man-hours were spent on compliance-related activities.[1]

Audience analysis is extremely important in reporting to government agencies. For example, a particular agency may require that figures be presented in a way that is unlike anything you are accustomed to. Knowing what they want will help you organize your records in an appropriate way and file the report correctly — thus eliminating the possibility of having to redo the work. It may also guarantee that your organization will not receive a reprimand or a threat by the agency to withhold funds, suspend a license, or take legal action.

Although many reports to government agencies are form reports, some — such as seeking a license to build a chemical disposal plant or to construct a nuclear facility — require persuasive writing in response to certain questions on the application forms. You probably know that some agencies, as well as the individuals who comprise them, have certain preconceived ideas about what is important, how the world ought to turn, how they should spend the money they have been allocated, or how they should carry out their responsibilities to the public. One of the first rules of persuasion is to learn what your audience believes, thinks, and feels about the topic under discussion (audience analysis). Then you can persuade by showing the audience how well your ideas fit into their current philosophy. This method of showing the audience how they can benefit from your suggestions is especially effective when persuading a government agency to grant you a license. Before attempting to apply, analyze all the printed materials — instructions, application forms, examples, and so on — that the agency has published on the topic. This will help you to understand the philosophy of the agency and to gear your request to it. If your company has personal contact periodically with a representa-

PERSUASION IN GOVERNMENT REPORTING

[1] R. J. Reynolds Industries, *Annual Report, 1979.*

EXHIBIT 12–1
OSHA Report: *Injuries and Illnesses*

Bureau of Labor Statistics
Log and Summary of Occupational
Injuries and Illnesses

NOTE: This form is required by Public Law 91-596 and must be kept in the establishment for *5 years*. Failure to maintain and post can result in the issuance of citations and assessment of penalties. *(See posting requirements on the other side of form.)*				**RECORDABLE CASES:** You are required to record information about every occupational **death**; every nonfatal occupational **illness**; and those nonfatal occupational injuries which involve one or more of the following: loss of consciousness, restriction of work or motion, transfer to another job, or medical treatment (other than first aid) *(See definitions on the other side of form.)*	
Case or File Number	**Date of Injury or Onset of Illness**	**Employee's Name**	**Occupation**	**Department**	**Description of Injury or Illness**
Enter a nondupli-cating number which will facilitate comparisons with supplementary records.	Enter Mo./day.	Enter first name or initial, middle initial, last name.	Enter regular job title, not activity employee was performing when injured or at onset of illness. In the absence of a formal title, enter a brief description of the employee's duties.	Enter department in which the employee is regularly employed or a description of normal workplace to which employee is assigned, even though temporarily working in another department at the time of injury or illness.	Enter a brief description of the injury or illness and indicate the part or parts of body affected. Typical entries for this column might be: Amputation of 1st joint right forefinger; Strain of lower back; Contact dermatitis on both hands; Electrocution—body.
(A)	(B)	(C)	(D)	(E)	(F)
					PREVIOUS PAGE TOTALS ➝
					TOTALS (instructions on other side of form.) ➝

OSHA No. 200

☆U.S. GOVERNMENT PRINTING OFFICE: 1978—261-018:653

EXHIBIT 12–1 (Continued)

U.S. Department of Labor

For Calendar Year 19 _____   Page ____ of ____

Company Name

Establishment Name

Establishment Address

Form Approved
O.M.B. No. 44R 1453

Extent of and Outcome of INJURY						Type, Extent of, and Outcome of ILLNESS											
Fatalities	Nonfatal Injuries					Type of Illness							Fatalities	Nonfatal Illnesses			
Injury Related	Injuries With Lost Workdays				Injuries Without Lost Workdays	CHECK Only One Column for Each Illness *(See other side of form for terminations or permanent transfers.)*							Illness Related	Illnesses With Lost Workdays				Illnesses Without Lost Workdays
Enter **DATE** of death. Mo./day/yr.	Enter a **CHECK** if injury involves days away from work, or days of restricted work activity, or both.	Enter a **CHECK** if injury involves days away from work.	Enter number of **DAYS** *away from work.*	Enter number of **DAYS** of *restricted work activity.*	Enter a **CHECK** if no entry was made in columns 1 or 2 but the injury is recordable as defined above.	Occupational skin diseases or disorders	Dust diseases of the lungs	Respiratory conditions due to toxic agents	Poisoning (systemic effects of toxic materials)	Disorders due to physical agents	Disorders associated with repeated trauma	All other occupational illnesses	Enter **DATE** of death. Mo./day/yr.	Enter a **CHECK** if illness involves days away from work, or days of restricted work activity, or both.	Enter a **CHECK** if illness involves days away from work.	Enter number of **DAYS** *away from work.*	Enter number of **DAYS** of *restricted work activity.*	Enter a **CHECK** if no entry was made in columns 8 or 9.
(1)	(2)	(3)	(4)	(5)	(6)	(a)	(b)	(c)	(d)	(e)	(f)	(g)	(8)	(9)	(10)	(11)	(12)	(13)

INJURIES

ILLNESSES

Certification of Annual Summary Totals By _____ Title _____ Date _____

FOLD

OSHA No. 200   **POST ONLY THIS PORTION OF THE LAST PAGE NO LATER THAN FEBRUARY 1.**

tive of the agency, cultivate a good rapport with him or her in order to learn more about how the agency determines which ideas are accepted or rejected. Then adjust your arguments to the agency's philosophy.

There are three kinds of appeals you can use in persuasion: the ethical appeal, the emotional appeal, and the logical appeal. The ethical appeal is your credibility — your personal appeal that is a culmination of all your past activities and actions that are known to your audience. This is the one appeal with which you cannot use the audience's motives to change their thinking; *you must change*. Study these examples of the ethical appeal. The last time the Environmental Protection Agency (EPA) sent a young man to inspect the company's records, you became angry with him and told him he was too young to know anything. This representative will remember your comment, and your ethical appeal will be low with him. If you need his support or the approval of his agency, he will probably not respond favorably. Similarly, if your company has been cited and fined by the agency numerous times for violations, the company's appeal will be less than that of a company that has always met the EPA standards.

Unlike the ethical appeal, the emotional appeal allows you to use the audience's motives to change their position on a topic. If, after analyzing your audience, you recognize that they are motivated by fear, sympathy, jealousy, or love of money, for example, you can appeal to those emotions to achieve your goals. This works well in consumer advertising, in direct mail contribution campaigns, and the like, but it usually is not the best means of appealing to a government agency.

Usually the best appeal is the logical one. You study the agency's guidelines and look for sound reasons why your company should be granted a request. This, like the emotional appeal, is based on the motives of the audience. In this case, the agency believes it has established logical guidelines; you merely prove that your request fits them. In planning your argumentation, you should write a *brief*, which consists of your proposition plus the reasons to support it; the two parts are usually joined by "since" or "because." Here is an example:

> XYZ, Inc. should be granted a license to build a nuclear facility at Arrowhead because
>
> 1. Population is growing in our service area at the rate of 5 percent per year.
> 2. Demand for electric power is increasing at the rate of 7 percent per year.
> 3. Our oil-fired facility is old and will not be able to provide electric power to meet the projected demand by 1990.

Your arguments should, of course, show how this request will benefit the public, since the agency represents the public; you should never say how the proposed ideas will benefit the company, even though we all know that no company will engage in an unprofitable business. Once your reasons are clear, you must support them with facts, figures, and other kinds of evidence to complete your logical argumentation. Careful planning of your arguments and a clear statement of them in the report are often the keys to getting a request approved by a government agency.

Businesses must comply not only with federal regulations but also with many state and local ones. For example, a restaurant must pass inspection by the board of health in the state in which it operates. If it wants to sell liquor, it must acquire a license from and follow the rules set down by the Alcoholic Beverage Commission. The restaurant must also abide by local regulations such as those concerning zoning and noise pollution, not to mention the reporting and paying of local, state, and federal taxes. So you can see why business is sometimes hostile to government agencies.

STATE AND LOCAL REGULATORY AGENCIES

Government agencies have long been ridiculed for being unable to explain things clearly and concisely so that businesses could comply with their regulations. In closing this chapter, we are including as Exhibit 12–2 a routing slip — perhaps created by some wag, but at least anonymous to this author — that shows the kind of verbosity and incoherence to *avoid* in your business reporting.

Just as the private sector uses reports to collect information on which to base decisions, so too does the federal government. Furthermore, just as private enterprise is organized into various functions, so too is the federal executive branch broken into executive departments. Also as in private businesses, the work load in these departments is delegated — in this case to regional, then to state offices.

SUMMARY

In the private sector when information reaches the top of the hierarchy, decisions are made and passed back down. So too with government. Laws are passed, private enterprise learns of them, and the government regulatory agencies enforce them.

Some of the general responsibilities of government regulatory agencies are to ensure the continuation of the free enterprise system by preventing monopolies, to protect the nation's citizens from unscrupulous business schemes, to ensure safe and healthful working

EXHIBIT 12–2
Department of Transportation Route Slip

DEPARTMENT OF TRANSPORTATION ROUTE SLIP	DATE 09–08–78
NAME TO: _____ NHG	**ORG/RTG SYMBOL** _____

☐ PER YOUR REQUEST
☐ FOR YOUR INFORMATION
☐ PER OUR CONVERSATION
☐ NOTE AND RETURN
☐ DISCUSS WITH ME
☐ FOR YOUR APPROVAL

☐ FOR YOUR SIGNATURE
☐ COMMENT
☐ TAKE APPROPRIATE ACTION
☐ PLEASE ANSWER
☐ PREPARE REPLY FOR SIGNATURE
  OF _____

REMARKS:

Regarding your recent inquiry, the answer to your question, in most cases, is yes. However, there are exceptions to the general rule and you should not consider the affirmative reply as binding in all situations. You will recognize the exceptions when the answer does not come to you immediately. Those situations must be handled on an individual basis since they require a firm and positive reply.

I trust the above is responsive to your inquiry. In the event you feel the need for further clarification, I suggest you consider rephrasing your question.

FROM: K	TELEPHONE NO.	ORG/RTG SYMBOL

FORM DOT F 1320.9 (5-67) FORMERLY FORM OST F 1320.1   GPO 904.204

places, and to guarantee equal job opportunities for all who wish to work.

Because business is heavily regulated, many employees are needed to keep records and file reports with the agencies to ensure compliance with the laws. Many of the reports are complicated, and one employee may be specially trained to file only that one report.

The government publication, *Catalog of Federal Paperwork Requirements — By Industry Group,* shows how many different reports a company must file.

Many government reports, such as applications for licenses, must be persuasive. The most important aspect of persuasion is to know your audience — in this case, the agency — well enough to estimate what they want. Then, knowing their philosophy, you can submit a persuasive report.

1. Select a government agency that interests you. Then proceed with one or more of the following activities:

    LEARNING ACTIVITIES

    a. Obtain the address of the office of information for the agency you are interested in (consult the *U.S. Government Manual*) and write a letter requesting the brochures and other information.

    b. Use the *U.S. Government Manual* and other publications to gather information about the agency. Prepare an informational report on your findings.

    c. Call the personnel department of a company near you that reports to the agency of your choice and ask for the name of the person who files the reports. Arrange an appointment to interview this employee about his or her responsibilities, feelings about the agency, and the like. Write up a short informational report for the interview. Below are some questions you may want to ask:

        (1) What is your official title? How long have you worked for this company? How did you happen to be selected to prepare the reports to this agency?

        (2) What kind(s) of reports does your company have to submit to the agency? How often does it require this information? What does the regulatory agency do with this information? Do you ever get any feedback — other than when the report is not submitted correctly?

        (3) Is the report sent in on a form? Does it require any sentence or paragraphed information, or just figures, check marks, and a few words? Is it difficult to complete correctly?

    (4) Where does the report go? Do you submit it to a regional office or directly to the headquarters of the agency?

    (5) What is your impression of this agency? Is it necessary to report to it, or is it a waste of the consumer's dollars and your time?

    (6) How do you think this agency will be affected by the present administration's budget cuts?

    (7) Can you show me the form(s) that are used to submit report(s)?

2. Go to your library's government documents section and use the *Catalog of Federal Paperwork Requirements — By Industry Group* as the basis for a report on the agencies to which a particular industry must report. In your report describe:

    a. The particular industry you chose and its SIC number.

    b. The number and name of all the different agencies to which the industry reports.

    c. The kinds of reports submitted (their name or purpose).

    d. The uses of the reports by the agency (to grant a license or permit, for internal use, for recordkeeping purposes, and so on).

    e. How often the reports are filed (periodically? as needed?).

3. Read the article "How to Outsmart the Bureaucrats," by Jack Anderson, in the July 27, 1980 issue of *Parade* magazine (Sunday supplement to many newspapers), page 18. Anderson offers some practical advice on dealing with regulatory agencies. Prepare a memo report for your instructor on the content of the article.

4. Select a government agency that is not listed in the charts in this chapter and prepare an oral report on it. Indicate whether the agency is under the jurisdiction of one of the major departments or whether it is an independent government establishment. Also explain the purpose of the agency, its benefit to the public, how long it has been in existence, who must report to it, and so forth.

Other Kinds of Business Writing

LEARNING OBJECTIVES

After reading this chapter, you should be able to:

- Prepare a *formal definition* for a technical term;
- Write an *informative abstract;*
- Describe the purposes of *job descriptions* and what to include in one;
- Define the term *house organ* and tell what formats are commonly used;
- Describe how *minutes* and *proceedings* are written;
- Explain the purpose of *press releases;*
- Differentiate between *trade* magazines and popular magazines and explain the characteristics of the former.

As you move up the hierarchy in your organization, you may have to write other kinds of business communications besides letters, memos, and reports. This chapter will discuss some of these.

FORMAL DEFINITIONS OF SPECIALIZED OR TECHNICAL TERMS

Sometimes in reports, articles, news releases, and so on, you will write for lay people who do not know the technical terms you use and take for granted in your work each day. In such cases, you must define these terms before you can commmunicate effectively.

A formal technical definition consists of three parts: the term, the genus, and the differentia. The *term* is the word you want to define. The *genus* is the class, category, or group that it fits into; for example, is it a machine? a process? an object? After you have assigned the word to a category, you must distinguish this item from all others in that same category; this is the *differentia*. For example, if it is a machine, you must distinguish it from all other machines. The following two examples show how a term is defined:

          Term   **Genus**
           ↓   ↓

A *cerebral vascular accident* (stroke) is a *physical condition* in

    Differentia
       ↓

which *the blood supply to the brain is reduced as a result of intracerebral hemorrhage, insufficient flow of blood to the brain, or any type of clot in the blood system.*

    Term   **Genus**   **Differentia**
      ↓   ↓   ↓

A *peizometer* is a *device* used for *measuring groundwater pressure during and after construction of an earthen embankment.*

Usually you will have to expand your formal definition to make it completely clear. You may describe what the item does, how it looks, its principles of operation, how it is used, and so on. Look at Exhibits 13–1 and 13–2 to see how the two formal definitions mentioned earlier were expanded to clarify the terms.

As we read in Chapter 6, an illustration can sometimes clarify written information; this holds true for definitions as well. The definitions in Exhibits 13–3, 13–4, and 13–5 were expanded and coupled with illustrations to make sure lay people would understand them.

INFORMATIVE ABSTRACTS

Another kind of writing that you may routinely do is preparing an abstract. You may be asked to abstract an article that your superior has heard about but has not had time to read, or you may have to abstract a

EXHIBIT 13–1
Expanded Formal Definition

A cerebral vascular accident (stroke) is a physical condition in which the blood supply to the brain is reduced as a result of intracerebral hemorrhage, insufficient flow of blood to the brain, or any type of clot in the blood system. Symptoms to recognize in a stroke are unconsciousness, uncontrollable bladder, unresponsiveness to verbal or painful stimuli, fixed or partially dilated eyes, and dusky-colored skin. Other signs include a rise in blood pressure and pulse, a drastic rise or fall in temperature, and paralysis of the right or left side of the body (depending on the part of the brain affected). Physical and supportive therapy are used in rehabilitation. Exercises in physical therapy are used to maintain muscle tone and prevent muscle spasm; supportive therapy is used to keep the patient comfortable and to help him or her accept physical limitations.

EXHIBIT 13–2
Expanded Formal Definition

A piezometer is a device for measuring groundwater pressure during and after construction of an earthen embankment. These devices take two general forms: a gas-actuated closed system and an open system. The gas-actuated piezometer charges a buried receptacle with nitrogen gas. This nitrogen acts on a movable diaphram within the receptacle and produces a readout on a portable console. The open system is read by dropping a cable into a standpipe. When the cable touches water, an electrical circuit is activated and produces a reading on an ammeter. Both of these devices provide valuable aid in evaluating groundwater pressure on dams and roadways.

EXHIBIT 13-3
Definition Clarified by an Illustration

A *hi-cone* is a *translucent plastic device* used in the canned-drink industry *to hold together six cans (6-pack) for convenient handling.* It is used predominantly by beer and soft-drink companies; however, there is some limited use in other industries where certain canned products can be handled more conveniently. For instance, outboard boat motor oil is sometimes packaged with hi-cones in 6-packs.

HI-CONE

EXHIBIT 13-4
Definition Clarified by an Illustration

Paper micrometers are *instruments* used for *measuring the thickness of paper or paper products in units of 1,000th of an inch* in order to determine the relative weight or bond of the paper. The two types of micrometers are the spring-operated type with a dial (pictured below) and the caliber type, which has a finely threaded screw turned for accurate measurement. The spring-operated type is the most commonly used by printers because of its compact size. This device is easily carried in the printer's apron or pocket.

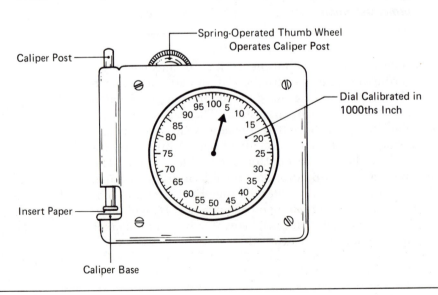

EXHIBIT 13-5
Definition Clarified by Illustrations

The Ljungstrom®
Air Preheater

How it works

The Ljungstrom air preheater is a machine designed to recover the heat that would otherwise be lost to the stacks of steam generating plants and process furnaces.

In the preheater, this waste heat is captured before it reaches the stack and is transferred to the incoming cold air.

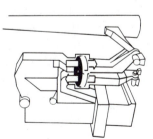

In some instances the air temperature can be raised to over 1,000°F by the air preheater.

The more heat added to this cold combustion air, the greater the savings in fuel that would have been required to heat this air in the boiler or furnace.

Thus, the main advantage of preheated air is the saving of costly fuel. However, its numerous indirect benefits are equally valuable.

Thousands of specially formed steel heating elements absorb the waste heat flowing through half of the preheater structure and release this heat to the incoming cold air as it passes through the other half of the structure.

The heating elements are arranged in a cylindrical shell called the rotor.

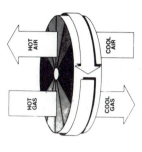

Spaces between the elements allow the air and gas streams to flow across the surface of each sheet. The rotor revolves slowly within the preheater structure - carrying the elements alternately through the air and gas streams so the transfer of heat is continuous.

⊏⊨ AIR PREHEATER
COMBUSTION ENGINEERING, INC.

Source: C-E Air Preheater, Combustion Engineering, Wellsville, New York.

complex 250-page ruling for a client so it is more understandable. An *informative abstract* is a brief summary of the most important information from a report, magazine, or newspaper article. Generally it should be 10 to 20 percent of the length of the original article.

At the beginning you should indicate that it is an abstract and give the title of the article or report, the author's name, the name of the publication, the date, and the pages on which the article appears. The rest of the abstract should show the main ideas gleaned from the original. Usually you can study the section headings in an article or report to find the most important ideas. These should be included — along with some supporting details — as the body of your abstract.

You should *not* give your opinion or your analysis; the abstract is merely a brief summary written in easy-to-understand language. Also, resist the temptation to lift entire portions from the source. Instead, read completely through the material first; then reread it, section by section, and write down the main ideas in your own words. Exhibit 13–6 is an example of an abstract of a magazine article.

MINUTES OR PROCEEDINGS OF A MEETING

Most of us dread the thought of being asked to take notes for the official record of a meeting; but it is not a difficult task if you prepare for it and follow some simple guidelines for taking notes and for writing up the material.

Types of Meetings

Meetings can be held any place that is comfortable and free of distractions. There are several types of meetings. The *informational meeting* is held to give information to the group. It may be a lecture or a presentation, complete with audiovisual support such as slides, videotapes, overhead transparencies, and the like. Questions may be asked by the group, and there may be some discussion, but one person or a small team will control the meeting. *Opinion-seeking meetings* are held when a superior or a co-worker wants the opinions or ideas of others in the group. The person who calls the meeting directs it early on, but, through open-ended questioning and expressing true interest in others' opinions, relinquishes the floor to benefit from the suggestions of others. In the end, though, the person who calls the meeting makes the decision, based on the feedback obtained from the group. The *problem-solving meeting* is called to present facts to the group so they can be considered and discussed and a decision reached. This is the most democratic type of meeting because everyone has an equal opportunity to influence the group if he or she understands the dynamics of small group behavior. This type of meeting results in a decision that is reached by group consensus.

EXHIBIT 13–6
Informative Abstract of a Magazine Article

INFORMATIVE ABSTRACT
of
''How Good People-Handlers Motivate Others'' by Bernard L. Rosenbaum, <u>Nation's Business</u>, March 1978, pp. 78–80.

This article states that industrial psychologists have identified five important principles of motivation. <u>Number 1: Building People's Self-Esteem</u>. When people feel confident, they perform better; it's up to the good people-handler to make people feel that what they are doing is right. An example is given: an executive complains to a supplier who made some mistakes in a shipment to his company. The article suggests that instead of complaining first, he should have concentrated on the things the supplier had sent that were correct. Then he should have mentioned the errors. People tend to fulfill the roles other people assign to them. So if you want people to do what you want, treat them as you <u>expect</u> them to behave.

<u>Number 2: Focus on the Problem, Not the Personality</u>. Rather than judging an employee, merely describe the <u>behavior</u> you would like changed. For example, if an employee has been late a lot lately, don't accuse, ''I guess you don't care about this job anymore.'' Rather, state the behavior: ''You've been absent four times this month.'' The person is less likely to become defensive if you say the latter.

<u>Number 3: Use Reinforcement to Shape Behavior</u>. The idea is to reinforce desirable behavior and ignore undesirable behavior. An example: A committee chairman talks and talks and talks at a meeting, boring the other members. However, after the meeting the members--following tradition--congratulate him on his speech. Therefore, they reinforce the trait--long-windedness--that they don't like.

Four concrete suggestions are made under point three:

1. Respond to both small and large units of behavior. Start by rewarding even the smallest piece of desirable behavior and go from there.

EXHIBIT 13–6 (Continued)

---

2. Use more reinforcement at the start because it's harder to <u>start</u> behavior change than to keep it going.
3. Respond immediately to desirable behavior so the person knows what he or she has done that you like.
4. Make sure your positive responses are accepted as positive by the recipient.

<u>Number 4: Actively Listen</u>. When someone has a complaint or is angry, listen. Then <u>repeat</u> what you think the individual is feeling. This is feeding back what the person has told you; the individual knows you have heard and understand how he or she is feeling. Don't include your opinion until the person has said all he or she wants to say and you have repeated the feelings the person expressed.

<u>Number 5: Set Solid Goals: Keep Communicating</u>. This principle means that you should set specific, achievable, clearly understood goals. Instead of saying, ''Let's get together again soon to talk about this some more,'' be specific: ''Let's talk about this some more at 10:00 next Tuesday.'' Keep working at a goal until you have reached it.

Many major corporations are using these five principles of good motivation with great success.

Usually a specific group will conduct a meeting. It may be a meeting of a local business or professional society. Or a manager may call a meeting of department heads, or the chairman may call a meeting of all the members of the board. These are examples of small group meetings. On occasion, though, a larger group may convene. For example, a plant manager may call together all hourly workers to inform them of a new dental plan that the company will implement or to discuss an upcoming union vote. At any rate, a good meeting will result if, beforehand, the person calling it sends out a clear statement of the purpose of the meeting so that those who wish to attend can prepare ideas, questions, or comments to bring up. A good manager will include an *agenda* with the announcement of the meeting.

What to Include in the Proceedings

The person who keeps the proceedings of a group is usually called the *recorder*. In many business meetings, parliamentary procedure is not followed, so the recorder must be careful to summarize all the important information including agreements, disagreements, compromises, and recommendations. If the group is to report — orally or in writing — to a higher authority or to a larger group at a later date, the recorder often writes the report. In groups where parliamentary procedure is not followed, the group leader will sometimes tell the recorder when something should go on record; at other times the recorder must make this decision. At any rate, the recorder should include the following details of the proceedings unless a special format is suggested:

1. The heading ("Proceedings" is suitable);

2. Date and time of the meeting;

3. Name, group number, or other designation for the group;

4. Meeting location;

5. Name of the group leader;

6. Task given to the group.

At the end of the meeting, the recorder should orally summarize the proceedings; the group may want to add, change, or delete some items. Exhibit 13–7 is an example of the proceedings of a group as the recorder submitted them to the group's leader.

Some organizations, such as business and professional societies, may use parliamentary procedure, in which case the official records of a meeting are called the *minutes*.

What to Include in the Minutes

The purpose of taking minutes is to provide a written record of business conducted by a group. Minutes are useful in the future if there is a question about what actually occurred at a meeting.

As with any written document, minutes usually have a heading; in this case "Minutes" is a good heading. Begin the narrative by giving the date, time, and place of the meeting and who called it. If the group is small, also list those who were present at the meeting and those who were supposed to be present but were not, with the exception of your superior. He or she has the option of not attending. The rest of the minutes should detail the business that was conducted. For example, record who participated in discussion, what they said, and the final outcome of the discussion and/or voting.

To ensure that you get all the important information down, plan ahead and devise some shortcuts of your own to abbreviate certain information. For example, check the names of those who will attend and assign their last name initial in your notes when they speak at the meeting. The result might look like this:

B.: We tried that back in '76, and it didn't work.

EXHIBIT 13–7
Proceedings of a Meeting

PROCEEDINGS

Marketing Group B
March 13, 1983
Conference Room C, 10:00 a.m.

<u>Group members</u>: Bakker, Claus, Sexton, Wilson, Wirt
<u>Task</u>: To study progress on plan to distribute Product X–101.
Agreements reached in the group center on two areas: Sales and
Advertising.

I. <u>Sales</u>
  A. Market surveys should be completed by April 17.
    1. Bakker disagreed on the time frame; his group needs
        more time.
    2. Wirt pointed out that Pro–Tech is rumored to have a
        similar product scheduled to go on the market in
        November/December; we must compete.
    3. Bakker agreed to try to meet the deadline.
  B. Brochures for retail outlets have been designed. Claus
      has had problems with printer; they have promised the
      brochures by March 27. Brochures will be mailed the week
      of March 30–April 3. All agreed timing was poor on
      these, but it's the best we can do. We will not contract
      with Unique Printing again.
  C. Demonstrations of the product are scheduled for the
      weeks of April 6–10, 13–17, and 20–24.
    1. Presentations will be given in southwest regions,
        week one; in the east and southeast regions, week
        two; and in the central regions, week three. All
        sites are go.
    2. Sexton's group has prepared its presentations; a dry
        run will be made before this group at the next
        meeting, March 27.
II. <u>Advertising</u>
  A. Negotiations for filming commercials are complete.
      Wirt says Willmora will have uncut version for his
      approval on April 10.

EXHIBIT 13–7 (Continued)

---

        1. He has begun negotiations for airing on national TV;
           target: early May.
        2. He wants to run commercial during evening news on
           Tuesdays and Thursdays.
     B. Brochures to be distributed at demonstration sites have
       been designed. Claus assures that Unique will have them
       finished by March 30. Sexton's group will have one week
       to become familiar with them before demonstrations
       begin.
Meeting adjourned at 11:15.
Next Meeting: March 27.

Other shortcuts involve devising abbreviations for technical terms that will come up often. And, of course, make use of such common abbreviations as *mtg., dept., mkting., prod.,* and so on.

Since people dislike reading verbose documents, your final draft should be as brief and as concise as possible. Use an outline form to present much of the material so it can be skimmed briefly. As soon as possible after the meeting you should write up the minutes from your notes; you may make copies for everyone attending the meeting for their own records unless, of course, the group is a mass meeting. Exhibit 13–8 is an example of the minutes of a meeting.

JOB DESCRIPTIONS (POSITION DESCRIPTIONS)

Job descriptions are being used more and more because they spell out for both the employee and the employer what is expected on the job. A job description is not written for a job applicant, although one is often posted when a company fills a position from within its ranks. More importantly, the job description is used by the personnel department to locate the right person for a new position and to help in administering wages and salaries uniformly.

Job descriptions are not always written by the personnel department, however, since it would be difficult for anyone in that department to know the specifics of every job in the company. Instead, the description is written either by someone who supervises a particular

EXHIBIT 13–8
Minutes of a Meeting

MINUTES
Executive Committee Meeting
Cleveland Gold Chapter
National Association of Accountants
May 16, 1983

The executive committee of the Cleveland Gold Chapter met at 6:00 p.m. in the Addison room of the Sheraton East before the monthly chapter dinner meeting.

The meeting was conducted by President Jeanne Fulsome.

I. Minutes of the April meeting were read by Secretary Mary Gawrych and approved by the committee.

II. Treasurer Bob Reid reported $965.52 in the chapter's account. The committee approved the following receipts and disbursements:

    A. Receipts

        1. Members' dinner fees—April meeting $320.00

        2. Half–year membership fees from five new members   75.00

    B. Disbursements

        1. Sheraton East—April dinner meeting $315.00

        2. Gratuity for guest speaker—April meeting   50.00

        3. Dues to national headquarters for new members   50.00

        4. Bache Florists—floral arrangements—April meeting   50.00

III. No old business was carried forward, so new business was conducted:

    A. Vice–President Bill Greer reported that he is working with Ben Housiadas from the Red Cross in setting up the blood drive on October 18. The blood drive committee is making final plans and will report to the executive committee in June.

    B. Bill also announced that Mayor Sara Kurkowski has agreed to present a proclamation at the October 16 meeting declaring the week of October 16–22 as National Association of Accountants week.

EXHIBIT 13–8 (Continued)

> C. Jeanne announced names of members of nominating
>   committee who will present to the executive committee
>   a slate of candidates for offices at the July meeting.
>   Voting for new officers will take place at the
>   September dinner meeting.
> IV. The committee meeting adjourned at 6:30 p.m.
>
> Secretary,
>
> *Mary Gawrych*
>
> Mary Gawrych

job and has done the job or by someone in the personnel department who interviews the supervisor or the employee who does the job to get an accurate description. Many personnel departments will devise forms such as Exhibit 13–9 to keep an accurate record of managers and their subordinates, particularly in upper and middle management.

Since a job description will be kept on file for a long period of time and since it will be used whenever a vacancy occurs in that job, it should be written in the impersonal style as opposed to the personal style. Study the two examples below:

Impersonal style: The applicant must be able to present self in a professional manner at all times when representing the company.

Personal style: You must be able to present yourself in a professional manner at all times when representing the company.

Because this is a description of a particular job, it should include the following:

1. Company's name and the heading "Job Description" or "Position Description."

EXHIBIT 13–9
Form Used to Record Organizational Relationships

DATE:
INCUMBENT:
POSITION:
DEPARTMENT:
LOCATION:

Superior and
Companion
Positions

Incumbent
and Peer
Positions

Subordinate
Positions

2nd Level
Subordinate
Positions

3rd Level
Subordinate
Positions

2. Date on which the description was written or revised; this is often found in one corner written like this: REV 1/80.

3. Title of the job being described.

4. Brief statement of purpose/function of the job; for example, tell what the employee does, whether it is a line or staff position, the number of people (if any) the applicant will supervise.

5. Title of immediate supervisor.

6. Specific responsibilities of the employee on the job.

7. Any special skills, education, materials, or supplies needed.

Although there is no "correct" format for a job description, it should be easy to read, with generous amounts of white space between parts. Exhibits 13–10, 13–11, and 13–12 are examples of job descriptions.

PRESS RELEASES

In any organization, establishing goodwill and promoting the company — not only with customers and suppliers but also with the community at large — is an important task. Usually the director of corporate communications in a large company handles all kinds of publicity for the company. In smaller companies this job may be done by someone in the personnel department who is usually responsible for employee communications as well as public relations. Often these people have degrees and experience in journalism.

If you have to publicize information for your company, you should send a *press release*, also sometimes called a news release, to all the newspapers, radio, and TV stations in the area, telling them the facts. They will then use the information as they have time or space to devote to it.

A press release is usually written on letterhead or other special stationery that clearly shows the name of the company or organization; the heading "Press Release" is often used to show that this is not routine information. The *current date* and the *date on which the information can be released* to the public should be indicated clearly. Often the information is "hot" news, and the release will merely say "For Immediate Release" rather than giving a specific date.

The first paragraph should *answer the five W's* of journalism: *who, what, when, where, why* (or *how*), and the remaining paragraphs should give further details. Exhibit 13–13 is an example of a press release, and Exhibit 13–14 is the newspaper article that resulted from it.

EXHIBIT 13–10
Job Description

JOB DESCRIPTION

<u>JOB TITLE</u>: Director of Physical Plant.
<u>JOB PURPOSE OR SUMMARY</u>: The Physical Plant Department has
as its essential purpose building operation and maintenance,
supplying of custodial services, responsibility for
operations relating to utilities, maintenance of furnishings
and grounds, and the apparatus used in these efforts,
purchasing and account management, personal relations with
the staff and the public, as well as safety and security as it
relates to all of the above.
<u>DIRECTLY SUPERVISES</u>: One maintenance mechanic, a
groundsman, four full-time custodians, as well as contractual
and part-time help.
<u>JOB CONTENT AND RESPONSIBILITIES</u>:
    PERSONNEL: Interviewing, hiring, in-service training,
    work scheduling, and maintaining records of approval or
    disapproval on employees' work efforts, attitudes, and
    dependability.
    SECURITY: Close up (or down) the building nightly and week
    ends. Be aware of, correct, or reduce effects of any
    emergencies that might arise.
    TRANSPORTATION: Delivery and/or moving of furniture,
    stock, freight, and supplies; receiving of any of the
    above, as well as equipment and apparatus to stock,
    storage, or final destination.
    PURCHASING: Supplies, equipment, and contractual
    services.
    PREVENTIVE MAINTENANCE: Writing specifications and
    supervision of procedures, tests, and maintenance of all
    functional equipment on campus.
    DESIGN OF FURNISHINGS, APPARATUS, ADDITIONS, AND
    CONVERSIONS: As needed by faculty, staff, and
    administration.
    WRITING: Reports and/or memos relating to Physical Plant
    facilities, abilities, and characteristics.
    SPECIFYING: Work and material requirements for in-plant
    and contractual work, as well as supervision during

EXHIBIT 13–10 *(Continued)*

```
       construction and inspection after completion and
       assumption of responsibility for any corrections,
       deletions, or payments made.
       COORDINATING: With university and design architects and
       general, electrical, and mechanical contractors, efforts
       relating to the rectification of inadequacies of the
       contractors' job performance as stipulated in the
       specifications and required under the warranty.
       TIME: Availability at all hours for emergencies,
       questions on problems, and for staff services when staff
       personnel are unavailable or handicapped doing more
       necessary, difficult, or grimy work.
       DIVERSIFICATION: Work in association with all faculty and
       administrators on many facets of concern as they relate to
       the Physical Plant.
```

ARTICLES FOR A TRADE PUBLICATION

A *trade publication* is a magazine, newsletter, or paper published for a specific industry or for a specific job within an industry. Examples include such diverse publications as *Hospital Topics*, for hospital administrators; *Women's Wear Daily*, for fashion merchandisers and others in the garment industry; and *Textile Chemist and Colorist*, for chemists and colorists.

Generally, the purpose of these publications is to keep readers informed of new developments in their field. The audience, of course, is very specialized, and articles are often written in technical language.

Once you have some experience and have found a new idea or observation you would like to share with others in the field, you may want to write an article for publication. Getting an article published is prestigious both for the author and the company for which the author works. Rather than simply submitting an unsolicited manuscript, however, it is best to inquire first. Send a short letter to the editor giving the title, length, and the opening paragraph of your article and asking about the possibility of publishing it. You will be notified if the publisher wants to read the entire manuscript.

Before writing an article, make a careful analysis of the publication you have in mind. The place to begin the analysis is the *mast-*

EXHIBIT 13–11
Job Description

BELDEN CORPORATION
<u>POSITION DESCRIPTION</u>

   I. TITLE: Sales Representative III

  II. ORGANIZATIONAL UNIT: Sales Department

 III. PRIMARY FUNCTION:
To provide complete sales and marketing services to all customers and prospective customers in the assigned territory, in accordance with sound business principles and specific sales and marketing policies. Also, to secure sufficient sales volume to meet or exceed established quota requirements as specified in the division profit plan and accomplish other divisional sales and marketing objectives.

 IV. ORGANIZATIONAL RELATIONSHIPS:
A. Line: Reports to Field Sales Manager.
B. Function or Staff: Cooperates with and communicates to the Marketing Department, Sales Service Department, Advertising Department, Sales Training Manager and the Engineering Department.

  V. SPECIFIC RESPONSIBILITIES:
A. Maintains effective line of communication with the Field Sales Manager at all times.
B. Plans, organizes, and executes daily sales call activities.
C. Conveys and explains company policies and procedures to all customers and prospects in a positive, constructive manner.
D. Educates and informs customers and prospects of new products and programs through:
  1. Distributor sales meetings.
  2. Personal contact with customer personnel in purchasing, engineering, research and development, quality control and production.
  3. Sales development calls.
  4. Value Analysis Team calls.
  5. Coordinating special engineering, management or marketing presentations.

EXHIBIT 13-11 (Continued)

6. Distribution of flyers, reports, or other printed materials.
7. Any other pertinent communications media.
E. Provides assistance and guidance to all customers to maintain a sufficient inventory of products through:
   1. Regular sales calls at intervals commensurate with potential maximum sales volume.
   2. Specific inventory control techniques when applicable.
F. Provides sales aids to all customers through:
   1. Catalogs, price bulletins, and technical literature.
   2. Advertising and sales promotional materials.
   3. Attendance at trade shows and local shows.
   4. Referrals.
G. Provides basic data for management decision making by filing written reports as follows:
   1. Daily call reports.
   2. Weekly plan sheets and two-week route sheets.
   3. Four-month route sheets.
   4. Descriptions of new product requirements.
   5. Reports concerning competitive propositions including products, catalogs, price bulletins, and policy statements.
   6. Weekly expense reports.
   7. Potentials of customers and prospects through reviews of quotas and planned objectives.
   8. Various other miscellaneous correspondence to ensure to company personnel and the customer that effective communication is taking place.
H. Plans, organizes, and executes customer sales meetings and seminars.
I. Plans, organizes, and executes missionary and resale calls.
J. Plans and executes effective field training of new sales representatives and evaluates performance at end of training.

EXHIBIT 13–11 (Continued)

K. Plans and executes effective design engineering calls and problem–solving calls by appropriate company personnel.

L. Plans and executes effective visits to key accounts by company management personnel.

M. Makes recommendations to marketing on new product requirements.

N. Makes recommendations to management on ways to improve sales representative productivity and effectiveness.

O. Makes recommendations to management on more innovative approaches to sales meetings and seminars.

P. Operates within all prescribed company policies, procedures, and expense budgets.

Q. Maintains strong image of professionalism in all activities.

R. Participates in trade and professional associations in order to keep up to date on all new developments and activities.

Source: Reprinted by permission of Belden Corporation, Geneva, Illinois.

head, usually found on one of the first pages just inside a magazine, or on page two of a newspaper. The masthead will usually be set in different type and will also tell some or all of this information:

Name of the publication;

Publisher's name and address;

The magazine's audience;

Subscription rates;

Names of the departmental editors and their staff;

Other information such as whether or not they accept unsolicited manuscripts.

EXHIBIT 13–12
Job Desription

EXEMPT POSITION DESCRIPTION

Position Is: New _____   Changed ___X___   Date ___4/76___

Title __Accountant II__   Grade Assignment __6__

Division __C–E Air Preheater__

Unit or Department __Finance Department__

Reports to __As Assigned__
                    TITLE

Exemption Status	
Executive	☐
Professional	☐
Administrative	☒
Outside Sales	☐

PRINCIPAL DUTIES

Under general direction perform duties of an accounting nature such as the following: examine accounts payable checks and vouchers and verify them as to the proper account numbers; receive and record cash receipts; prepare weekly, monthly, and yearly accounting reports; develop and analyze data related to specific accounting problems; prepare sales register; audit expense reports and payroll register.

Prepare and review long–range plans, operating forecasts, and sales tax returns.

Responsible for wage, nonexempt, and exempt payrolls. Administer costing of fringe benefits as required.

Responsible for accounts payable and cash forecasting projects. Prepare monthly financial statements.

EXHIBIT 13–12   (Continued)

SCOPE AND IMPACT (*As applicable*)

Sales/service volume $ _____   Other income _____

Costs or expenses supervised $ 20,000 _____

Assets controlled $ payroll, accounts payable   Description _____

_____

Personnel: Total number of employees reporting directly or through subordinates 3 ____

Positions reporting directly _____

COMPLEXITY OF TASKS

1. Prepare exhibits; make recapitulations of monthly statistical reports and provide data.

2. Assist in studies and budget preparations, and develop data as requested by controller.

3. Examine and audit internal accounting records.

4. Complete outside audit functions as required.

5. Prepare income tax information for corporate tax preparation.

EDUCATION, EXPERIENCE, AND SPECIAL SKILLS REQUIRED

Bachelors degree and three years experience or equivalent.

Source: Reprinted by permission of Combustion Engineering, Stamford, Connecticut.

EXHIBIT 13–13
Press Release

Press Release
Matthews, Cremins, McLean

For Immediate Release

9/22/78

MCM NAMED TO HANDLE AREA McDONALD'S ACCOUNT

Matthews, Cremins, McLean, already Charlotte's top billing advertising agency, announced that as of October 1, it has been appointed to be the agency of record for McDonald's Hamburgers' Central Co-op Group, bringing MCM's new business additions in the last 60 days to more than $2 million.

McDonald's Central Co-op Group includes the Charlotte, Greensboro, and Winston-Salem markets in North Carolina and the Rock Hill and Lancaster markets in South Carolina.

According to Max Muhleman, executive vice-president and general manager for MCM, the agency will handle all local aspects of public relations, promotion, and advertising for the Central Co-op Group of stores.

In addition to the McDonald's account, MCM has acquired in the past two months Paramount Pictures Corporation and Beck & Gregg Industries of Atlanta, an association of over 500 ARMA hardware stores in the Southeast.

''Coincidental with the opening of our Southfield, Michigan, branch office on August 1, we initiated an intensive new business campaign aimed at major clients which we feel uniquely qualified to serve,'' Muhleman said. ''We are

EXHIBIT 13–13   (Continued)

delighted to have been selected by such quality advertisers as McDonald's, Paramount and B&G/ARMA.''

MCM is best known for its association with the National Automotive Parts Association (NAPA). The agency had handled local and national advertising for the giant auto parts association since 1972, winning a special award from Advertising Age in 1976 for creating a high public awareness of NAPA products and service.

MCM has also been active in NAPA's stock car racing promotions, including the NAPA National 500, which is being run at the Charlotte Motor Speedway Sunday, October 8.

Muhleman also announced, effective immediately, two MCM executives will be promoted to new positions.

John Pace, formerly an account executive, will now become production manager for the agency. His duties will include production and coordination of all advertising materials distributed by the agency to all clients.

Pace came to MCM in 1976 from Garner Associates, where he had been an account executive. Before turning to account service, Pace had an outstanding background in television and radio production in the Air Force and with Jefferson Pilot.

Tricia Miller, formerly media director for the agency, now becomes a member of the account executive staff and will be handling account responsibilities with most if not all of MCM's newly acquired accounts in addition to NAPA.

Ms. Miller joined MCM in 1974, coming to MCM from the research department of Jefferson Pilot.

####

Source: Reprinted by permission of Matthews, Muhleman, McLean, Charlotte, North Carolina.

Annually, the publication must also print information on circulation figures as required by the government. The masthead will help you decide to whom to send a manuscript or letter of inquiry.

EXHIBIT 13–14
Newspaper Article Based on Press Release in Exhibit 13–13

THE CHARLOTTE OBSERVER Sun., Oct. 8, 1978 **5B**

McDonald's Picks MCM

Matthews, Cremins, McLean (MCM) has plucked itself another plum. The latest for the advertising and public relations agency is the McDonald's Central Co-Op Group, which includes McDonald's hamburger stores in Charlotte, Winston-Salem, Greensboro, Rock Hill and Lancaster.

According to MCM Executive Vice President Max Muhleman, the account, which includes all PR, promotion and advertising for the stores, brings to $2 million the new business added within the last 60 days.

In addition to McDonald's, the agency has picked up Paramount Pictures Corp. and Beck & Gregg Industries of Atlanta within the last two months. The latter is an association of more than 500 ARMA hardware stores in the Southeast.

Source: Reprinted by permission of the *Charlotte Observer*, Charlotte, North Carolina.

Next, study the layout of the publication, the kinds of articles (hard news, folksy, and so on) it publishes, its regular columns or features, the writing style, the length of the articles (number of words or pages), length of sentences and paragraphs, and the word choices used. Try to use a similar style when writing an article for a specific publication. You should include the following on the first page of your manuscript:

1. Name of publication (in *top right-hand* corner of the page);

2. Number of words in the article (just *under the name of the publication*);

3. Title of the article (centered about *2 in. down on the page*);

4. Your byline (your name and title *under the title of the article*).

The rest of the manuscript — typed, double-spaced — will contain your article. Exhibit 13–15 shows an example of an article submitted for publication.

EXHIBIT 13–15
Article Submitted to Trade Magazine

Submitted to:
The Business Forms Reporter
500 words

Dealer or Direct? How to Answer the Question
by
David D. Jordan

During my travels throughout the United States, the most frequent question asked of me has been: ''Which is better, selling as a dealer representative or as a direct salesman?'' Most people who ask that question are aware, of course, that I have done a great deal of both during the past 18 years. I can only answer such a question, however, on the basis of what I have observed about those I have known in this industry and of my own personal experience.

DIRECT SALES—-There is a kind of comfort in working for a manufacturer in a direct sales setting. One is constantly aware of the resources that have been organized into the manufacturing plant to provide the salesman with the technical tools of his trade to produce the product which he sells. Therefore, there is a direct link between the salesman getting the order and the machinery operator getting paid. There is a team spirit at work, and there is moral support for the man on the firing line.

The plant is there to back you up with a special delivery. Also, the necessity to meet certain competitive pressures, particularly price, may cause the plant to grant the direct salesman pricing concessions that would not ordinarily go to a dealer.

Manufacturers are often well financed, make profits, and provide benefits to their employees. There are usually group insurance plans, retirement or pension and profit—sharing plans and stock purchase plans to enable the employee to own a ''piece'' of the company.

EXHIBIT 13–15   (Continued)

There are also sales managers, and thus the opportunity to advance. There are sales reports, expense reports, forecasts, rules, regulations, working hours, scheduled vacations, assigned territories and limitations on personal freedom, such as dress codes, hair codes — even auto codes. But, alas, also the direct salesman gets paid less than the dealer representative.

DEALER SALES——The most attractive aspect of being in dealer sales is the higher pay. Commissions are much more generous, and product diversity is, by its very nature, far greater than in direct plants. After all, the direct company wants their salesmen to concentrate on the products they manufacture to the exclusion of everything else.

How, you ask, does this extraordinary diversity help one make more money? Simple. When a dealer enters an account, he does not have to call on just the purchasing agent or whoever purchases just the business forms. He can call on the shipping department for tags and tickets. The dealer can see the computer manager about continuous forms or tab cards. The dealer can visit the various departments concerning their printing needs or even the comptroller about the company's annual report. There is hardly any area where the professional dealer will not be welcome.

Secondly, a dealer is his own boss. He reports to no one but himself. No supplier can give him or his company a quota to sell. All he has to sell is as much as he wants in order to live as comfortably as he wants. Neither is there anyone to ''cut'' his territory when he comes in over quota, thus giving over business he has developed to some less experienced person who probably doesn't deserve it anyway.

Reports? File a tax report every three months.

Vacations? Come and go as your business will permit. One of the most exciting things about being a dealer is the complete freedom to set your own schedule. Play golf with a client. Some direct companies frown on such practices; however, dealers don't have to worry about company rules——they are the company.

EXHIBIT 13–15 (Continued)

SUMMARY--Obviously, being a dealer does involve some special responsibilities. One of the most important personality characteristics of a good dealer is that of being a self-starter. Therefore, anyone wishing to enter the Business Forms industry as a dealer would probably be better off getting his or her training with a good manufacturing concern.

One note of caution. Most manufacturing concerns have a ''no-compete'' clause in their employee contract. Read it over carefully. You may seek this training and not be able to use it.

ABOUT THE AUTHOR
David D. Jordan, Vice-President of Precision Business Forms, Inc., a manufacturer of business forms in Charlotte, N.C., is responsible for all sales, dealer and direct, for that company. Jordan has been Dealer Sales Manager at Jordan Business Forms, Inc., the largest independent business forms manufacturer in the United States and has also worked as an independent business forms dealer for 10 of the last 18 years.

Source: Reprinted by permission of David D. Jordan.

ARTICLES FOR A HOUSE ORGAN

A *house organ* is a magazine, newspaper, or newsletter that is regularly published for and contains information concerning *employees* of an organization. Its purpose is to create company loyalty, improve morale, and provide information to employees. House organs may be handled by a director of corporate communications in some organizations, or in others by an associate in the personnel function who handles all types of employee communication. The house organ may be published in-house if the company has its own facilities, or by a printing company outside the organization. The content of the house organ is interesting because it reflects the size and atmosphere of a company. For example, a small company's house organ may deal almost exclusively with news about the local employees, their interests, hobbies, activities, accomplishments, and so forth. Larger companies, on the other hand, have many employees and can feature only those who have gained special recognition or promotions within the company. In addition to features about employees, the publication usually has one

EXHIBIT 13–16
Column from House Organ: Written by Employee/Reporter

SECOND FLOOR

Orval Gilliland, Reporter

Our "Glorious Leader," good ole J.B., has taken a week of his vacation. "Just did some work around the house," said he. Came back to work sunburned, nose peeling, tired and worn out. Now I ask what kind of vacation is this??? Undoubtedly one of the best. At least it's a change of pace. John tells me his garden needs some rain. A good rain certainly would be a welcome luxury, and maybe, just maybe, John would bring some of his less fortunate fellow employees a good mess of peas!!

Hubbie Dubbie Dillman has also taken a week of his vacation and like John did some painting and other work around the house. In case you didn't know, Hubert puts in a lot of time on his job as head of the Order Processing Department. He stops every morning at the post office, picks up the mail and by 7:30 is usually at his desk getting ready for another day's business. Remember, he is working when most of us are beginning to think about coming to work!

Our good friend Frank Morgenroth continues to be good ole steady Frank. Every day on the job he is even-tempered and always willing to help wherever he can. Frank took the grandchildren to the circus recently. From all reports, a good time was enjoyed by all. Don't think there was a tummy ache in the group. Keep in mind, Frank does a good job painting, electrical repairing and is very good at baby sitting!!

Keith Dorsey doesn't like hot weather at all and that's for sure. Every time he emerges from unloading a truck he is wet, really soaked, and to complicate matters his corn hurts! Any suggestions for him? The best one yet is to go barefoot — Oh, Brother! Not with those big feet.

Fred Clark continues to make good coffee and keep things neat and orderly. During our June open house, Fred made countless cups and helped the caterer with the noon meal. Early in the spring, Fred suffered a fall resulting in some broken ribs which necessitated his being off work about six weeks. We miss Fred when he isn't here, and we are glad to have him back with us.

Kent Phenis is back working this summer helping wherever he is needed. Kent has quite an extensive collection of comic books. Some, we understand, are very rare and valuable.

Source: Reprinted by permission of the Adam H. Bartel Company, Richmond, Indiana.

EXHIBIT 13–17
Sample House Organ: Newspaper Format

The
BARTEL LANTERN

Volume 7, No. 2

Summer, 1976

Independent Associated Distributors

We Are Pleased To Present: Mrs. Paul Lingle

This is the fourth of a series of articles in the Bartel Lantern, saluting Outstanding Women Leaders of Richmond. We are indebted to Frances Eward for the following excellent contribution to our publication.

Some know her as Mrs. Paul Lingle, others as Sandy Lingle. This, in itself, proves that she, in this day of "the liberated woman," is capable of pursuing with considerable grace and skill a four-fold role: wife, mother, professional piano teacher, and community leader.

Listed in this year's "Who's Who Among American Women," Sandy Lingle is the first woman ever to serve as president of the Richmond Symphony Orchestra Board of Directors in its 18-year history.

Our "Eyes and Ears" in the New York Market

All my life I have heard, from various members of the AHB executive team, the phrase "going to New York." Such trips invariably included, I realized, valuable contact with our office there, the Independent Associated Distributors. This spring, finding myself in New York, I decided to visit this office and inquire the ways in which it contributes to the smooth and successful functioning of our business.

Taking a taxi to 101 West 31 Street, I found myself in the heart of the famed textile business district and, before I left, I found that the office of Independent Associated Distributors itself has a heart — a big one, in the persons of Fred J. Dufek and George W. Vorisek.

"What is the function of your office?" I asked them. In reply, they mentioned many ways in which they serve their members and handed me a booklet prepared by

Pennsylvania area, to know that the design, cutting, and assembly of fabrics accounts for a yearly amount of some five billion dollars.

And now let me tell you a little about Fred and George. When you walk into their office, you feel at home. This is partly because of the friendly welcome of their secretary, Betty Weinstein, who, with Hilda Meyerson, makes up the office staff. It is partly because of the decor of the rooms themselves. Family pictures reflect close ties. An American flag relates partly to Fred's training during World War II as a bomber pilot. Sea shells remind you that here in the midst of New York traffic you are both near the sea and with two men who love it and the out-of-doors generally. On a gaily colored table cloth there is an artistic creation done by George — a sea gull perched on drift wood. Later on you see whimsical figures made of varishaped stones. These are the creations of Fred. You hear of Fred's activities in the volunteer fire department in his home town on Long Island, of the charitable and

Source: Reprinted by permission of the Adam H. Bartel Company, Richmond, Indiana.

or more articles about some aspect of the company's business. Since the audience for a house organ is diverse, the articles use popular diction rather than highly technical language.

In large companies managers usually submit the names of employees who are to receive recognition in upcoming issues of the house organ. In small companies the person who handles the publication may ask employees in the organization to act as reporters and to provide articles about their particular departments each time the house organ is published. If you should serve as a reporter, you will need to gather information and write a column periodically. Usually, if you follow the five W's of journalism in the first paragraph of your column, you will create a *news story.* If you want to create a *feature story* (a human interest story), you will begin with an attention-getting device in the first paragraph. When writing for a house organ, you should use the personal style and select words and phrases to sound warm, friendly, and conversational.

The newsletter, paper, or magazine will have a title that reflects the name of the company, its product or service, or some other connection to the company. The volume number indicates the number of years the publication has been in existence, and the issues during each year are numbered. The date of publication is also shown on the front page. Exhibit 13–16 (see p. 335) shows a column from the publication of a small company that uses employees as reporters, and Exhibit 13–17 shows part of the same publication. As you can see, this small wholesale business uses the newspaper format to good effect with its employees.

If you advance in your company, you will probably prepare at least one of these other kinds of business writing. In closing, let us remind you that the more adept you are at expressing yourself on paper, the more valuable you become to your company. Write on!

SUMMARY

Often in business you will write more than just reports. This chapter discusses other kinds of business writing. One of these is the *formal definition,* which you may need to write to clarify a term for a reader. It consists of three parts: the term, the genus, and the differentia. The *term* is the word to be defined, the *genus* is the category or class it fits into, and the *differentia* is the part that shows how this word differs from all others in the same category or class. Sometimes an illustration coupled with a formal definition is the best way to make sure lay people understand a technical term.

If your superior does not have time to read a report, magazine, or newspaper article, you may be asked to write an informative *abstract* of it. An abstract is a summary of the important ideas in the article; it should never include your analysis or recommendations but should merely present the most important facts.

You may also need to record the *proceedings* or take *minutes* of a meeting. There are several kinds of meetings: informational, opinion seeking, and problem solving. The *recorder* should include the date, time, location, who attended, and what occurred at the meeting, including disagreements, agreements, recommendations, and so on.

Job descriptions are used by personnel departments to place the right person in the job and to administer wages and salaries. A good job description will give the company name; the date the description was written or updated; the title of the job; a statement of purpose for the job or how it fits into the overall organizational picture; the number of people the employee will supervise (if applicable); to whom the employee reports; the specific responsibilities of the job; and any special skills, education, materials or supplies needed.

If you work for a small company, you may handle public relations, in which case you will need to write *press releases*. A press release is an article that is sent to newspapers and radio and TV stations to announce some important news about the company. The media will decide how much of the released information they will air or publish. The press release should contain the five W's of journalism: *who, what, when, where, why* (or how). It should indicate that it is a press release and provide the date the information was released and when it may be publicized.

Once you have become experienced in your field, you may have ideas you would like to share with others. A *trade publication* is a magazine, newspaper, or newsletter for a specific industry or job within an industry. Since the audience is very specialized, the language used is technical. If you have an article for publication, you should first write to the editor to ask if it can be used. If so, you should submit it in the following format: Put in the upper right-hand corner the name of the publication and the number of words in your article; center the title of the article two inches down from the top of the page; put your byline just under the title; and type the rest of the article, double-spaced. The *masthead* inside the front page of the publication will tell the name of the editor, where the magazine is published, and its address.

A *house organ* is a newspaper, magazine, or newsletter that is published regularly for and contains information about the employees in an organization. In larger companies the director of corporate communications or someone in the personnel function is responsible for the house organ. These publications take many forms, and sometimes an employee will act as reporter for a particular department or section and contribute a regular column. When writing for a house organ, use the personal style and choose words that sound warm, friendly, and conversational.

1. Prepare a formal definition for a specialized/technical term you understand well and expand it to clarify the term. Use an illustration to further enhance your definition.

2. Analyze the minutes of a meeting of an organization you belong to. Discuss the analysis in a brief memo report addressed to the president of the organization.

3. Prepare a job description for some job you have done and of which you have a thorough understanding. Be sure to use some headings to indicate important aspects of the job.

4. Refer to your work experience and select an event that was important to your company (celebration of a 30th anniversary, building a new plant, performance of a service to the community) and write a press release for the local papers and radio and TV stations about it.

5. Most of us are experts in some field, and probably there is a business connected with that field of expertise. Write an article suitable for publication in your field. Be sure to identify the publication for which you are writing.

6. Make a study of a trade magazine in a field that interests you and prepare an oral report to your class in which you show a copy of the publication and discuss the following:

   a. Who publishes it and how often it is published.
   b. Who (what industry) reads the magazine.
   c. What its regular features/columns are.
   d. The kinds of articles and advertising that appear in it.

7. Obtain a copy of a house organ and analyze it. In a brief memo report, describe:

   a. The name of the publication and the company that publishes it.
   b. The format (magazine, newsletter, newspaper).
   c. The kinds of articles.
   d. The writing style and how it reflects the company that publishes it.
   e. The ways in which the publication attempts to build morale and create company loyalty.

8. Several members of the class should obtain copies of different types of house organs—newsletters, newspapers, magazines—from companies of various sizes. Each person should analyze one, answering the questions in activity 7, above. Each should present an oral report of the analysis to the class, showing an example of the publication.

9. Choose a business topic that interests you. Use the *Business Periodicals Index* to find a good article on the topic and make a photocopy of it. Then write an abstract of the article and submit both the photocopy and the abstract to your instructor.

10. Study the masthead of five different trade publications (available in your library). Analyze the kinds of information that appear there, including the number of subscribers, and submit your analysis in a memo report to your instructor. Be sure to identify the five publications by name and also by the audience each one serves.

APPENDIX

A Brief Guide to Grammatical Usage in Business Writing

In this appendix we will consider the grammatical conventions of good business writing. We will set down some general rules to follow and show examples of each rule. Of course, there are often exceptions to any rule, so we will indicate exceptions and cautions by using this symbol: ▲

I. In general, write out in words the numbers one through ten; write in figures those numbers over ten. **FIGURES**

Examples:

We will train three more employees for a similar project in April or May.

Send the report to the Eastern Regional Office, One Haedenford Place, Suite 311, Darien, CT.

We cannot refund money on merchandise returned later than 30 days after purchase.

The proposed site of the new warehouse is 1054 West Sixth Street.

Order a 16-ft. I-beam for project #10156.

Research in digestibles shows that pork is 98 percent digestible.

We have opened a second office at 239 South 32nd Street.

▲ **Caution:** To maintain consistency when writing several figures, write all of them in the same form, even if some are less than ten.

Example: Currently only 15 percent of our loans carry interest rates under 8½ percent.

▲ **Exceptions:**

Write dimensions in numbers regardless of the "one through ten" rule:

The market price of first grade 2 × 4's fluctuates daily.

The finished stock should measure 2 in. × 14 in. × 1.5 in.

When any number begins a sentence, write it out in words, or recast the sentence to avoid beginning with the figure:

Fourteen employees had a perfect attendance record last year.

Days of the month and years are always written in numbers:

. . . on July 2, 1984 . . .

. . . by the 3rd of August . . .

II. In general, write sums of money in figures, but use the decimal point only if a cents amount exists.

Examples:

. . . at $1.65/100 . . .

. . . at $245 per employee . . .

. . . at only $0.85 a share . . .

▲ **Exceptions:**

When writing about large sums of money or other large figures that have several zeros, use a combination of words and figures to prevent misreading:

Our assets now total $10 million.

The U.S. trade deficit last year was over $20 billion.

COMMAS

I. When joining two sentences with a coordinating conjunction (*and, but, or*) to form a compound sentence, use a comma before the conjunction.

Examples:

The starting pay is good, but salary increases come only with advancement.

Our engineering staff has studied your problem, and we recommend replacing the unit rather than trying to repair it.

▲**Caution:** Do not use a conjunction to join sentences that are not closely related in meaning.

> *Incorrect:* We hope the report is informative, and please let us know if you need further assistance.
>
> *Correct:* We trust the report is informative. Please let us know if you need further assistance.

▲**Caution:** Not all sentences with conjunctions need commas — only those that join two or more *independent clauses:*

> These cases include felonies that carry penalties of two years to death and civil cases amounting to $5,000 or more.
>
> Warehouse and assortment stores keep costs to a minimum and pass savings on to the consumer.

II. When a sentence *begins* with a subordinating conjunction (*if, when, as, since, because,* and others), use a comma after the subordinate clause.

Examples:

Since businesses are run for profit, reduction of operating costs is a primary concern.

If you have some experience, the starting salary range is $18,000 to $20,000.

▲**Caution:** If the subordinate clause comes at the end of the sentence, it is in its natural order, and no comma is used:

> Prevention of accidents is important in reducing operating costs since accidents cost the company money.
>
> The starting salary range is $18,000 to $20,000 if you have some experience.

III. Use a comma between elements in a series of items.

Examples:

When credit is tight, the small business person faces many problems: profit losses, layoffs, cancellation of plans for growth, and even bankruptcy.

Answers to these questions were obtained from trade journals, from an interview with a local businessman, and from correspondence with a small-engine manufacturer.

▲**Exception:**

When there are commas *within* any of the elements in a series, the commas separating the elements are changed to semicolons to prevent misreading:

Our plants in Darlington, SC; Norfolk, NE; and Jewett, TX are currently being expanded.

IV. Use a comma between elements when the sentence might be misread without the comma.

Examples:

Because of custom and power, senior partners get the largest offices.

In 1982, 496,310 people in the state will be employed in the professional, technical, managerial, and official category according to U.S. Department of Labor statistics.

▲**Caution:** Do not use a comma between the month and year in dates:

. . . in June 1982 . . .
. . . by January 1983 . . .

V. Use a comma after conjunctive adverbs (*however, therefore, moreover*) when they are used as transition words at the beginning of a sentence.

Examples:

The insurance industry is still expanding. Therefore, it is a good place for young graduates to begin their careers.

Ordinary sand can be used. However, we have found that it does not withstand pressure as well as the glass beads do.

VI. Use commas before and after any element that interrupts the natural flow (S-V-O) of a sentence.

Examples:

We are, however, issuing you a credit memo for $315.86.

The file folders, on the other hand, will be bright green so they can be seen easily.

Joseph Buchanan, the new vice-president of finance, came to us from AM International, Inc.

VII. Use the comma to set off a name when addressing the person directly.

Examples:

As you know, Mr. Hanover, the deadline for receiving proposals was May 8.

VIII. Use a comma to separate two adjectives that modify the same noun. If you can mentally insert the word *and* between the adjectives and if the sentence still reads sensibly, you need a comma between them.

Examples:

The brown tones give a serene, sophisticated appearance to the office.

The new design has clean, uncluttered lines.

I. Use a semicolon to join two closely related sentences that ordinarily would be separated by a period.

SEMICOLONS

Examples:

Employees do not need to report the change in their status; the personnel department will automatically make the changes.

By 1946 few homemakers were making their own soap; quality commercial soaps had become dependable and inexpensive.

An alkaline solution will turn red litmus blue; therefore, sodium hydroxide must be an alkaline solution.

▲**Caution:** *Never* join two complete sentences with a comma.

    Incorrect: Our president began as an engineer in this plant 30 years ago, today he is just as concerned about the way our product is engineered as he was then.

    Correct: Our president began as an engineer in this plant 30 years ago; today he is just as concerned about the way our product is engineered as he was then.

II. Use semicolons between items in a series if any of the items has commas within it.

Example:

Paralegals may receive training in one of four areas: litigation; corporation law; real estate and mortgages; or estates, trusts, and wills (probate).

COLONS

I.   Use a colon after the salutation in business letters.

Examples:

Dear Mr. Bronson:

Dear Dr. Jackson:

II. Use a colon at the end of a phrase that indicates a *list* of items will follow.

Examples:

The titles — in order of lowest to highest rank — are as follows: Personnel Representative, Personnel Supervisor, Personnel Superintendent, Personnel Manager, and Corporate Personnel Director.

When interviewing for a sales representative position, you should:

1.   Dress conservatively;
2.   Be enthusiastic;
3.   Exhibit confidence;
4.   Demonstrate a willingness to learn;
5.   Be willing to relocate.

III. Use the colon as a stylistic device (to add interest and variety to your writing) at the end of a statement when you plan to follow the statement with something that exemplifies it.

Examples:

The major producers of these machines are two companies, both located in Italy: the Lonattia Company and Matec, S.P.A.

The applicant did not demonstrate two important qualities essential to this job: self-confidence and an outgoing personality.

▲Caution: Do not use a colon after the expression "such as" even though you follow it with examples:

The purchasing function contracts for printing supplies such as paper, ink, and printing plates, as well as for major equipment such as computer-controlled cameras and photocopy machines.

DASHES AND PARENTHESES

I.   These two marks of punctuation are seldom used in business writing since they are stylistic devices. However, you may need them when you wish to include some information that is of secondary importance, that is an afterthought, or that is an offhand example.

The dash is the more flamboyant mark and will cause the information inside it to stand out — to assume importance. The parentheses, on the other hand, will cause the information within them to diminish in importance. In the examples below notice that the information within these two marks of punctuation can be omitted without altering the basic meaning or structure of the sentence.

Examples:

Supermarkets and combination stores are now adding specialty departments — deli, wine shop, bakery, cheese shop, floral boutique, and general merchandise — to attract more customers.

Reminder: No shipments should be scheduled to arrive when the plant is closed for vacation (July 1–15).

Lamb must compete with less expensive meats (chicken, ground beef, and pork) for the consumer's food dollar.

II. In legal documents such as contracts, use parentheses to enclose dollar amounts or other quantities written in numbers after the same quantity is expressed in words.

Examples:

The purchaser agrees to deposit five hundred dollars ($500) in an escrow account.

Total cost of the seminar is three thousand six hundred dollars ($3,600).

BRACKETS

Use brackets to enclose your own explanatory comments within material you are quoting.

Examples:

"The cost [of compliance with government regulations] is twice the amount we spend for employee benefits."

"Some degledations [sic] spent as much as $3,000 per person at the convention."

APOSTROPHES

I. Use an apostrophe to form the *possessive* case of nouns.
   A. To form a singular possessive, always add *'s* to the singular form of the word.

Examples:

> . . . this company's revenues . . .
> . . . Gus's report . . .
> . . . an employee's response . . .
> . . . a dollar's worth of polyvinyl chloride . . .

B. To create the plural possessive, first write the plural form of the noun. If it ends in *s*, add only the apostrophe. If the plural form does *not* end in *s*, add both the apostrophe and *s*.

Examples:

companies	Most companies' pension fund . . .
engineers	All engineers' hours will be extended . . .
men	Two men's quick thinking saved . . .
women	The women's support group . . .

PRONOUNS

I. The *personal pronouns* are grouped into three categories or *cases*. The *nominative* (or subjective) case pronouns should be used when the pronoun is the subject or predicate nominative of a sentence or clause. *Objective* case pronouns are used as direct objects, indirect objects, or objects of prepositions. *Possessive* case pronouns are used to show ownership.

A. Nominative case pronouns:

	Singular	Plural
1	I	we
2	you	you
3	she, he, it	they

Examples:

We appreciate the department's support.
This is she speaking.

B. Objective case pronouns:

	Singular	Plural
1	me	us
2	you	you
3	him, her, it	they

Examples:

Please let us know your decision by April 15.
Between you and me, this plan is unsound.

C.   Possessive case pronouns:

	Singular	Plural
1	my, mine	our, ours
2	your, yours	your, yours
3	his, hers, her, its	their, theirs

Examples:

Our products are guaranteed for six months.

We are still awaiting their approval.

II.   *Relative pronouns* include *who, whose, which,* and *that.*
   A.   Use *who* to refer to people.

Example:

Jerry Haskins is the representative who handles the Corwin account.
   B.   Use *which* or *that* to refer to things.

Example:

The part that (or which) you requested should arrive by air tomorrow.

   C.   *Who* is used informally these days, as both a nominative and an objective case pronoun. However, if you know your audience expects the more formal usage, use *who* for nominative case and *whom* as the objective case pronoun.

Examples:

Who (or "whom") would you like to assist you?

Who (or "whom") should I ask about this Radnor contract?

In this section we will look at some words that are often misused in business writing.

USING WORDS CORRECTLY

   I.   *Amount and Number.* Use *amount* when referring to things in bulk or mass — things you can't count. Use *number* for things you can count.

Examples:

Incorrect: The result is an increasing amount of jobs that are hard to fill.

Correct: The result is an increasing number of jobs that are hard to fill.

Correct: What amount of money is needed to open an account?

Correct: The number of dollars lost to white-collar criminals increases each year.

II. *Fewer and Less.* Use *fewer* when referring to things you can count. Use *less* with things in bulk or mass — things you can't count.

Examples:

Incorrect: We have had less accidents involving company cars this year than we had last year.

Correct: We had fewer accidents involving company cars this year than we had last year.

Incorrect: Less applications taken by phone means less money spent returning phone calls.

Correct: Fewer applications taken by phone means less money spent returning phone calls.

III. *As (as if) and Like.* *Like* is a preposition and is therefore used with a noun; *as* is a subordinate conjunction and is therefore used to introduce a clause. Do not interchange them. Also, do not substitute *as* for *because* or *since* (other subordinate conjunctions).

Examples:

Incorrect: (colloquialism): I feel like (that) we should not invest in AML Corp.

Correct: I believe (that) we should not invest in AML Corp.

Correct: This copier is like the one we used to have.

Incorrect: As we did not receive your deposit before May 15, we must charge the full fee.

IV. *Cooperation and Assistance. Cooperation* should generally be used with one's subordinates because the connotation of the word is one of common effort and therefore engenders a feeling of sharing. If you need help from a co-worker or a superior, it is tactful to use the words "assistance" or "help."

Examples:

Thank you for your cooperation. (in messages to subordinates)

I appreciate your assistance. (in messages to co-workers or superiors)

V. *Advice and Advise. Advice* is a noun meaning a recommendation or suggestion; *advise* is a verb meaning to offer a suggestion or recommendation.

Examples:

Our corporate counsel advises us not to discuss the case with the press.

Consumers are not heeding the advice given on the label.

VI. *Among and Between.* Both of these words are prepositions. Use *among* when talking about three or more people or things; use *between* when discussing two people or things.

Examples:

The workload has been divided among the three secretaries.

Our final choice is between Frank Jacobs and Gene Nugent.

VII. *Complement and Compliment. Complement* means to complete or supplement; *compliment* means to flatter or praise. Both words function as either noun or verb.

Examples:

This new product complements our line of health care items.

The *Wall Street Journal* article was a compliment to our good management for the past five years.

VIII. *Criterion and Criteria.* These words have a Greek derivation; *criterion* is singular; *criteria* is plural. *Phenomenon* and *phenomena* operate the same way. *DATA* is a word that may be either singular (one fact or one figure) or plural (several facts or figures). Use *data is* for the singular and *data are* for the plural.

Examples:

Examine the third criterion more carefully.

The criteria for our decision are as follows.

Our data on the Clayton sample are inconclusive.

IX. *Disinterested and Uninterested. Disinterested* means unbiased or objective; *uninterested* means unconcerned or lacking interest in.

Examples:

The bargaining agent was the disinterested third party in the negotiations.

John seems uninterested in the welfare of his subordinates.

X. *Elicit and Illicit. Elicit* means to draw out (usually a comment or remark); *illicit* means illegal or unlawful.

Examples:

That statement may elicit a negative response from stockholders.

In many countries bribery is considered a necessary part of doing business, not an illicit activity.

XI. *Imply and Infer. Imply* means to hint at or make allusion to something; *infer* means to draw a conclusion from what has been said or implied. You imply something and I infer your meaning.

Examples:

He implied that earnings per share would be less than last quarter.

I inferred that the company had been affected by the economic slowdown.

XII. *Moral and Morale. Moral* is a noun meaning a basic principle or lesson, or an adjective meaning ethical. *Morale* is a noun meaning a psychological state of mind.

Examples:

We have a moral responsibility to the investing public.

Morale has been higher since we instituted the work team system on the assembly line.

XIII. *Respectfully and Respectively. Respectfully* means with deference to or with respect for, while *respectively* means in the order listed.

Examples:

We respectfully submit our recommendations for changes in the proposed plan.

Larry Figbaum and Janice Hartis were named vice-president and treasurer, respectively.

XIV. *Stationery and Stationary.* Use *stationery* when you mean writing paper; use *stationary* when you mean permanent or unmoving.

Examples:

Our stationery requisition is pink.

The new building was designed without stationary interior

walls so changes in office locations could be made more easily as we grow.

XV. *Than and Then.* Use *than* when you are comparing things; use *then* when you mean next (in relation to time), or at that time.

Examples:

Amco charges one cent less per foot than Pickens does.
Cut the cord, then wrap it with electrical tape.

Capitalize proper names, job titles, courtesy titles, earned degrees, product brand names, names of specific departments, names of organizations, names of specific geographic areas, names of eras or decades, and so on.

CAPITALIZATION

Examples:

the "Big Eight" accounting firms
Jay Hanrahan, Manager of Data Processing, said . . .
   (But — The manager of data processing said . . .)
The engineering department
Savin Copiers
Bachelor of Arts degree in Business Administration
The Southwest
Governor James O'Connor
Taylor wines
Judge Blankenship
Beecher, Rowe and Company
Mrs. Swensen
Amana Radarange

Caution: Do not capitalize general directions — east, west, north, south:
   Our plant is located west of Interstate 90.

Caution: Do not capitalize general descriptive words that follow capitalized words unless they are a part of a title, trademark, or brand name:
   Kodak photographic products (But — Kodak Ektachrome 400)
   the economics of scale (But — an Economics course)

GLOSSARY

Abstract a brief summary of the main ideas from a report, magazine, or newspaper article; an abstract is usually 10 to 20 percent of the length of the original item.

Abstraction, levels of the degree of generality of a word; the opposite of concrete (specific) words. "Young man" is abstract; "James Harvey, Jr." is concrete.

Active voice a term used to describe verbs; it is a relationship between a subject and verb in which the subject performs the action described by the verb.

Analytical report any report that gathers and interprets information for the reader.

Annual report a professionally designed brochure that is compiled and presented yearly to show the financial activities of a company during the past year. See also **Corporate annual report**.

Appraisal, performance a document detailing the recent past performance of an employee on the job and suggestions for improving individual productivity.

Authorization an official request — orally or in writing — for a report. If in writing, the authorization or a copy of it may be included in a long formal report.

Bar chart or graph an illustration that uses horizontal bars to show two variables — usually quantity and time.

Brief a formal statement of logic consisting of a proposition, the words *since* or *because*, followed by the reasons to support the proposition. Example: The product did not sell because the packaging was not sophisticated enough for our target market.

Business directory a special reference that lists companies, products, names of officers, addresses, financial data, and other information about various companies.

Colloquial diction words or pronunciations that are peculiar to and used only in a particular limited region or area. Examples: *y'all*, *you guys* for the plural *you*.

Concrete word the degree of specificity in a word; the opposite of abstract words. Example: lending institution is abstract; North Coast National Bank is concrete.

Connotation the emotional reaction — positive, negative, or neutral — that a word or phrase evokes in a reader or listener.

Corporate annual report the professionally designed brochure that is compiled for and presented annually primarily to stockholders; it is a public relations tool that shows the financial as well as other activities of the company during the past year.

Cutaway drawing a type of illustration that shows the interior of an object by removing its outer layer; it can show inner construction or other details.

Deductive organization method by which the conclusion is presented first and the supporting facts, next.

Definition, formal an explanation of a technical or specialized word in which one presents three parts: the *term*, the *genus*, and the *differentia*.

Diction, levels of four categories of words in our language that have specialized uses; the categories are slang, colloquial, popular, and learned dictions. See entries under each category.

Differentia the part of a formal definition that explains how the word being defined is different from all others in the same class or category.

Downward communication messages coming from one's superiors.

Emotional appeal one of the three methods of persuasion; it manipulates the audience's emotions (fear, anger, love, hatred) as a basis for convincing them of a point of view.

Ethical appeal one of the three methods of persuasion; this appeal comes from the speaker, whose past actions and activities cause the audience to like or dislike, believe or disbelieve, accept or reject the speaker and his ideas.

Ethos from a Greek word meaning "custom"; this word describes one kind of appeal — the ethical appeal — that is used in written or oral persuasion. See also **Ethical appeal.**

Exhibit any illustration that is a sample of an item or is a photocopy of an original report, contract, or letter.

Exploded drawing a type of illustration in which a portion of the drawing is enlarged to show greater detail.

Feasibility report a type of report in which one tries to show that one alternative is preferable to another; also a report that attempts to show whether or not one particular alternative is worthwhile, cost-effective, and the like.

Figure a method of labeling illustrations; if the illustration is not a table or an exhibit, it will be labeled as a figure. See also **Table** and **Exhibit.**

Flow chart an illustration that uses symbols to show steps in a process, how a paperwork system operates, or other types of activities that require a particular sequence; also a method of showing the steps in the logic used in writing a computer program.

Form report any report that is submitted on a carefully organized and designed piece of paper; a form report has categories that require the use of check marks, numbers, words or short phrases rather than complete sentences.

Formal definition See **Definition, formal.**

Genus one of the three parts of a formal definition; the genus separates the term from all others into a specific class or category.

Government regulatory agency any of the several bodies established by the federal government to act as a liaison between the public and private enterprise; general areas of agency responsibility include maintaining the free enterprise system, protecting the working public's health and safety, protecting the investing public from unscrupulous schemes, monitoring equality of work opportunity for all who want to work, and so forth.

House organ any type of employee communication that is published at regular intervals and contains articles about and for the employees; it may use the newsletter, newspaper, or magazine format; its main objective is to boost morale and build loyalty to the company.

Impersonal writing style a kind of writing that does not attempt to involve the reader personally; it is characterized by the use of the impersonal pronoun *one*, by nouns such as *the manager, the stock broker, the loan officer* and by the third-person pronouns *she, he, they, his,* and so on.

Index a type of publication that lists all magazine articles, all newspaper articles, or all books published on specific topics in a given time period; indexes are used to find numerous sources of information on a particular subject.

Inductive organization method by which facts are presented first and a conclusion, based on the facts, is presented next.

Informational report any report that presents only facts, figures, and observations on a topic. No analysis or evaluation of facts is made, and no recommendations are offered in this type of report.

Interview report any report whose basis for fact is a question/answer exchange between two people. Interviews may be conducted to gain information (informative interview), to judge someone's ability to do a job (job interview), or to find out why an employee is leaving the company (exit interview).

Jargon language that tries to impress rather than to communicate; it consists of many learned words strung together with prepositions and other parts of speech, making it difficult to comprehend.

Job description a document used by personnel departments to match the right employee to the right job and to aid in administering wages and salaries; it describes a particular job, the educational and/or other qualifications needed to perform the job, the responsibilities it entails, and so on.

Lateral communication communication between or among people at the same level in an organization.

Learned diction a category of words that is used by the best educated people in our country; these are words you have seen and possibly have a general understanding of but never use in your own speech or writing.

Letter report a format used for reports that are five pages or less in length and are compiled for someone outside your own organization. The format uses the traditional letter heading, inside address, salutation, and closing; a subject line gives the topic of the report, and the body of the report uses headings to show the most important ideas.

Line chart a type of illustration that uses lines to connect points plotted on two axes to show two variables, often time and quantity.

Logical appeal a method of persuasion that uses reasoned statements and facts to appeal to an audience.

Logos the Greek word meaning speech or ratio; used to describe one of the types of persuasive appeals. See **Logical appeal**.

Long formal report a format used for reports that are more than five or six pages long; it is more formal than other formats and consists of prefatory parts (letter of authorization, transmittal, table of contents, synopsis), the main body of the report, and end parts (notes, bibliography, appendix); it is used for reports within or outside the organization.

Memo report a format used for reports that are five pages or less in length and are used within the organization; it consists of the traditional memorandum heading (Date, To, From, Subject) with the subject line telling the topic of the report. The body of the report has section headings to show the important ideas in the report.

Methods and procedures reports a document that discusses step by step how a procedure is to be performed or how a particular job is to be done.

Minutes (of a meeting) a brief description of the topics covered, discussion, voting, or other details of a meeting; minutes are kept as a written record of such activities for future references.

Nonverbal communication any method of communicating without the use of words or language.

Passive voice a term used to describe verbs; it is the relationship between a subject and verb, in which the subject does not perform the action expressed by the verb but rather is acted upon by someone or something.

Pathos a Greek word meaning suffering; also used to describe one of the three types of appeals in persuasion. See also **Emotional appeal**.

Performance report or appraisal a document that discusses the recent past performance of an employee on the job and suggests ways to improve individual productivity.

Periodic report any routine report that is submitted at regular time intervals — daily, weekly, monthly, semiannually, and the like.

Personal writing style a type of writing that attempts to personally involve the reader; it is characterized by the use of first- and second-person pronouns (*I, you, we, our, yours, us*).

Pictograph an illustration that is part picture, part graph; it can be used to show the composition of an item, the ingredients that comprise the item, or the percentages of each ingredient in the item.

Pie chart   a circular illustration that is used to show the percentages of various parts that comprise the whole pie (100 percent).

Popular diction   a category of words that would be easily understood by most people in our country. These are the words used by the mass media — radio, TV, and newspapers. It is also the level of diction to use in business writing.

Population   the entire group of subjects a researcher wants to study in a primary research project.

Press release   a brief news item containing information that a company would like publicized. News releases are prepared by the director of corporate communications and sent to local TV and radio stations and to newspapers: the media determine how much of the information to publicize.

Process chart   a method of showing the steps in a process by using symbols for each different kind of activity performed by the employee; process charts are most often used by industrial engineers to improve productivity.

Progress report   a report of the activities that have been completed on one phase of a long-term project; the report briefly mentions past progress, gives greater detail about the current phase and any complications that have arisen to change plans for the project, and desribes what remains to be done on the project.

Proposal   a document that seeks approval and/or funding for a particular project; it should include objectives, methods for reaching those objectives (research method), timetables, a budget, personnel requirements, and so forth.

Proxy   literally a document giving someone power to vote for you; if, as a stockholder, you cannot attend the annual stockholders meeting, you can vote for members of the board by returning your proxy statement to be counted in the voting at the meeting.

Radial communication   the process of communicating parts of a larger message to various levels of the organization, giving the persons at each level only the information relevant to their jobs.

Random sampling   a means of testing an entire population by testing a few subjects; everyone within the given population has an equal chance of being selected for the test.

Recommendation report   a document that presents facts or observations, analyzes those facts or observations, and makes specific recommendations based on the facts and analyses.

Recorder   the person who takes notes on the proceedings at a meeting; he or she may also present the report to superiors or to a larger group meeting.

Regulatory agencies   see **Government regulatory agency.**

Rendering   a drawing made by an architect of the interior or exterior of a building or of a landscape design.

Sampling   a means of examining an entire population by examining at random subjects taken from the population.

Slang   the level of diction characterized by the use of vivid expressions; slang has a short life span and is usually understood by a limited group of people who create and use it.

Specialized words   technical words used by employees who do a particular kind of work (computer programmer, plumber, printer, and so on); these are not understood or used by the general public.

Statement of purpose   the thesis statement in a report; it tells the purpose for submitting the report and what aspects of the topic will be covered in the report.

Strong verbs   one-word verbs in the active voice that are used to create direct, forceful messages.

Suggestion report   a report that is submitted to recommend some kind of change; it is initiated by the employee and may be accepted or rejected by management.

Synopsis   a brief summary of important parts in a report or a magazine or newspaper article. See also **Abstract.**

Table   an illustration that arranges numbers in rows and columns for ease in reading and understanding them.

Technical words   see **Specialized words.**

Term   the first of three parts of a formal definition; the term is the word to be defined.

Tone   the total impression that a piece of writing makes on the reader; tone is the result of choices made in content, organization, words, sentence patterns, and paragraph arrangement.

Trade publication   a magazine, newspaper, or newsletter published regularly for a specific industry, trade group, or organization; it uses technical language and covers job-related topics.

Transmittal   a letter or memo used as a formal means of turning over a long report to the reader; it says "Here is the report you asked for." It may also explain how the research was done and any problems that were encountered.

Upward communication   message coming from one's subordinates.

Verbal   any kind of communication that involves the use of words, language, or symbols for words.

Voice   a grammatical term used to describe action verbs; the relationship between the verb and its subject. Verbs may be in active or passive voice. See also **Active verbs** and **Passive verbs**.

Weak verbs   verbs that consist of more than one word; generally weak verbs contain unnecessary words that, if eliminated, make the sentence more direct and forceful. Examples of weak verbs are "placed an order" and "keeps records of." Examples of strong verbs are: "ordered" and "records."

BIBLIOGRAPHY

Air Products and Chemicals, Inc. 1979 Annual Report.

Annual Report for Year Ending August 31, 1979, Mecklenburg Unit American Cancer Society.

"Annual Reports 1980." *Financial World* 149 (June 15, 1980):63–69.

"Annual Report Survey Results." *Public Relations Journal* (August 1980):18

Barnard, P. J., et al. "Effects of Response Instructions and Question Style on the Ease of Completing Forms." *Journal of Occupational Psychology* 52 (September 1979):209–226.

Beaulieu, R. "Easier Look at Performance Appraisals." *Training and Development Journal* 34 (October 1980):56–58.

Belden Corporation 1975 Annual Report.

Bohl, Marilyn. *Flow Charting Techniques.* Chicago: Science Research Associates, 1971.

Boner, J. R. "Putting Sparkle in Those Annual Reports." *International Management* 35 (September 1980):44–45.

Brinkerhoff, D. W., and Kanter, R. M. "Appraising the Performance of Performance Appraisals." *Sloan Management Review* 21 (Spring 1980):3–16.

Cornelius, E. T., III, et al. "Methodological Approach to Job Classification for Performance Appraisal Purposes." *Personnel Psychology* 32 (Summer 1979):341–357.

Dowst, S. "Use the Users to Test Your Office Forms." *Purchasing* 89 (October 23, 1980):80–81.

Dunk, William. "28 Trends in Annual Reports." *Public Relations Journal* 36 (August 1980):10–13.

"Editors Polled on Acceptability of News Releases." *Editor and Publisher* 112 (November 10, 1979):30.

Engraph Annual Report 1977.

Ewing, David. *Writing for Results: In Business, Government, and the Professions.* New York: Wiley, 1974.

Flesch, Rudolph. *How to Write Plain English.* New York: Barnes and Noble Books, 1979.

General Motors Annual Report 1979.

George, Claude S., Jr. *Supervision in Action: The Art of Managing Others.* Reston, Va.: Reston Publishing Co., 1977.

Ghorpade, J., and Atchison, T. J. "The Concept of Job Analysis: A Review and Some Suggestions." *Public Personnel Management* 9, no. 3 (1980):134–144.

Gibaldi, Joseph, and Achtert, Walter S. *MLA Handbook for Writers of Research Papers, Theses, and Dissertations.* New York: Modern Language Association, 1980.

Goodman, R. "Annual Reports Are Serving a Dual Marketing Function — Report of a Survey." *Public Relations Quarterly* 25 (Summer 1980):21–24.

Grazulis, C. "Communicating Corporate Attitudes Through Annual Reports." *Personnel Administrator* 24 (July 1975):51–55.

Greyhound Corporation 1975 Annual Report.

Guillet, D. R. "Forms Design: It's Really a System." *Administrative Management* 40 (November 1979):48–50.

Hamelink, J., and Hamelink, J. "A Numeric Plan for Performance Appraisal." *Training and Development Journal* 34 (October 1980):88–89.

Jacobi, Ernst. *Writing at Work: Do's, Don'ts, and How To's.* Rochelle Park, N.J.: Hayden Book Co., 1976.

Jordan, Lewis, ed. *The New York Times Manual of Style and Usage.* New York: Times Books, 1979.

Kershaw, J. "Some Good Ideas for Designing Better Business Forms." *Office* 90 (September 1979):119–120.

Kirk, N. A. "Legal Restraints in Forms Design." *Journal of Systems Management* 30 (June 1979):38–42.

Kish, Joseph L. "Simplify Forms to Increase Productivity and Reduce Cost." *Graphic Arts Monthly* (January 1980):162j–162k.

Miller, Casey, and Swift, Kate. *The Handbook of Non-Sexist Writing for Writers, Editors, and Speakers.* New York: Barnes and Noble Books, 1980.

R. J. Reynolds Industries 1979 Annual Report.

Schindler-Rainman, Eva, et al. *Taking Your Meeting Out of the Doldrums.* Columbus, Ohio: Association of Professional Directors, 1975.

Second National Bank Annual Report 1975.

Statistical Abstracts of the United States. Washington, D.C.: U.S. Government Printing Office, 1979.

Stinson, J., and Stokes, J. "How to Multi-Appraise." *Management Today* (June 1980):43.

"Ten Commandments of Valid Performance Appraisal." *Personnel* (September 1979):45–48.

This, Leslie. *The Small Meeting Planner*. Houston: Gulf Publishing Company, 1979.

Venolia, Jan. *Write Right! A Desk Drawer Digest of Punctuation, Grammar, and Style*. Berkeley, Calif: Ten Speed Press, 1982.

Weiss, Allen. *Write What You Mean*. New York: AMACOM (American Management Associations), 1977.

Wexley, K. N., et al. "Attitudinal Congruence and Similarity as Related to Interpersonal Evaluations in Manager-Subordinate Dyads." *Academy of Management Journal* 23 (June 1980):320–330.

Winstanley, N. B. "How Accurate Are Peformance Appraisals?" *Personnel Administrator* 25 (August 1980):55–58.

Zelko, Harold P. *The Business Conference: Leadership and Participation*. New York: McGraw-Hill, 1969.

Index

Abstract: informative, 308; sample, 313

Abstract in long report. *See* Long formal report

Abstract words, 93

Accountant's Index, 52

Accuracy in reports. *See* Reports

Active voice (of verbs), 97

Agricultural Marketing Service. *See* Government regulatory agencies

Air Products and Chemicals, Inc., 281

American Cancer Society, 277

Among, correct use of word, 351

Amount, correct use of word, 349

Animal and Plant Health Inspection Service. *See* Government regulatory agencies

Annual reports, understanding, 281. *See also* Corporate annual report

Annuals. *See* Secondary sources of information

Apostrophes, using, 347–348

Architects' renderings, use of, in reports, 120. *See also* Illustrations in reports

Area Labor Summary, 55

Audience analysis, 17–18

Audiences: primary, 18; secondary, 18

Bar charts or graphs. *See* Graphs; Illustrations in reports

Bartel Company, Adam H., 335–336

Basic sentence pattern. *See* Sentences

Before-after design. *See* Experiments

Belden Corporation, 324–326

Best's Insurance Reports, 52

Between, correct use of word, 351

Bibliography. *See* Long formal report

Binders and paper used in reports. *See* Nonverbal elements in reports

Blueprints, use of, in reports, 121. *See also* Illustrations in reports

Brackets, use of, in writing, 347

Brief-writing, 302

Bureau of Alcohol, Tobacco, and Firearms. *See* Government regulatory agencies

Business communication media, 4

Business directories. *See* Secondary sources of information

Business library, how to use, 51

Business Periodicals Index, 51

Business services. *See* Secondary sources of information

Catalogue of Federal Paperwork Requirements—By Industry Group, 298
Cause/effect plan of organization, 25–26
Chronological plan of organization, 24
Civil Rights Act of 1964, 148; Title VII of, 148
Colloquial diction, 95
Colons, using, 346
Column charts or graphs. *See* Graphs; Illustrations in reports
Combustion Engineering, 327–328; C-E Air Preheater (subsidiary), 311
Commas, using, 342–345
Commendations. *See* Reports
Commodities Futures Trading Commission. *See* Government regulatory agencies
Communication: lateral, 5; radial, 6; upward, 5
Company records. *See* Primary sources of information
Comparison/contrast plan of organization, 24–25
Computer graphics. *See* Illustrations in reports
Conclusion, defined, 15
Concrete words, 93
Conference Board, 52
Connotation: defined, 92; in annual reports, 283
Consumer Product Safety Commission. *See* Government regulatory agencies
Controlled before-after design. *See* Experiments
Corporate annual report, 276; and board of directors, 280; color in, use of, 282; compilation of, 283; cover of, 278; and financial data, summary of, 278; financial highlights in, 280; financial statements in, 280; letter from certified public accounting firm in, 280; letter to stockholders in, 280; nonverbal elements in, 281; paper in, quali-

Corporate annual report (*continued*) ty of, 282; photographs in, use of, 282; suggestion in, use of, 281; table of contents of, 278; verbal elements in, 283
Cutaway drawings in reports, 122. *See also* Illustrations in reports

Daily reports. *See* Reports
Dashes, use of, 346
Data. *See* Primary data
Decision-making process, 4–9
Deductive logic, 22
Deductive organization, 22
Definition, formal, 308; clarified by illustration, 310–311; differentia in, 308; expanded, 309; genus in, 308; term in, 308
Dichotomous question. *See* Survey questions
Differentia. *See* Definition, formal
Disinterested, correct use of word, 351
Duke Power Company, 66–67, 121
Dun and Bradstreet: *Middle Market Directory,* 53; *Million Dollar Directory,* 52

Economic Almanac, 52
Economic Regulatory Administration. *See* Government regulatory agencies
Employee publications. *See* House organ
Employment interview, 166, 167–175; illegal questions in, 167–168; questions to ask in, 169–171; tips for, 168
End material. *See* Long formal report
Environmental Protection Agency. *See* Government regulatory agencies
Equal Employment Opportunity Commission (EEOC). *See* Government regulatory agencies

Exit interview, 175–177; format and contents of, 176

Experiments, 45; before-after design of, 45–46; controlled before-after design of, 45–46. *See also* Primary sources of information

Exploded drawings in reports, 122. *See also* Illustrations in reports

Factor plan of organization, 27

Federal Aviation Administration. *See* Government regulatory agencies

Federal Communications Commission. *See* Government regulatory agencies

Federal Deposit Insurance Corporation. *See* Government regulatory agencies

Federal Energy Regulatory Commission. *See* Government regulatory agencies

Federal Grain Inspection Service. *See* Government regulatory agencies

Federal Maritime Commission. *See* Government regulatory agencies

Federal Register, 55

Federal Trade Commission. *See* Government regulatory agencies

Fewer, correct use of word, 350

Food and Drug Administration. *See* Government regulatory agencies

Food Safety and Quality Service. *See* Government regulatory agencies

Findings, research, 15

Figures in reports, 112–127. *See also* Illustrations in reports

First-degree heads. *See* Outline, organization of

Flow charts. *See* Illustrations in reports

Formal outline. *See* Outline, organization of

Form report, 63–68; examples of, 64, 66–67; training subordinates in use of, 65

Forms design, 139

Function plan of organization, 27

General Motors, 281, 283

General theory of sampling. *See* Sampling

Genus. *See* Definition, formal

Government Printing Office, 54

Government publications. *See* Secondary sources of information

Government regulatory agencies, 291–303; Agricultural Marketing Service, 295; Animal and Plant Health Inspection Service, 295; Bureau of Alcohol, Tobacco, and Firearms, 297; Commodities Futures Trading Commission, 295; Consumer Product Safety Commission, 295; Economic Regulatory Administration, 298; Environmental Protection Agency, 295; Equal Employment Opportunity Commission, 148, 295; Federal Aviation Administration, 298; Federal Communications Commission, 296; Federal Deposit Insurance Corporation, 296; Federal Energy Regulatory Commission, 296; Federal Grain Inspection Service, 295; Federal Maritime Commission, 297; Federal Trade Commission, 55, 296; Food and Drug Administration, 296; Food Safety and Quality Service, 295; Internal Revenue Service, 297; Interstate Commerce Commission, 297; Mine Safety and Health Administration, 297; Nuclear Regulatory Commission, 297; Occupational Safety and Health Administration, 296, 300–301; organizational structure of, 291; purpose of, 294; Securities and Exchange Commission, 53, 285, 297; U.S. Coast Guard, 298; U.S. Customs Service, 297

Graphs: bar, 115; column, 116; line, 118; pie, 112, 114–115
Greyhound Corporation, 279

Hedging in reports, 101
House organ, 334–336
Hypothesis, defined, 15. *See also* Conclusion, defined; Inference; Findings, research; Recommendation, defined

Illustration, defined, 109
Illustrations in reports, 109–127; architects' renderings, 120; bar charts, 115; blueprints, 121; column charts, 116; computer graphics, 127; cutaway drawings, 122; exhibits, 110, 112; exploded drawings, 122; figures, 112–127; flow charts, 124; line charts, 118; maps, 119; organization charts, 124; photographs, 120; pictographs, 124; pie charts, 112, 114–115; tables, 109, 110
Imply, correct use of word, 352
Indexes. *See* Secondary sources of information
Inductive logic, 22
Inductive organization, 22
Industrial engineer, 191
Infer, correct use of word, 352
Inference, 15
Informal outline. *See* Outline, organization of
Information interview, 35–37, 178; preparation for, 36
Internal Revenue Service. *See* Government regulatory agencies
Interstate Commerce Commission. *See* Government regulatory agencies
Interviews. *See* Employment interview; Exit interview; Information interview
Interview styles, 168; distributive, 168; reflective, 168; stress, 168

Investors' newsletters. *See* Secondary sources of information
Ivey's Carolinas, 144

Jargon, defined, 96
Job description, 317; samples of, 322, 324, 325, 327
Johnson, H. Webster (business libraries), 51
Journal of Economic Literature, 52

Kiplinger Washington Letter, 54
Kish, Joseph L., Jr. (forms design), 139–140

Lateral communication. *See* Communication
Less, correct use of word, 350
Letter report, 72–76; complimentary close in, 74; heading in, 72, 76; inside address in, 72; salutation in, 74; sample, 75, 77; subject line in, 74
Library. *See* Business library
Line charts or graphs. *See* Graphs; Illustrations in reports
Listening responses, 37
Listing. *See* Nonverbal elements in reports
Long formal report, 76–79, 229–263; abstract (summary, synopsis) in, 231; appendix in, 236; bibliography in, 234–236; body of, 231–232; defining problem in, 228; end material in, 76, 232–235; letter/memo of authorization in, 230; letter/memo of transmittal in, 231; prefatory material in, 76, 229–231; purpose of, 229; sample, 237–253, 254–265; source notes in, 232–234; table of contents in, 230; title page in, 230

Mean, statistical, 50
Median, statistical, 50

Memo report, 68–72; conclusions and recommendations in, 71; section headings in, 70–71; statement of purpose in, 68

Mine Safety and Health Administration. *See* Government regulatory agencies

Minutes of meeting, 312, 315

Mode, statistical, 51

Monthly Catalog of U.S. Government Publications, 55

Moody's Bond Survey, 54

Moral, correct use of word, 352

Morale, correct use of word, 352

Multiple-choice questions. *See* Survey questions

News release. *See* Press release

Nonsexist language, 102

Nonverbal communication in annual reports, 281

Nonverbal elements in reports, 103; capital letters, 103; lists, 104; paper and binders, 104; underlining, 103; white space, 103

Nuclear Regulatory Commission. *See* Government regulatory agencies

Number, correct use of word, 349

Numbers, using in reports, 341–342

Occupational Safety and Health Administration. *See* Government regulatory agencies

Open-ended questions. *See* Survey questions

Order of importance plan of organization, 27

Organization, methods of. *See* Cause/effect plan of organization; Chronological plan of organization; Comparison/contrast plan of organization; Deductive organization; Factor plan of organization; Function plan of organization; Inductive organization; Order of importance plan of organization;

Organization, methods of (*continued*) Place or location plan of organization; Problem/solution plan of organization; Quantity plan of organization

Organization chart, theme park, 7

Organization charts in reports. *See* Illustrations in reports

Outline, organization of, 22–29; and body, 21; and cause/effect plan, 25–26; and chronological plan, 24; and comparison/contrast plan, 24–25; and conclusion, 29; deductive, 22; formal, 23; and heads, 22; inductive, 22; informal, 23; and introduction, 21; and order of importance plan, 27–28; and place or location plan, 26–27; preparing, 21–31; and problem/solution plan, 23; and quantity plan, 28–29; standard structure for, 21; technical structure for, 21

Parentheses, using, 346

Passive voice (of verbs), 97

Performance appraisal. *See* Reports

Personal observation. *See* Primary sources of information

Persuasion in government reports, 299

Photographs in reports, 120. *See also* Illustrations in reports

Pie charts or graphs. *See* Graphs; Illustrations in reports

Piedmont Natural Gas Company, 142, 153

Pilot survey, 43

Place or location plan of organization, 26–27

Population in surveys and questionnaires, 40

Position description. *See* Job description

Prefatory material. *See* Long formal report

Press release, 321; sample of, 329–331

Primary audience. *See* Audiences

Primary data, 48–51; interpreting, 50–51; organizing, 48–49; tabulating, 50–51

Primary sources of information: company records, 38; defined, 35; experiments, 45; personal experience, 45; personal observation, 45; questionnaires and surveys, 38–39

Problems, steps to understanding, 14–15

Problem/solution plan of organization, 23

Proceedings of meetings, 314, 316

Process chart, 190; example of, 192; symbols used in, 190–191

Pronouns, using, 348–349

Proposals, 212, 215–222

Quantity plan of organization, 28–29

Questionnaires, 38–45; and defining population, 40; and gathering data, 40; writing, 39–40

Questionnaires and surveys, 38–45; pilot survey, 43

Radial communication. *See* Communication

Random sampling. *See* Sampling

Ranking method. *See* Survey questions

Rasberry, Robert W. (annual reports), 281

Readers' Guide to Periodical Literature, 51

Recommendation, defined, 15

Report, defined, 4

Reports: accuracy in, 10–11; analytical, 10; commendation, 152; daily, 141; feasibility, 210, 215–220; form, 63–68; formats for, 80–86; and government regulatory agencies, 291–303; informative, 10; interview, 166–178; letter, 72–79; long formal, 76–79, 229–263; managerial, 138–200; memo,

Reports (*continued*) 68–74; methods and procedures, 190–200; monthly, 141; need for, 4; objectives of, 9; performance, 64, 148–160; periodic, 138–160; progress, 178, 184–190; proposals as, 212, 215–222; recommendation, 207, 210; role of, 5; suggestion, 207, 208–210; uses of, 5; weekly, 141

Representative sample. *See* Sample, representative

Respectfully, correct use of word, 352

Respectively, correct use of word, 352

Reynolds Industries, R. J., 279, 299

Sales report, example of, 81–86

Sample, representative, 41

Sampling: general theory of, 41; random, 41–43; stratified random, 41

Secondary audience. *See* Audiences

Secondary sources of information, 50–56; annuals, 52; business directories, 52–54; business services and newsletters, 54; government publications, 54–56; indexes, 51; other, 56–57

Second-degree heads. *See* Outline, organization of

Securities and Exchange Commission. *See* Governmental regulatory agencies

Semicolons, using, 345

Sentences, 99–101; active voice in, 97; basic S-V-O pattern in, 99; and empty beginnings, 98; enlarged with modifiers, 99–100; important ideas first or last in, 98; passive voice in, 97; simple structure of, 99

Sexist language, defined, 102

Short reports, defined, 76

Solving problems, steps to, 14–15

Specialized language, 95

Standard Industrial Classification Code, 55–56

Standard Industrial Classification Manual, 55

Standard Metropolitan Statistical Area (SMSA), 55

Standard and Poor's: *Register of Corporations, Directors, and Executives*, 53; *Stock Reports*, 53

Statement of purpose, 19–20

State regulatory agencies, 303

Statistical Abstracts of the United States, 52

Stockholders, letter to. *See* Corporate annual report

Stratified random sampling. *See* Sampling

Strong verbs. *See* Verbs

Survey questions, 42–43; dichotomous, 43; multiple-choice, 43; open-ended, 42; and ranking method, 43

Tables, 109–110. *See also* Illustrations in reports

Technical outline. *See* Outline, organization of

Technical term, defining. *See* Definition, formal

Theme park, organization chart for. *See* Organization chart, theme park

Thesis statement. *See* Statement of purpose

Third-degree heads. *See* Outline, organization of

Thomas Register of American Manufacturers, 53

ThomCat, 53

Tone, defined, 92

Trade publications, 323, 332–334

Uncertainty reduction, 5

Underlining. *See* Nonverbal elements in reports

Uninterested, correct use of word, 351

Upward communication. *See* Communication

U.S. Coast Guard. *See* Government regulatory agencies

U.S. Customs Service. *See* Government regulatory agencies

U.S. Master Tax Guide, 54

Value-Line Investment Survey, 54

Variable, manipulating in experiments, 45

Verbal, defined, 92

Verbs: strong, 96–97; weak, 97

Voice (of verbs), 97; active, 97; passive, 97

Wall Street Journal Index, 52

Weak verbs. *See* Verbs

Weekly reports. *See* Reports

White space. *See* Nonverbal elements in reports

Wolf Associates, 122

Word processing in reports, 127

Writing style, 100; impersonal, characteristics of, 100; personal, characteristics of, 100